# THE CLINICAL DETECTIVE

*TECHNIQUES IN THE EVALUATION OF SEXUAL ABUSE*

## Aaron Noah Hoorwitz

W.W. NORTON & COMPANY · *NEW YORK* · *LONDON*

Printed in the United States of America.

First Edition

**Library of Congress Cataloging-in-Publication Data**

Hoorwitz, Aaron Noah.
   The clinical detective : techniques in the evaluation of sexual
abuse / Aaron Noah Hoorwitz.
      p.      cm.
   Includes bibliographical references.
   ISBN 0-393-70124-7 : $27.95
   1. Sexually abused children—Mental health.   2. Child molesting—
Diagnosis.   3. Interviewing.   I. Title.
   [DNLM:   1. Child Abuse, Sexual—diagnosis.   2. Interview,
Psychological—methods.   WA 320 H789c]
RJ507.S49H66   1992      618.92'8583075—dc20      91-27039

W. W. Norton & Company, Inc., 500 Fifth Avenue, New York, N.Y. 10110

W. W. Norton & Company, Ltd., 10 Coptic Street, London WC1A 1PU

1 2 3 4 5 6 7 8 9 0

*To the student in each of us*

# Contents

*THE*
*CLINICAL*
*DETECTIVE*

# PART 1

# *Stages of the Interview Process*

"But haven't I told you enough about the case for us to figure out whether this child is lying about being sexually abused?"

"No, I'm afraid not."

"But I thought you have this long list of variables that differentiates between true and false recantations of abuse. Can't you just tell me the variables?"

"I could, but it wouldn't do you any good."

"But why? I interviewed these people for hours. I have tons of material."

"Most of it is useless."

"But I'm a skilled clinician. You've said so yourself. What did I do wrong?"

"It would take me several days to tell you."

"I don't have days. Give me a hint. In five words or less."

"You lack skill in evaluation."

"And sexual abuse too?"

"Yes, that too. And other things. But you kept me to five words. And you seem to be in such a rush."

"But why is all my interview material useless? Why can't you just tell me the variables and let me decide if I can use them? After all, I am a professional."

"A little knowledge is a dangerous thing. It would be like putting a lethal weapon in the hands of a child."

"That's kind of insulting. Do you mind making yourself clear?"

"If you have the time."

"Just get to the point if you don't mind. Don't you think I behave in a responsible and ethical fashion?"

"I think you try, but I don't think you realize that you'll be making a recommendation that could wreck people's lives. The basis of your recommendation should be a complicated and careful process of thinking, which involves many considerations, only one of which is an examination of the strengths and weaknesses of the child's statement."

"But that's what I'm asking your help with. The variables that will help me to evaluate those strengths and weaknesses in her statement."

"I know, but, you see, that analysis is the very end point of a longer evaluation process. It depends on how you went about doing the interviews. What questions you chose to ask. And more importantly, how you went about asking them."

"And you say my interview material is useless? Why?"

"Because you didn't use interview techniques that would magnify the strengths and weaknesses of the child's statement."

"My interview technique is bad? What's wrong with it?"

"It wasn't confrontative enough, for one thing. But I thought you didn't have time to hear this. I thought you were in a rush."

"I am, but I need to figure out where to go from here. Can you help me or not?"

"Well, yes, maybe. It will take some training, though, and that would take some time."

"I don't have much time. How much time are you talking about?"

"Weeks, months, years, I don't know. It depends on you."

"I don't have that much time. I need to get back to the court in a week."

"How fast do you read?"

"Why? Did you write an article on this? Would it take me long to read it?"

"No, I'm writing a book on this. The manuscript that's completed might be helpful, if you can read real fast."

"I can't read books fast. And they aren't very practical."

"This one is. It tells you what to do."

"I get bored with textbooks. My eyes cross when I read the literature reviews and all the research."

"There isn't any of that."

"Then it will probably depress me with case histories about sexual abuse. All the horrible things that those monsters do to kids. I don't need to get all depressed when I'm trying to hurry and get this report done."

*"I'm afraid it's not as depressing as most books, and maybe that's a drawback. You see, it doesn't focus on case histories. It focuses on you."*

*"On me?"*

*"On the clinician. On what you do. On techniques. On figuring out what to do first, second, and last. It takes you by the hand and brings you through it all, step by step."*

*"Sounds too good to be true. And I'd really like to read it some time. But couldn't you make this a little easier on me? Would it hurt so much to just tell me how to patch up the botched job I did? I could even get the people back for another interview."*

*"You'd have to do the whole thing from scratch."*

*"From scratch? My God, what else did I do wrong?"*

*"Everything. You didn't ask very many of the right questions. Instead you treated it like any other case. You didn't even interview the right people. And the ones you interviewed, you interviewed in the wrong order. That's the very beginning point of the evaluation process and you didn't get that right either. You have to do first things first to get it all to come out right in the end."*

*"Anything else I did wrong?"*

*"Yes, you failed to appreciate exactly in what ways you are a good clinician, so that you could remain within your limits of expertise."*

*"Is that a polite way of saying that I don't know how much I don't know?"*

*"Yes."*

*"And I suppose your manuscript starts out with that very point."*

*"First things first."*

*"Okay, you win. Let me take a look at the manuscript."*

# CHAPTER 1

# *What You Need to Know First*

"I'm not sure what to do with this case." The clinician paused, with wrinkled brows and pursed lips. "I just don't feel comfortable putting it on the waiting list."

"Why not?" asked the supervisor.

"I'm not sure it should sit there and wait, and I'm not sure that the therapist who ends up with the case will be any more clear than I am about what needs to be done. And I don't know whether to prioritize it over other cases on the waiting list."

"What's so confusing?"

"Well, I'm not sure it's appropriate for therapy. Instead, maybe it needs a sexual abuse evaluation. But I'm really not sure."

"Why can't you tell which it needs? Didn't you get enough information on the phone? Maybe you need to see them in person first."

"I did see them. They didn't call. They just showed up for an intake. Clark Mitchelson* from D.S.S. walked them straight over from a Family Court hearing. He said the judge wanted treatment for them."

*All names are fictional.

"Did the judge order treatment or suggest it?"

"I'm not sure, but Clark said that the judge wanted the child seen here."

"For what purpose?"

"Uh, I'm not sure."

"Who are we supposed to see? Just the child? Or the alleged offender too?"

"I don't know. But they all came. The mother, the stepfather, and the grandmother."

"Why the grandmother?"

"That's who Heather is staying with right now."

"Well, okay, so what's the problem?"

"Heather said that her stepfather's been having oral sex with her for the last three years."

"When did she make the disclosure? And to whom?"

"To a worker at the shelter for battered women. Heather and her mom were staying there a couple of weeks ago after a fight between the mom and the stepdad."

"Okay, what does the stepfather say? Does he say he abused her or that he didn't?"

"He denies it."

"And Heather's mother? What does she say?"

"She wasn't sure who to believe. So she asked her own mother to take care of Heather for a while. But then Heather started changing her story to say that . . . "

"Wait, I don't understand. You mean Heather went to stay with her grandmother? Straight from the shelter? And then changed her story?"

"The mother called the grandmother from the shelter and asked if Heather could stay with her for a while, and the grandmother said that would be fine. So the grandmother picked her up and she stayed with her for about a week with no problems. Then Heather started changing her story and saying that . . . "

"Who did she tell when she changed her story?"

"The protective worker. Clark. She told him that she lied about the sex abuse so that she could get her stepdad out of the picture, in order to keep her mom from getting hit. But Clark thinks she might be lying because they've been putting a lot of pressure on Heather to change her story, and . . . "

"Who is they? Who's pressuring her?"

"The mother and the stepdad. His job is on the line because he's missing time from work with all these interviews and if he loses his job mom doesn't know how she'll make ends meet. Besides, the parents aren't fighting anymore and are back together. So Clark thinks they've been pressuring Heather to change her story because they want to get her back."

"So she changed her story and D.S.S. isn't sure she's telling the truth now."

"Right, but they figured they didn't have enough evidence to push their case when they went to court today. They figured that Heather would just get sent home."

"So what's the problem?"

"Well, today in court Heather changed her story again. She showed up with the worker from the shelter. The one whom she disclosed to in the first place. Heather said in court that it really was the truth, that her stepdad did abuse her."

"So what did the court decide?"

"I don't think they decided anything. Clark isn't sure whether the sex abuse actually happened and neither is the judge, so the only thing they decided was to adjourn the case until counseling could get started."

"Counseling for what? For what problem?"

"For sexual abuse."

"But how can we treat her for sexual abuse if she wasn't abused?"

"But maybe she was."

"Maybe she was, maybe she wasn't."

"I think she probably was. Clark thinks so too. He said he'd ask us for a report later, after the counseling gets underway."

"But what kind of report? About counseling? About whether sexual abuse occurred?"

"I think he wants some evidence that he can use to keep Heather from going back to the stepfather. Until he gets that, I guess she can go back if she wants to. So I told him we could probably do that."

"That we could do what? You mean give an opinion that she was abused?"

"Yeah, I guess."

"If we did that, we'd be putting the family in jeopardy, splitting them up, making it difficult for them to make ends meet. Do you have enough justification for that? I mean, what's the basis for your opinion that Heather was abused?"

"I'm not sure I do have enough justification. But can we just let her go back home to be abused again? I guess that's why I'm asking you about it."

" You mean you want me to help you to figure out if you have enough justification for giving an opinion like that?"

"Yeah, I guess maybe that is what I want. I guess that would help."

"Well, okay, then, who did you interview?"

"Everyone."

"Who first?"

"Mom and stepdad."

"Why them first?"

"I usually see parents first to get a background on the case."

"Individually or together?"

"Together."

"And they both denied the possibility that sexual abuse could have occurred?"

"Exactly. They totally denied it. They both said she concocted the whole story about oral sex. That she lies all the time about everything and that she's been a discipline problem lately. They claim that she's probably making this allegation because in the past month or so they've become more strict with her."

"But you think Heather is telling the truth?"

"Yes. She told me her stepfather made her give him blow-jobs. Millions of times, she said. And I believe her. She sounded real to me."

"Why?"

"She just sounded like she was telling the truth. And kids who are sexually abused don't lie about it."

"How did she sound like she was telling the truth? What was it about the way she told you that convinced you?"

"I don't know. I just knew it."

"How? What did she do to convince you? How did she act?"

"She looked me right in the eye and said it right out, I guess. Like she wanted me to believe her. The worker who was with her thinks she was telling the truth too."

"What worker?"

"From the shelter. The one whom she disclosed to in the first place."

"You mean she was in the interview with you and Heather?"

"Yeah, she . . . "

"Why did you let her sit in?"

"Heather seemed to want her there."

"How did she get so involved?"

"She said that Heather needed an advocate, for support. This worker, she said she was abused herself as a child and that kids feel most supported by people who have the same kinds of problems."

"Did she say much during the interview?"

"Well, yes, I guess she kind of encouraged Heather to tell me about the millions of blow-jobs."

"Okay, so Heather ended up saying something about millions of blow-jobs. Can you give me a sense for when this sexual abuse was supposed to have started?"

"Clark said it started three years ago."

"Clark said?"

"Yeah, Clark told me."

"But did you ask Heather?"

"No."

"Did it just suddenly start out with oral sex? Or was there a progression to oral sex? You know, mild caresses? Mutual masturbation? When did the oral sex actually begin? Was there any attempt at anything further?"

"I don't know. All I know about is the oral sex. I didn't ask about the other kinds."

"How frequently did it occur? Once a day? Once a week? Once a month? Where was the mother when it was happening?"

"I don't know any of that. I didn't ask."

"Where did it usually occur? In the car? In the house? Certain rooms in the house?"

"I guess I don't know any of that either."

"Well, then, how badly did it affect her? How severely was she traumatized? What were the specific effects on her?"

"I don't know."

"You don't know whether she was affected or not?"

"Well, uh, no, I guess not."

"Why not?"

"I didn't ask her those questions. I didn't think to do it."

"Did you ask Heather why she changed her story?"

"No. I didn't think to ask. Sorry."

"What else did you ask her about the abuse?"

"Not much. I didn't want to harass her. I just let her talk so that she could feel comfortable."

"So that's all she said about the sexual abuse? That her stepfather made her give him blow-jobs? No other details?"

"No, nothing, I guess I didn't ask."

"Why not?"

"I'm not sure. Maybe because she was uncomfortable about it. But maybe because I was uncomfortable asking. I'm not sure."

"Okay, then, at least you could probably tell me something about her adjustment."

"Her adjustment? You mean whether she's on target in her development?"

"Yeah, you know, the kinds of things you would ordinarily find out in an intake. Is her development and adjustment within the broad limits of normal? Any peculiarities in peer relationships, school achievement, behavior at school, bonding, impulse control . . . "

"No, no, I forgot to ask those questions, too. I don't know why, because I always ask those questions. I guess I must have been distracted by the issue."

"The issue of sexual abuse?"

"Right. And this is really kind of embarrassing, with all that I forgot to ask."

"I'm sorry. I'm not trying to embarrass you. I'm just trying to get a grasp on this case."

"Right, and you can't get a grasp on it because I guess I don't know much about the case at all, do I? But I can't assign it to the waiting list for counseling, can I?"

"No, you're making a good decision about that."

"At least I made one good decision."

"Right. If you put it on the waiting list, it would just sit there for a while."

"And then whoever got it would be just as confused as I am."

"That's right. It still wouldn't be clear what it is we're supposed to do."

"And it still wouldn't be clear whether Heather's telling the truth or whether she's lying?"

"Yes, and even if it is the truth, we still don't know how badly the abuse affected her, so we don't know what kind of treatment would be best for her."

"Well, one thing's clear. I won't put it on the waiting list."

"No. It needs a sexual abuse evaluation to figure out what's what."

\* \* \* \* \*

The young clinician in this case was myself, a number of years ago. My conduct in this case was typical of that of many mental health professional who do not yet possess knowledge and experience in the area of sexual abuse. I was also not yet skilled in the art of conducting a fine-tuned and economical evaluation. The questions that were put to me by my supervisor were intended to help me to learn; they were not intended to put me down or threaten my sense of professional adequacy. Unfortunately, the kinds of questions my supervisor asked, when not answered in a complete fashion, do tend to threaten one's sense of adequacy.

In my defense, and in defense of other inexperienced clinicians, I can say that I failed to ask questions which I might have ordinarily asked, such as about mental status and developmental adjustment, because I was distracted by the inflammatory nature of sexual abuse issues. I was distracted also by my misperception of an urgent need to respond to the court and to the Department of Social Services. My misperception of urgency was due to an inability to prioritize problems, that is, to differentiate between serious and moderate problems and to see each case in a wider perspective. My ability to put this case in perspective was severely limited by the limited experience I had at the time.

I was not able adequately to answer the other questions because I did not possess the expertise in the area of sexual abuse that would enable me to elicit the most relevant information in my interviews. As a result, my conduct on this case was a comedy of errors. Specifically, I failed to determine whether the court's direction to obtain mental health services was an order or merely a suggestion; that is, whether we, as well as the clients, were under a legal obligation to comply with a court order. Similarly, I failed to insist on a clarification of the purpose of the referral; that is, whether the court wanted counseling for the clients or an evaluation that would attempt to determine whether or not sexual abuse had occurred.

Examples of my ineptitude do not stop there. I should not have interviewed the parents together because doing so fosters the parents' tendency to collude in maintaining the denial of any abusive episodes. I was also much too passive in my interview of the child, asking her to say only what she was comfortable enough to say on her own. While I told my supervisor that the child was uncomfortable, it is likely that I, the clinician, was more uncomfortable than she was, and for reasons which were not at all clear to me at the time.

I took the child's statement at its face value, believing the early lore in the literature that children do not lie about sexual abuse. In believing the child, I did not give sufficient weight to the effects of family disruption should the stepfather be innocent, in order to balance those effects against the effects on the child of abuse, effects which I had failed to ascertain.

Finally, I did not inquire sufficiently into the child's possible motivations for lying. Specifically, I did not question the child further about whether she had made this allegation to protect her mother from the stepfather's physical abuse, whether she had done so in reaction to parental strictness, or whether she had other reasons. Further, I failed to inquire into reasons why she changed her story twice.

None of this can be held against me or against others who are as inexperienced as I was at that time. Most mental health professionals have not been trained to respond appropriately to the peculiar needs of sexual abuse cases. It is essential that those with a lack of expertise in a particular area recognize the limits of their expertise and seek help when they exceed those limits. Although I did exceed the limits, I recognized that in some vague way and was able, at least, to prevent counseling from getting underway. As a result, no real damage was done. I have seen many other therapists, in similar situations, who have proceeded forward to conduct their brands of therapy in the false belief that they were being helpful.

There are too many cases in which therapists who are well skilled in a particular form of therapy neglect to adequately treat the effects of sexual abuse. Sometimes, it is because they have too much respect for their own brand of therapy and not enough expertise in the area of sexual abuse. Sometimes it is because they do not inquire into the specifics of the abuse. Such inquiry may be neglected when their brand of therapy does not dictate that they look into the matter further, perhaps because they believe their focus should be more on the systemic structure of the family, or on the parents' families of origin, or on the intrapsychic tensions of the child. The training they received can result in an unproductive approach to problems of sexual abuse.

There are also therapists who neglect to ask about the specifics of the abuse because they are uncomfortable with, and sometimes even appalled by, the issue of sexual abuse. They feel especially uncomfortable asking questions which might bring them into direct contact with the intimate details of actual abuse. On the other hand, there are therapists who fearlessly plunge right into the intimacies of what happened. Lately trained in treatment methods for sexual abuse, they get right down to business and begin treatment, but often without adequately questioning whether the abuse actually occurred. This, too, can be a mistaken course of action, because without conducting an adequate evaluation it is impossible to determine whether sexual abuse is the problem to treat or whether there is a more pressing problem that deserves a higher priority.

Even when sexual abuse is the target of treatment, an evaluation is first necessary, prior to implementation of any therapeutic intervention. An evaluation is necessary to determine the extent of the abuse and the severity of its effects. These effects need to be reliably assessed in every case, not only to dictate the best type of treatment for each particular client, but also to provide guidance and consultation to the various helping agents involved, such as the courts, the Department of Social Services, the District Attorney's office, the police, and any other service providers.

In almost every case, it is crucial to have some kind of an opinion as to whether the alleged abuse occurred. Many mental health professionals shy away from this, saying that they are therapists, not investigators. They are correct about this. They are, primarily, therapists. However, to be good therapists they must, to some extent, be good detectives. Or good investigators. Or, in the parlance of our field, they must be good evaluators. That is to say, they must be capable of arriving at an understanding of what the problem is that they are attempting to treat.

Are they treating a child who has been sexually abused and suffering from its effects? Or a child who has not been abused but has made false allegations for specific reasons? The child may require some sort of treatment in either case, but the course of treatment should be drastically different in each of these cases. Treatment for pathological lying is quite different from treatment for sexual abuse.

Therefore, it is necessary for the mental health professional to make some determination about whether the abuse occurred at all and, if it did, to what extent and with what effects. To do so requires the expertise to determine whether children who make allegations of abuse are credible and whether children who make such allegations and recant them are credible in their recantations.

All of this knowledge and expertise would have been useful to me when I conducted the intake described above. And I think that much of it can be useful to many clinicians who have basic skills and good intentions, but who lack the specialized knowledge that would enable them to ask the necessary questions and make the appropriate decisions in the conduct of their evaluations.

\* \* \* \* \*

How one knows what to do in such cases is the topic of this book. My purpose is to lead the reader by the hand, step by step, through the complicated process of a sexual abuse evaluation. I will begin with very basic questions concerning who to interview first and what kinds of broad topics to address in those interviews. Matters will become more complex as we proceed to interview techniques, taking a microscopic look at the multitude of ways that the interview process can be fine-tuned or ruined by the clinician's words and behaviors. Eventually we will arrive at the most complex stage of the evaluation, the end point, where information is pulled together and evaluated to formulate conclusions and recommendations.

As we proceed from first steps to last, it will be evident at various points that evaluations of this kind are often investigative in nature, sometimes requiring skills of detection. However, it will also be evident that the quality of the evaluation process depends primarily on the best use of techniques and reasoning processes characteristic of good clinical work in general. After all, an investigation or an evaluation of a sexual abuse allegation is not only useful for providing guidance to the courts, the police, or the Department of Social Services, but also valuable to any therapist treating problems related to sexual abuse, sexual exploitation, or sexually inappropriate behavior.

A competent evaluation is crucial for any therapeutic intervention, in regard to any problem. How can one know how to go about intervening if one does not understand the problem? A thorough evaluation ensures that a complete understanding of the problem will at least be attempted and provides an optimal context and starting point for therapeutic treatment. It sets the stage for treatment, punctuating the importance of the problem, the need for therapy, and the roles and responsibilities of the various players involved.

Therefore, this book is intended to be of some help both to those who treat the problem of sexual abuse and to those who evaluate it. It may be of some interest, as well, to attorneys, judges, and child protective workers who must make decisions about how specific cases will be handled at each stage in the life of a sexual abuse problem. But most of all, I hope it will be helpful to therapists and clinicians who wish to fine-tune their interview technique, evaluation skill, and clinical judgment in regard to any kind of problem.

Unlike many other books on major topics, I will not begin with a review of the literature or a scholarly discussion of what is known in the field. My intent is more practical; it is a supervisory rather than a scholarly intent. It is an intent to teach clinical practice. I do hope the reader will acquire knowledge represented in the research and literature on sexual abuse, but it is not my exclusive intent to teach this. Some of what is known in the field will emerge gradually, as cases are presented and the reader is confronted repeatedly with the question of what to do next in each specific problem.

However, I have deliberately avoided referring to literature because I do not wish to clutter these pages with references requiring clarification of conflicting findings or controversial ideas. Clarifications of this kind are not germane to the points I want to make. Examining controversial literature can seductively lead to a multiplicity of tangents which, though worthy of careful consideration, could make for heavy reading. I fear that a complicated narrative of this kind would either bog down or waylay my efforts to lead the reader down a very particular kind of path, a path which is complicated enough as it is. Since a scholarly narrative is not my purpose, I consider it to be a "primrose path of dalliance," which I intend scrupulously to avoid in this particular piece of work.

For similar reasons, results of recent research on sexual abuse are not used to organize or guide the topics presented here. This is not intended as a sign of disrespect for research. On the contrary, I consider research to be essential to this field of knowledge, particularly in regard to certain topics emphasized in the book, such as interview technique or differentiation of true and false statements. The most promising research is now focusing on topics of this kind and is beginning to catch up with clinical practice. However, good research tends to lag behind clinical practice because it is difficult to design, time-consuming, and expensive to conduct. My goal in this book is to teach clinical practice, unhampered by the controversies of research questions, despite the fact that this practice is, at this point, much more of an art than a science.

Therefore, I have written this book in a style that permits me to provide the kind of direct, practical, and informal guidance that I would with a student to whom I was teaching the art of evaluation. As we proceed through each successive phase of the evaluation process, I will try to help clinicians to navigate their way through the confusing array of options that arise at each step.

\* \* \* \* \*

Before proceeding further, I think it would be a good idea to address the feelings of disgust that the topic of sexual abuse elicits in a great many people. It is essential to confront this issue clearly and honestly if one is serious about working with problems of sexual abuse. It is important to address it at the outset because it can color and contaminate the reader's understanding of the remainder of this book. These feelings of disgust are so strong that otherwise compassionate, liberal, and open-minded individuals can be heard denouncing sexual abuse as the ultimate expression of evil. This wish to condemn and to punish is experienced by many of us. I have heard it expressed by friends, relatives, acquaintances, administrators in public service, network anchorpersons, and even colleagues.

Those who feel this way tend to view sex offenders as monsters, ogres, or inhuman creatures. They see very little affinity or similarity between these offenders and themselves, preferring to view these offenders as aliens from another planet. They tend to liken their acts to the most heinous acts possible, such as murder and torture. But most of all, the sexual offense is incomprehensible, not accessible to ordinary understanding, inexplicable. How can a human being do such a thing to a child? And this mystery remains its most distinguishing feature. As a result, most people feel repulsed, disgusted, and alienated. They do what they can to distance themselves, as far as possible, from the offense.

I would like to make two major points about this. First, clinicians who feel this way about sexual abuse—or anything even close to this—have an increased likelihood of conducting poor evaluations, as well as poor therapy. Second, it might be useful for clinicians to explore the source of this repugnance toward sexual abuse. After all, it is a repugnance that is commonly experienced, and therefore expectable; yet, it can seriously interfere with clinical effectiveness. The remainder of this chapter is devoted to addressing this issue.

This feeling of repugnance may at times be due to a clinician's own unresolved feelings about abuse that she experienced in her childhood. This was the case with the worker I permitted to be present during my intake interview with Heather in the example which opened this chapter. Having gained better judgment about this issue since that interview, I do not appreciate the presence of such persons during my sexual abuse evaluations.

Since that time, a number of colleagues have asked to be present during my evaluations, and I have been selective about whom I will and will not allow. When the request is made with an attitude reflecting the wish to learn more, and there seems to be no hidden agenda, I usually agree. However, I deny the request when I observe an avid, eager interest which suggests an agenda other than solving the problem at hand. Consider the following illustration.

"Aaron, maybe it would be a good idea if I sat in on this one with you. She's a therapy case of mine and she'd be more comfortable, since she knows me already."

The request in itself seemed entirely reasonable, but her nostrils were flaring and her eyes were bugging out of her head. My impression was that she wanted in on this because she had a bone to pick. She especially wanted to be present for the interview with the alleged offender, whom she had not met. However, I definitely did not want her to be present, fearing that her presence would compromise my effectiveness in the interviews. I was convinced that, even if she were to remain silent during the interview, her feelings would have been loud and clear, since something out of the ordinary was already being conveyed to me.

I found out later, from her, that she had indeed been sexually abused herself as a child and that she was enraged at her client's father. If I had allowed her to be present during the interview, her nonverbal communications would have put off the offender, and I would never have been able to get all the details of the offense that I was actually able to obtain. He would not have felt understood and would have held back. She would have let him know, even if only by her body language, that she found him repugnant.

If she were interviewing the child, she might have been too eager to believe the child's story and not as likely to remember to test the child's memory, to uncover evidence of post-traumatic stress disorder, to determine whether there existed a coherence of details about the event, to inquire into possible motivations for lying, and to push the child to disclose details of the event. This example illustrates the handicapping effects of unresolved issues in an evaluator who has been sexually abused herself. Yet, many others, who have not been abused, also harbor a secret and unresolved repugnance for sexual abuse.

Mental health professionals who feel this repugnance are often responsible for conducting therapy in the area of sexual abuse, and sometimes tend to do so in a vague, ambiguous, and circuitous manner. Although the presenting problem is sexual abuse, they often talk about everything but sexual abuse. When I have had occasion to evaluate their clients, I usually elicit a great many intimate details about the abuse, with the effect that the victim feels both a great deal of pain and tremendous relief. That is, the session is usually not only informative for the purposes of investigation but also therapeutic.

At those times, I usually ask the child whether she has been talking to her therapist about these matters. If she says no, I encourage her to do so. I have been surprised to find that many of these children have not been talking about the sexual abuse, except in a vague, cursory, offhand fashion. When I encourage them to bring it up and to talk about it as they did with me, they tell me they would be uncomfortable doing so with their therapist because the therapist doesn't seem to want to discuss it. Since this could be only a child's distorted rendition of events, I have sometimes checked with the therapists, only to find that "there are so many other problems which are more pressing, it's hard to get the time to focus on the abuse" or "it's too painful for her to confront it head on, so I'm moving slowly, waiting until she's ready to talk about it."

I think that the child is sometimes more ready to talk about the abuse than the therapist. When other problems are more pressing or more important than the problem of sexual abuse, then certainly the therapist needs to focus on those first. However, when they are not more important, but simply more current, then those other problems may constitute a convenient excuse for the therapist to avoid confronting the pain of sexual abuse. Perhaps when we can understand this pain and understand our repugnance, we will be free to listen to the child tell her story and help her to go over the details of what happened to her as much and as often as she needs to.

Not only can this feeling of repugnance interfere with our work with children, but it can be disastrous to our effectiveness in interviewing offenders. It is with the offender that repugnance is most keenly felt. It is ironic that such feelings, which are impossible to fully disguise, will render inaccessible the very information the evaluator or therapist is after: the offender's most intimate thoughts, feelings, and memories about the sexual abuse. Only when one is empathic with the offender's point of view will these kinds of details be disclosed. By empathic, I do not mean approving. One can disapprove of the sexual offense while at the same time understanding and empathizing with the offender's experiencing of the event, seeing how one might, under certain conditions, do the same.

What stops us from experiencing this empathy? And what causes us to experience a feeling of repugnance instead? The source of this problem may be our failure to understand and fully accept our own capacities and talents for hurting others, as well as our desire to be better than we really are. We like to think of ourselves as kind and generous and incapable of hurtful deeds.

Yet, history and experimental research have repeatedly shown that, under given circumstances, most of us will engage in shameful and hurtful actions, of which we would never have believed ourselves capable. The Sondercommandos, Jews themselves, buried Jewish bodies, dug out gold teeth, and committed other acts they surely never imagined they would commit. In experiments, most students administered electric shock, at dangerous levels, to a man they believed to have a heart condition when circumstances were deliberately manipulated to achieve this result; yet most of them, when asked if they would do such a thing, believed themselves incapable of it.

Aren't many other acts possible as well? Ask a war veteran about this. He might feel comfortable enough to tell you about his actions if he is not too fearful of your condemnation or repugnance for him. The kind of empathy I am talking about is possible only when one can truly understand the reasons and circumstances that can account for one human being's hurting another, and when one understands that many of us—our friends, neighbors, and relatives—might, under the right circumstances, be capable of the most heinous deeds imaginable.

It could be that many of us are capable of sexual abuse under the right circumstances. What might these circumstances be? Imagine a close friend and neighbor, alone with his 14-year-old stepdaughter, a young woman who flirts with him and who he mistakenly believes wants his caress as much as he wants hers.

She enjoys the feeling that she is the only one who understands him, and therefore has spent a lot of time listening to his problems about work and about his unhappy marriage to her mother. Her desire for his company has always made him feel special, a feeling he can no longer obtain from a wife who has little interest in him. Sexually interacting with his stepdaughter may be his easiest path to feeling affirmed, and at the same time an easy way to get even with his wife. He doesn't possess the esteem or the skills that would tend to lead him to explore other options for meeting these needs. In addition to these circumstances, his use of alcohol impairs his clarity of thought and reduces his ability to inhibit his impulses.

If he were to sexually molest his stepdaughter, I do not think that this act of abuse would be inexplicable, given the various circumstances. On the contrary, it would be quite understandable. It is possible to empathize with him and to understand from his point of view how this could happen — how it could happen to our neighbor, our relative, our friend, and maybe even to ourselves.

To experience true empathy for the man who commits an act of this kind is not the same as approving or excusing the act. One can strongly disapprove, yet at the same time experience full empathy. While empathy and understanding don't mitigate or soften our stance of disapproval, they can prevent the development of feelings of repugnance when such feelings are born of a need to distance from the act.

Repugnance and disgust are engendered in our flight from the possibility that our friends might also commit such acts. These feelings of disgust are feelings which comfort us because they blind us from seeing that we may ourselves harbor secret or unconscious fears of committing such acts. Repugnance helps to cement in our minds the belief that sex offenders are inhuman aliens who are unlike ourselves.

The inability or unwillingness to accept this side of human nature leaves part of ourselves inaccessible, unavailable for use in understanding ourselves and our clients. It renders us vulnerable, at inopportune moments, to unexpected feelings of repugnance, which can seriously interfere with our capacity to seek the kind of information we need to fully understand a problem.

\* \* \* \* \*

"This is depressing stuff. I thought you said this book wasn't depressing."

"What's so depressing?"

"That we have such a capacity for evil."

"The point I was making is that there's an incredible range in human capacity, for all degrees of helping and hurting."

"But all you've been emphasizing is the hurting. Our capability and talent for it."

"It's necessary to punctuate these capacities so that as clinicians we can recognize them in ourselves."

"But do you have to rub our noses in this dark side of our nature?"

"To do so can bring the dark side into the light so that it doesn't interfere with your attempts to help."

"Okay, I get the point. But isn't it a little one-sided?"

"How do you mean?"

"If our capacity for hurting is so immense, what about our capacity for helping? Isn't that just as immense?"

"That's what the rest of the book is about—ideas that are intended to enhance those capacities for helping."

# CHAPTER 2

# *Who to Interview First*

"But Earnie couldn't have done it," said Mrs. Paulson. "He's hardly ever alone with the kids. Isn't that right, Earnie?"

"Right," said Mr. Paulson. "I'm hardly ever alone with them."

"Are you aware of exactly what it is that your son said you did?"

"That Earnie was teaching him to masturbate in the bathtub," said Mrs. Paulson. "But Earnie couldn't have done it. He never gives the kids baths. He never even . . . "

"Mr. Paulson, did you ever give your son a bath?"

"Never," said Mrs. Paulson. "He never did. Not that I can remember. Did you ever, Earnie?"

"I can't remember. But I never touched my son. I'll tell you that. I don't know how anybody could think I would be such an animal."

"Were you ever accused of anything like this before?"

"Do we look like the kind of people that would molest children?" asked Mrs. Paulson.

"Do you realize how insulting all this is?" asked Mr. Paulson. "I don't even believe my son said those things."

"That's right," said Mrs. Paulson. "I told Earnie before that it must have been that social worker putting ideas in little Earnie's head and making him say yes and no to a lot of lies. I'd have to hear a tape recording of little Earnie to believe it."

* * * * *

"When did you do this interview? Is this the case that you asked for help with in the beginning? For determining whether the abuse occurred or didn't occur?"

"No, this was an interview I just taped today. And I'm not sure what I did wrong with it. Why did I have so much trouble?"

"I don't think you proceeded as effectively as you could have."

"I know that. But why not?"

"I think there were a couple of things that might have blocked you."

"What things?"

"Well, I think it was probably difficult for you to imagine these nice people, who are so similar to yourself in appearance and lifestyle, as capable of being guilty of the offense. They were indignant at being accused, and maybe you were a little bit indignant for them."

"But if they were innocent, they certainly have a right to feel indignant."

"Yes, they certainly do. And because their indignance seems so extremely reasonable to you, it interferes with good judgment and effective questioning."

"How was my judgment poor? And what was wrong with my questioning?"

"Well, you were awfully easy on them, and I think it was probably because they're so similar to yourself, and because you've been conditioned all your life to be so exceptionally courteous."

"But I interrupted them. Didn't you hear that?"

"Yes, but not enough. You let them run the interview because you were afraid of hurting their feelings. Can you own that?"

"Own what?"

"The feeling of having your hands tied because you didn't want to hurt their feelings."

"Well, yeah, now that I think about it, I guess you nailed me there. That's exactly how I felt. But what about the poor judgment?"

"You chose to interview them together. And you did so before you interviewed the child. I'm not sure why. Maybe it wasn't poor judgment, just inexperience. Or maybe it's due to your family therapy training. I don't know."

"Well, yeah, I was taught to interview spouses together the first time I see a case, and always before the child, in order to accord them their due respect as parents."

"Accord them their due respect as parents? I guess you can certainly do so, but possibly to the detriment of the child whose statement about an abusive parent may deserve the same respect that you ordinarily reserve for the parents."

"But if your primary alliance is with the child first, you might alienate the parents and they might not bring the child back for another meeting."

"Yes, that's important, if you're only dealing with a parent as the complainant. But if the court or D.S.S. is involved and asking for this to be done, then you don't have to worry about it as much. Your ultimate goals aren't as dependent on that alliance with the parent."

"So I should have interviewed the child first?"

"I'm not saying that exactly. There are no hard and fast rules here."

"But I don't want to show disrespect for the child either. Which do I do? See the child first? Or the parents?"

"You decide. There are disadvantages and advantages to each option."

"Well, what are the advantages and disadvantages?"

"It's best to see the child first when the child is the complainant, when she is really upset about the abuse and complaining about it. But the advantage to seeing a parent first is that you can form the alliance you were talking about. Also, a parent can give you background and history about a child's functioning and early development that the child herself can't provide very reliably."

"So who should I have interviewed first?"

"I'm not sure. That depends on what it was you were supposed to find out. What was it?"

"Well, I wasn't sure, at first. I thought I was supposed to figure out if abuse occurred, but as it turned out, Mr. Paulson had already admitted to the allegations in private to the D.S.S. worker. All the D.S.S. worker wanted to know was whether the child would benefit from counseling."

"When did you find this out?"

"When I interviewed the D.S.S. worker."

"You mean you interviewed him after all the other interviews?"

"Yeah, I guess I kind of wasted a lot of interview time, didn't I? This is embarrassing. It's so obvious now. I should have interviewed him first."

"So you've answered your own question about whom to interview first."

"But I still don't understand what was so bad about interviewing the parents together."

"Because when they're together, their denial of abuse tends to be more rigid."

"I guess I noticed that a bit. Each of the Paulsons seemed to reinforce the other's denial."

"And tended to inhibit one another from saying to you what they probably would say if you saw them each alone."

"I guess I should have seen them alone if I wanted to find out what was really going on."

"By seeing them together you practically guaranteed that you'd get a very unreal picture of events. Tell me what happened later when you interviewed them separately. What did you find out?"

"Well, okay, I guess your point is well taken. Mr. Paulson shared a lot more information, like about some of the allegations. He even admitted to some of them. And here I'd thought it was because I did a better interview, and that was the reason he finally opened up."

"You might actually have done a better interview, but ask yourself this question. Would he have even remotely considered disclosing these kinds of things in the presence of his wife?"

"No, I guess not, now that I really think about it. He really did open up, you know, about early sexual experiences with goats and ducks on the farm he grew up on."

"He had intercourse with the animals?"

"Right. I don't even want to mention what he used to do with those poor ducks and goats."

"I can imagine, but my guess is that he would have had a bit of difficulty mentioning it at all in the presence of his wife."

"Yes, he asked me not to tell her about it. He said it might offend her sensibilities."

"He used those words? 'Offend her sensibilities?'"

"Well, maybe not those exact words."

"Sounds like maybe it was your own sensibilities that were offended."

"I guess so. But I see your point about seeing them separately instead of together. I guess I did use poor judgment in that first interview. But how would I know in advance that this was poor judgment? I mean, I was taught to do it one way, and now you're teaching me another way. Is this an arbitrary decision? Do some clinicians do it one way and others do it the other way? Do you always interview people alone?"

"No, not at all. When people are in open disagreement, it's often more useful to see them together."

"Can you give me an example?"

"Sure. Like a rebellious adolescent and a parent."

"When people disagree?"

"Yes, when they disagree openly, overtly. Like two spouses in a custody dispute."

"What about an abusing parent in open conflict with a nonabusing parent? When the nonabusing parent isn't scared and is loud and clear in her complaints about him."

"Yes, that's possible, too. In any of these examples the disagreement is obvious. It's overt. The disagreements between the two people help you to examine what might be the reality in the exaggerated perspectives they each give."

"Exaggerated perspective? You mean each person is lying?"

"Not necessarily lying, but seeing things from his or her own perspective, which is necessarily distorted, and distorting it perhaps further by trying to vindicate his or her own position."

"Trying to snow you, you mean."

"Trying to stay out of trouble maybe, trying to show themselves at their best and to be viewed as acceptable people, which is only natural, it's only to be expected. But seeing them together enables the distortions of each of them to occur in the same room right in front of you, and that way it provides some checks and balances that prevent you from being taken in by one of them."

"From becoming triangulated and sucked in?"

"Exactly. And getting them to angrily challenge each other's exaggerations is the quickest way to obtain successive approximations to reality. Unless, of course, they're so angry and so far apart that neither of them can back down from an exaggerated accusation. Then all you have is a lousy interview with a lot of fighting."

"Wait, I'm getting confused here. You said first that it's better to put two people together if they're fighting, but then in the next breath you say it's not better."

"It's a question of how severe the disagreement is. If it's severe, it will only waste your time and be hurtful to them to sling mud at one another. It's better to see them alone."

"But what about the Paulsons? They weren't in extreme disagreement."

"No, not at all. There was probably covert conflict, as there is in almost any relationship, but overtly there was no conflict at all. And when you see people like that together, the lack of conflict becomes exaggerated. So you split them up and maximize the chances that what was covert will then become more overt in your individual interview."

"You divide and conquer."

"Exactly, when the conflict is not overt and there is a threat to the spousal system, as in a majority of cases of abuse or neglect."

"And you throw them together when the conflict is overt."

"Yes, but when it is so extreme that it appears that they are living on different planets instead of in the same house . . . "

"Then you see them separately, Okay, I think I've got all that. But I'm still confused about something. Who should I have interviewed first?"

"Like I said before, there are no hard and fast rules, but interviewing people in random or arbitrary sequences can waste time and cause problems, as you've seen for yourself in your interview."

"So how do you figure out who to see first?"

"By trying to follow some principles."

"Like what?"

"Well, like one we've already discussed."

"You mean don't interview an offender in the company of the spouse."

"Right."

"Okay, what other principles?"

"I alluded to another principle earlier when you asked if you should have interviewed the child first."

"And you didn't give me an answer, just a lot of double-talk."

"It's not exactly double-talk to say that there are advantages and disadvantages to each option. I said that you could interview the child first if she was the complainant. Generally, in any kind of case, it's always a pretty safe course to interview the complainant first."

"You mean the person who makes the complaint?"

"Exactly. And who was that in your case?"

"I'm not sure. The child?"

"Wasn't the D.S.S. worker the one who made the complaint? The one who wanted help? Help in figuring out if the child could benefit from counseling? Did any of the family members want your help?"

"No, none of them wanted to be there, not even the child. But isn't the patient the one you're supposed to see first? Isn't the patient the complainant? Does that mean the D.S.S. worker is my patient?"

"Yes, in a sense. The complainant is the person who makes the complaint. Ideally, that person is the one you see in one session after another, who you think of as your patient. However, in many instances, the complainant is not the patient."

"You mean like when a parent calls to ask for help for her teenage son?"

"Exactly. The parent is the complainant and the son is the patient, and it is quite possible that this patient wants no help at all because he is not the one complaining about a problem. To interview the son first would be a mistake for a number of reasons."

"He probably wouldn't tell you what the problem was because according to him there is no problem."

"That's right, so right off the bat you wouldn't have any sense of direction. On top of that, you couldn't really establish a therapeutic relationship or a mutual understanding about what kind of service to provide if the person is not asking for help of any kind."

"And this is the same thing that happens when a D.S.S. worker is the one who calls?"

"Yes, the D.S.S. worker is the complainant."

"Or the probation officer, if that's who's making the referral?"

"Exactly."

"Or the school guidance counselor or the judge?"

"Right. Those people are complaining about the problem, not the child or the parents, so your only real therapeutic relationship is with the complainants, not the child or parents."

"But what if the child wants help with a problem too?"

"Then the child is a complainant."

"And if the parents themselves are very concerned about the sex abuse and want help?"

"Then they're complainants too."

"Well, then, if everybody is a complainant, who would you interview first?"

"It's kind of a toss-up in that kind of situation, but probably the D.S.S. worker."

"Why?"

"Because that would enable you to get a general overview and give you some ideas about how to proceed next. The D.S.S. worker is in the best position to describe the background of the case, the status of the investigation or court process, what needs to be known at this point, what the positions or opinions are of the various professionals involved, and the possible directions the case might take."

"But what if the parents call on their own for either counseling or an evaluation, maybe because they asked a D.S.S. worker how to find help and the worker gave them your number? Wouldn't it be appropriate to interview the parents first, since they are the complainants?"

"Yes, of course. But if they call only because someone else tells them they have to, then talk to that someone else if you can. It can sometimes be a mistake to allow the complainant to elude the responsibility for making the complaint. As a result of this mistake, misunderstandings occur with regard to what's being evaluated. Look what happened to you with the Paulsons because you didn't talk to the complainant first."

"Okay, don't rub it in. So I wasted a little bit of precious time."

"Yes, in making your own determination of abuse, when in fact abuse had already been established. All they wanted were treatment recommendations."

"I know that. You don't have to keep saying it."

"And were you in a position to even make recommendations about treatment in the time you had left? Did you even answer the question that gave rise to the referral to you?"

"Well, no, not really, now that you mention it. I hadn't spent enough time with the child. But that was because I didn't know what was . . . well, I guess that's your point, isn't it? Unless I'm clear about why the complainant wants them to be seen, I might go off on a wild goose chase and not even address that reason."

"On the other hand, some referring sources, such as judges, are quite clear about their own inability or unwillingness to formulate the appropriate questions to ask and would prefer that the evaluator do this job for them."

"This is exactly what you just said you shouldn't permit."

"I know. And I've tried to pin judges and attorneys and D.S.S. workers down. But sometimes you just can't because they really feel that you have the greater expertise to think up the question that they want asked."

"But they're the complainants! Can't you just insist on a clear complaint? And not do anything until you get one?"

"You can, but sometimes it's a question of diplomacy and of how much outside of your own domain you're willing to go to oblige the complainant."

"By doing their job? By formulating the question that they're supposed to ask you?"

"Yes. If the evaluator insists on a question, and the judge or attorney can't come up with one, then the evaluator's position will be regarded as oppositional and nothing fruitful will be accomplished. On the other hand, an understanding can be established between the judge and the evaluator that the evaluator will accept the task of defining the question to be addressed when guidance is not provided."

"Hold on. This is getting really confusing. You're saying that you should go ahead and try to get the complainant to give a reason for the evaluation, but you're also saying that some complainants definitely don't want to provide this but want an evaluation anyway and want you to figure out the complaint."

"Yes. I think you've got it. It *is* confusing."

"Okay, then. I'm to assume that this arrangement works out okay, without the complainant making a complaint?"

"Often it does, but sometimes it's a real joke."

"A joke?"

"A total waste of time. For example, clients sometimes arrive for an evaluation appointment with previous instructions to say nothing about the alleged abuse."

"That sounds like a real bad joke, on you."

"It is. Picture this. I'm all set to begin, I've introduced myself, I've tried to make this client comfortable and explained the purposes of the evaluation and the lack of confidentiality, and I've even started to ask some questions about the client's history. Then, as soon as I get to any question about the abuse, the client suddenly says, 'Sorry, I can't talk about that. My attorney told me not to talk about the case.'"

"What do they think they're there for, then?"

"That's what I ask them."

"And what do they say?"

"They say they're there for an evaluation. And I say, yes, that's right and the evaluation is about the alleged abuse, and they say, "Sorry, I'm not supposed to talk about that." And sometimes it's even worse—they won't answer any questions at all because their attorney told them to say nothing."

"Makes you wonder why they even bothered to come at all."

"Exactly."

"So what do you do?"

"Usually, I send them home at that point, and tell the court that the court-ordered evaluation was an exercise in wasting time because the client complied with the order by showing up but refused to say anything. Refusing to talk in such an interview is certainly within the client's rights, but this refusal is the kind of thing that should have first been ascertained and addressed in court."

"But wait a second. Can't a person refuse to talk about a crime and still be evaluated, for example, an evaluation of his competency to stand trial, or an evaluation of mental status, or psychological testing?"

"Sure, and if that's what's desired, then we could do the testing and report the results and the client could remain silent about the alleged offense. But in my experience that is not what is usually wanted."

"What do they want, then?"

"They usually want to know whether some indications exist to suggest that the abuse occurred, what the risk is for further abuse, and what can be done to reduce the risk."

"Like what kind of treatment to provide? Or whether the offender should be removed from the home?"

"Yes, that's what they want to know. They need to make practical decisions and that's what they want help with. But, you know, we've kind of strayed from the point here, from the question you asked earlier about who to interview first."

"But I think the tangent is useful. It helps me to see all the complications that can come up when it's not really clear what the court wants from an evaluation. And the kinds of problems I need to anticipate when the complainant isn't there for the first interview."

"But is your question answered? About who to interview first? How to sequence your interviews?"

"Sort of. Like you said, there are no hard and fast rules. I suppose sometimes I could interview the clients without interviewing the complainant, like a judge. And sometimes I might choose to interview a parent before a D.S.S. investigator. And sometimes the child before the parent. But mostly I'd probably interview the D.S.S. worker first, then one of the parents, then the other one, and then the child."

"Sounds about right to me. But sometimes you might want to interview the child before the alleged offender."

"Why?"

"Because you can then confront the alleged offender with what you've learned from the child. Or with your opinion about what happened."

"Can't you just do another interview with the offender?"

"Sure, if you have the time."

"There's only one question I have left."

"What's that?"

"What is it I'm supposed to cover in each of these interviews? What is it I'm supposed to say?"

"Good question. That's what I wanted to get to next. Let me start out by showing you an excerpt from a dialogue between myself and a D.S.S. worker."

## INTERVIEWING THE INVESTIGATOR

"Okay, I think I've got all their names and ages now," I say to the investigator. "But why did you bring them in for an evaluation? What is it you would like me to address? How can I help?"

The worker answers, "Well, to be honest, I'm not exactly sure. The perpetrator admitted to it, but all he said was that he touched Cheryl, his stepdaughter, just one time, some time before Christmas, but he wasn't exactly sure when it happened. That's about all we know. There are some other details but not much of any substance."

"Have you talked to him about it? What did he tell you?"

"No, I got all that from the statement he gave the police when they arrested him."

"What are you doing on the case? What's going on at this point?"

"His lawyer didn't want me to talk to him. He's going to court on May 29. He won't talk to anyone now."

"So all you did was talk to the daughter?"

"Right. And to the mother. And to the police. I think he's trying to cop a plea to a lesser charge. I doubt he'll say anything to you either."

"What court is this appearing in? County Court? Family Court? A town justice? What?"

"The town justice, I think. But I'm not really sure."

"Not sure? Why not?"

"I can't remember."

"Okay, so what is it you're doing with the case? What do you want me to look at?"

"Well, he hasn't been allowed to go back into the house. We told him that he would have to leave voluntarily or we'd have to remove Cheryl. He left and so far he's staying out of the house, even though his lawyer told him it would be better for him to go back to the house and let us take Cheryl. That's basically where things stand. We've got him out of the house."

"How do you know that his attorney gave him this advice? You said you didn't talk to him. Did you talk to his attorney?"

"No, his wife told me."

"They're in contact with each other?"

"Every night. On the phone."

"Right, okay, so what is it you want from me? How can I help?"

"I guess we want to know if Cheryl needs some follow-up counseling and we want him to get some counseling too."

"So, are you saying that you want to return this man to the home? Is that what you're saying?"

"Yeah, if you think it's okay, if it's appropriate. That's basically what we want from you."

"To determine if it's appropriate? And to determine if Cheryl needs counseling?"

"Right."

\* \* \* \* \*

In the attempt to provide orientation and direction for an evaluation, this was neither the most ideal nor the worst presentation by a D.S.S. worker. In my experience, it is about par for the course. Ideally, the D.S.S. worker should be able to provide the reason for the referral and some background on the case. Relevant background includes ages and occupations of family members, the allegations, how the disclosure was made and to whom, the legal status of the case, and how the child has been faring since the disclosure. This is sometimes accomplished quite well by the D.S.S. investigator; sometimes it is not, as I will describe presently.

However, before proceeding, I would like to point out that any descriptions here of incompetence are not intended to single out D.S.S. workers in general as less professional or less competent than mental health workers; after all, the pages of this book are replete with illustrations of incompetence by mental health workers as well. It is necessary, though, to illustrate for mental health workers who are new to these kinds of evaluations the kinds of frustrations they are likely to face in the real world and to provide guidance in handling these frustrations. In doing so, I want to emphasize that many D.S.S. workers very often have their facts straight and their presentations coherent. In fact, their knowledge of the case may be so comprehensive that it is hard to see how you can be helpful.

On the other hand, due to an overwhelming workload or lack of training, they may not have the file on hand and as a consequence can't even provide correct ages of family members, occupations, and so on. Sometimes, even with the files, they may contradict themselves and not get their facts straight. Their description of a case may be based on a combination of direct observation and second- and third-hand information, so that it is necessary to ascertain carefully and painstakingly how each piece of data was obtained. Occasionally they have no idea at all what they want from the evaluation, as is illustrated below.

\* \* \* \* \*

"But what is the purpose of this evaluation. What is it I can do to be helpful? What is it you need to know?"

"I don't know."

"Then why did you bring these people here today?"

"My supervisor told me to."

\* \* \* \* \*

These kinds of situations can be frustrating, especially for mental health professionals who are new to the craft of evaluation and not yet accustomed to the slipshod and clumsy level of practice in the fields of human services and juvenile justice. It can be tempting to send an investigator back to do his homework and to get his act together. However, in the end it is more diplomatic, and more cost-effective, to do the best one can with what is offered. While it is useful to take measures to improve the kinds of information presented by these referring sources, to insist upon an adequate presentation is not likely to be perceived as helpful, and it certainly will not be helpful to the child who is a victim in one of these cases.

Even after speaking to supervisors about the importance of adequate referral information and instituting a referral form that asks in advance for such information in written form, one will still face frustrations. Investigators will still be unsure why they are there asking for an evaluation. They will still sometimes contradict themselves and fail to get their facts straight. And they will still sometimes fail to ask rudimentary questions that you think anyone would have thought to ask. It is better to get used to this kind of frustration and expect it, rather than to insist, idealistically, that it should not happen.

Another frequent reason for wanting to turn investigators away is that the reason for an evaluation appears on the surface to be inappropriate or trivial. The evaluator may feel misused because the evaluation appears to constitute a waste of time and expertise. As alluded to earlier, investigators may appear to have enough data, so that it is unlikely that you will add any more. Or it may seem that they just want your rubber stamp of approval. Or they may present you with a situation where it is highly unlikely that you will be able to add to the pool of useful data, such as asking you to evaluate a two-year-old child who is not capable of conveying a reliable message either in play or in words.

While you may not view your participation in such cases as useful, it may be viewed as essential by D.S.S. or by the court. Sometimes you will get more information than they can. Even when that's unlikely, they view this as one last chance to get that additional information. They reason that, if you can't get it, then it can't be had, and this provides a kind of closure to the case.

When your stamp of approval is desired, you may feel misused and prostituted. However, keep in mind that your credentials are greatly appreciated and can help, at times, to assure protection and treatment for a child who might not obtain these benefits without your participation. Finally, there are those times—a great many of them—when you are unable to add any data to what the investigators have already gathered. Yet, by virtue of your expertise and training, you can, after interviewing the parties concerned, add insight and a fresh, crisp perspective, which may give direction to the management of the case.

## INTERVIEWING THE PARENT AND THE OFFENDER

Since the emphasis in this book is on working with the child, the present section on interviewing the adults will be somewhat brief, without a great deal of illustration.

After interviewing the D.S.S. investigator, you might next interview one of the parents. The topics to be included in the interview with an adult will depend to some extent on who that adult is, whether nonoffending parent, offending parent, or nonfamilial offender. With parents of the child, it is useful to gather some information on the child that one would ordinarily obtain in assessing any child, such as a developmental history and a description of the child's current functioning.

With a nonoffending parent, it is essential to ascertain the degree to which that parent is able to support the child despite the possibility that the parent feels caught in a loyalty conflict between believing the child and believing the denial of the alleged offender. It is also important to explore possible hidden agendas, which may be motivating false allegations of sexual abuse. For example, a mother could be encouraging false allegations because this is her only solution for getting out of a physically abusive relationship with her husband. Or a custodial parent might be involved in a hotly contested visitation dispute and be using the allegation as a way to terminate visitation between the child and the alleged offender.

In interviewing any of the adults, one must ask questions with the intent of determining whether the abuse constituted a fixated offense or a regressed one—that is, whether the offender is fixated at an early stage of sexual development or whether he regressed to an earlier stage due to a constellation of stresses common to incest.

For example, in a stereotypical father-daughter incest scenario, a number of features may be present which are characteristic of regressed offenses. A dominant-dependent relationship between the spouses may have developed, about which both of the spouses eventually harbor a great deal of resentment and anger. Their inappropriate handling of this anger may eventually lead to the father displacing his anger toward his wife onto his daughter, who comes to represent the wife, especially if the daughter has been parentified and the mother has abdicated some of her traditional responsibilities to her. This child may also provide the only emotional affirmation to the father that he ever gets, since he may no longer receive this from his wife and may lack the self-esteem to seek sources of emotional and sexual gratification from outside of the family. The choice of his daughter as a sexual object can be understood as a stress-related regression from a relatively normal sexual development.

On the other hand, fixated offenders are those commonly thought of as pedophiles or child molesters. They often have immature sexual interests, histories of offenses with unrelated children, and may not be capable of establishing healthy and intimate sexual relationships with adults. Differentiating between fixated and regressed offenses is not always easy because an offense or an offender may not always be on one or the other end of the continuum, but somewhere in the middle.

In many offenses, whether they are fixated or regressed, there may be certain characteristics that commonly occur, such as low self-esteem, problems with impulse control, a tendency to displace anger, and an entangling of various needs. For example, the needs for sexual release, emotional affirmation, feeling effective and esteemed, and discharging anger or exacting revenge can all become entangled in the one economical act of sexual abuse rather than in separate and, therefore more costly, acts, projects, and relationships.

In order to gather enough information to determine this kind of knowledge, it is often useful to include in these interviews the kinds of interview formats that are common in many other kinds of assessments. That is, the evaluator should be prepared, if need be, to conduct a mental status exam, obtain a sexual and marital history, examine family roles, dynamics, and structure, and explore the client's history of alcohol and drug use.

At a later point in the interview with an alleged offender it is necessary to ask for an explanation of the allegations. When a person has admitted to the allegations, it is often useful to inquire into the intimate thoughts and feelings associated with the sexual acts. Doing so can help to determine whether those acts were planned or were due to an uncontrollable urge, whether the urge had ever been inhibited and, if so, by what thoughts or fears, and whether ideas were associated with the act that would help to account for and understand it.

In many cases, the alleged offender may adamantly deny the allegations. Sometimes the denial makes sense in view of many other characteristics of the case that are inconsistent with abuse or, for example, when a parent can otherwise account for an allegation in a manner that explains how it has been misconstrued as sexual abuse. However, when a child's statement or symptoms are convincing, and a parent adamantly denies the allegation and can give no adequate accounting for it, a dilemma exists for those who must make some decision about the case, such as the judge, the D.S.S. worker, the Law Guardian, and the evaluator.

On the one hand, the court can try to go along with the evidence provided by the child, even if it is flimsy evidence, and assume that the alleged offender is guilty without having adequately proven guilt. On the other hand, the court can assume innocence because guilt has not been adequately proven and thereby put the child at continued risk. This is often a difficult dilemma to resolve because no one wishes to interfere with an innocent parent's relationship with his child, and yet no one feels comfortable enough with the existing facts and suspicions to be confident that the child will be safe. An example may help to illustrate this dilemma.

A three-year-old boy whose penis was physically injured was unable to explain, due to his limited language capacities, exactly how the injury occurred, except to vaguely implicate his uncle, with whom he spent every weekend and with whom he enjoyed a rich and meaningful relationship. The medical opinion was that the foreskin of the uncircumcised penis was forcibly drawn back, causing excessive bleeding. While this could be caused by abuse, this kind of injury to an uncircumcised penis can also occur in innocent ways. The boy's uncle could have easily accounted for the injury, as well as the child's vague statements, by explaining that the injury occurred while he was washing the child's genitals in the bath.

However, when this possibility was posed to the uncle, he adamantly denied it. He even went so far as to say that he made it a practice to "never ever touch" the child's genitals, for fear of being accused of abuse, and instead always left the child's genitals unwashed. This situation left the court in the typical dilemma articulated above. As a result, litigation was prolonged for over a year, during which time the court permitted only minimal and supervised contact between uncle and nephew. This drastically altered the relationship between the child and his uncle and placed an excessive burden on the child's mother, a weekend waitress, who now had to find more costly alternatives for child care.

When this kind of dilemma can be anticipated during the interview, it can be useful to punctuate it for the alleged offender as a part of the interview process. This articulation of the dilemma is illustrated in the case of Jean, a three-year-old, who was suspected of being abused because she was masturbating daily and imitating sexual intercourse with playmates and with dolls. Her father suspected that she had been sexually abused while in the custody of her mother and the mother's boyfriend, so he withheld the child instead of returning her after his weekend visit. He obtained a temporary order of custody from a judge, who ordered that a mental health evaluation be conducted in the hope of shedding some light on the case.

After interviewing everyone of relevance, I was still unsure of what had actually happened. The only thing that remained clear to me was that the child was sexually preoccupied to a degree that fell outside of normal limits. However, this preoccupation could have been due to sexual play with other children, exposure to pornography, observation of adults engaged in sexual intercourse, or other sexually stimulating material, as well as being due to sexual abuse.

At the end of the interview, when the mother asked what my conclusions were, I told her I was unsure. When she asked what was likely to happen, I again told her the same, that I was unsure. When she asked why I was unsure, I explained the dilemma articulated above. I did so in order to be sure that she understood the realities of the situation and to give her an opportunity to decide to change her story in view of those realities. By threatening her with something that does not yet exist, the possibility exists that the person might be coerced into lying. This can be viewed as being similar to pushing someone to cop a plea to a lesser charge, although he never committed a crime in the first place. However, the dilemma articulated above is usually not clear to someone who may have committed a questionable act but who thinks that to deny it is her best course of action. When she can understand the dilemma and the realities it represents, she often sees other courses of action as being more desirable. A transcript of my discussion with the mother in the preceding case is presented below.

\* \* \* \* \*

"If you're not sure of what happened," asked Jean's mother, "then doesn't that mean that I'll get her back?"

"Maybe you will," I said. "I'll tell the judge I'm not sure, but then he's still stuck with the fact that Jean seems to have sex on her mind, and nobody knows why. Do you think the judge will think it's safe to give Jean back to you when he can't figure out what's causing her to have sex on her mind?"

"But I didn't abuse her. And neither did Ralph. My ex-husband just hates me and wants custody. He's jealous of Ralph and just wants to get even with me any way that he can."

"That might be so."

"Can't you just tell the judge that?"

"All I can say is that you told me and that it's a possibility, but I also believe that Jean was exposed to something that is causing her to have sex on her mind, and I don't know what that something is."

"So what will happen?"

"I don't know. That's really up to the judge. And I'm in the same dilemma as the judge is."

"What do you mean? I don't get it."

"I'm stuck with believing that something happened, but I'm not sure what it is. Maybe nothing happened at all when Jean was at your house."

"It didn't."

"Maybe. And maybe something happened somewhere else. But if

something did happen at your house, and if there was a way we could
know what did happen, then it might not be such a big deal, and then I
could tell that to the judge."

"What do you mean?"

"I don't know. It could be a specific event, or something she observed,
what somebody did or said to her. If there was something like this that
we could do something about, then I'd be able to say that I understood
what caused the problem and what needed to be done about it, and that
there was no longer any reason to keep Jean from you."

"Do you mean if I go and tell you that Ralph abused her, or if she
saw us having sex, I'd get her back?"

"No, I'm not trying to trick you. If Ralph abused her, then maybe it
would be best that Jean didn't come back. Or maybe it would be best for
her to come back if Ralph got therapy and changed. I don't know yet.
I'd have to be more clear about what it is that happened. Or if Jean saw
you having sex, then maybe it would be a simple matter of making sure
it didn't happen again."

"So you want me to say . . . "

"Wait, I don't want you to make things up. I don't want you to lie.
But if there really was something that you know about that happened
that could explain why she has sex on her mind, even if that something
puts you in a bad light, if there was a way for you to say, 'I'm sorry
for that happening and I won't do it again and this is how I'm going to
show you that it won't happen again,' and if I was satisfied with that,
then . . . "

"Then I could see Jean again? Have custody of her again?"

" . . . then I'd be able to say to the judge, okay, this is why Jean has
sex on her mind and we're going to do such and such to fix the problem
so there's no reason anymore to keep Jean from her mother."

"Is that what you want me to say?"

"No. I'm not trying to get you to say you did something that you
didn't do. For example, I'm not trying to say that you should tell me all
of a sudden that, like, you caught Ralph and Jean together doing . . . "

"Like caught them in bed together."

"Right. Because I don't know why it is that she has sex on her mind
all the time. That's what I'm trying to find out. But if you have any idea
what might be causing it, then it might be better for everyone if I knew
what it was."

"Because you could help?"

"Because if it's something that we could help with, and if everyone
believed that the problem could be helped, then I could say so to the
judge. But if there's nothing, then I would never want you to make
something up."

"Well, okay, then," she said, and sighed.

"Okay? What do you mean?"

"There was something."

"What?"

"It isn't easy to talk about. And I don't know if it's important."

"What?"

"Remember you asked before if Jean ever saw us?"

"Saw you?"

"Yeah, saw us."

"You mean having sex?"

"Yeah, well, maybe she did."

"Did what?"

"Saw us."

"You're saying she saw you have sex?"

"Maybe once. I'm not sure she did. It happened so fast."

"When?"

"One time, in the middle of the night, she woke up and when I looked up she was standing there so I sent her back to bed."

"Did you tell her to go back? Or bring her?"

"Brought her."

"So you had to get out of bed. What were you doing just before you got out of bed?"

"I was shocked, seeing her standing there in the door."

"So you didn't see her at first."

"No, I was shocked."

"So she might have been there watching for a while. You're not sure how long."

"No, but it couldn't have been too long, I would have seen her."

"What exactly was it that she saw you doing?"

"I was on top. God, I can't believe I'm telling you this."

"Having intercourse?"

"Yeah, that too."

"What else?"

"This is hard to say to you."

"Well, before you got on top, what exactly were you doing just before that?"

"Giving him head."

"And what exactly did she see, like where was she standing in the room? Let me make a drawing here. Show me how the room is arranged, so I can picture what her angle of vision was."

"Well, she was in the doorway on the right, and the bed was over here, so . . ."

"So she could have seen everything, right?"

"Right."

"And how long was she standing there?"

"Only a second."

"Did you notice when she got there?"

"No, when I saw her I jumped up."

"So she could have been there awhile?"

"Yeah, I guess, but I never really thought about it like that. God, I hope she didn't see it all."

"And what about other times you had sex. When did you usually do it?"

"Oh, I don't know. At night. And after dinner usually, before he went to work."

"And where would Jean be?"

"Upstairs playing. Or put to bed."

"And you would be where?"

"On the couch or in the bedroom."

"The couch is in the living room?"

"Yeah, but it wasn't like we did it right in front of her. She was playing in her room."

"But sometimes if she was playing, she could come down, couldn't she?"

"Whenever we heard her coming, we would stop or tell her to go back upstairs."

"Like if you suddenly noticed that she was standing on the stairs and watching you?"

"Yeah, we'd tell her to go back to bed."

"Sounds like this happened more than once. Quite a few times in fact."

"Not every night. Just once in a while. Besides, she's too young to understand what we were doing."

\* \* \* \* \*

While this kind of interview tactic is potentially leading and coercive, many people flatly refuse to respond to it, either because they are truly innocent or because what they have to say would be highly detrimental to their case. However, a significant number of people respond to this tactic in ways that permit a more adequate accounting of the allegations and some reasonable manner of handling the case. Therefore, it is worth illustrating this tactic here, while at the same time cautioning that it must be used judiciously.

\* \* \* \* \*

"Do you have more techniques like that? I loved it."

"Sure. There's a lot more on interview technique in later chapters."

"Techniques for interviewing adults, too?"

"The focus is primarily on the child, but many of the techniques are just as applicable to adults."

"Well, let's get to it. What are we waiting for?"

"Not quite yet. Be patient. Have you learned anything yet about who to interview first?"

"Yes, you made it crystal clear."

"And what questions to ask and what topics to include?"

"Yes, yes, I know all that now. Let's get on with interview technique."

"But what about the interview with the child? We didn't talk at all about what topics you would include in your interview. Or what questions you would ask. How would you go about it?"

"Uh, that's right. You didn't say anything about that yet."

"Well, that's what we'll turn to next."

"Good, I'm glad, now that you mention it. That would help me a lot, because I think maybe that's my weak point in all this."

"What is?"

"When I interview kids about sex abuse, I just don't seem to ask the right questions. I just did another interview today and it turned out awful. So, what are we waiting for? Let's get to it."

# CHAPTER 3

# Key Considerations in Interviewing the Child

"I don't know why I feel so inadequate when I interview children about sexual abuse. Usually I do a pretty good job with kids on other kinds of problems, so I just don't get it."

"Do you just feel inadequate? Or do you think that maybe you're genuinely doing an inadequate job?"

"Maybe a little bit of both. I'm not sure."

"What seems to go wrong?"

"Well, I seem to feel unsure of how to proceed from moment to moment during the interview."

"Unsure about what exactly? About what to do next?"

"Yes, maybe it's the choices I make in directing the interview. I feel so uncertain about those choices."

"Do they actually turn out to be the wrong choices?"

"It's hard for me to tell, so I'm always worried that they'll be the wrong choices. So then I get kind of stiff and uncomfortable."

"And then the child gets uncomfortable."

"Right, and nothing very productive happens, and I don't even know what went wrong."

"So you're saying that you need to get better at recognizing the choice points in an interview, in order to make the right choices instead of the wrong ones."

"Yes, I think so. But I need some help in recognizing when I'm making the wrong choices. Do you think you could look at this tape I did?"

"Is this the case you started out with? When you wanted help in deciding whether the child was telling the truth or . . . "

"No, this was one I did today."

"Okay, let's see it."

\* \* \* \* \*

"Hi, Jenny, why don't you sit right there. Is that okay? Are you comfortable?"

A nod of the head from Jenny.

"Jenny, do you know why you're here today?"

The clinician pulled up another chair and sat down so that they were toe to toe, making sure to maintain eye contact with Jenny, whose eyes looked everywhere but at the clinician.

"Jenny, do you know why you're here?"

"No," she whispered, shaking her head back and forth.

"Your mother didn't explain it to you?"

Another shake of the head.

"Well, it's to talk about something very, very important."

"Hmm-hmm," Jenny responded.

"Yes, we're here to talk about what you said your father did to you. You told your aunt some things about what he did, and then your mother talked to you about it, and then the police, and a lot of other people. And now they want to figure out what happened because they can't seem to understand it right. So they want me to talk to you and see if I can figure out what's wrong, and to figure out how you feel about it to see how bad you feel. Do you understand what I'm saying?"

Another nod of the head from Jenny.

"Well, what I want you to tell me is, what did he do?"

A long silence from Jenny.

"Jenny? What did your father do?"

Jenny remained silent for about 30 seconds.

Finally, she mumbled, "He touched me."

"Where, Jenny?"

Silence again.

"When did he touch you?"

Jenny shrugged.

"How many times did he touch you?"

Another shrug.

"Jenny, I know this is difficult, but it's very, very important to answer my questions. How many times did your father touch you?"

*  *  *  *  *

"So, what did I do wrong?"

"First, let me tell you what you did right."

"I did something right?"

"Yes, some portions of this interview were good, particularly in how you used language to convey your messages so that these messages could be understood by a seven-year-old."

"Like when?"

"Like in your statement about the purpose of the interview. I think you went on too long with this and used too many words all at once, but you explained the purpose with words and concepts that a child this age could comprehend. A lot of clinicians talk right over a child's head."

"Did I do anything else right?"

"Well, you had good intentions. Like when you tried so hard to establish rapport with Jenny."

"Thanks."

"But your focus on her was so complete and so intense that you intimidated her instead of making her comfortable. You can see that, can't you? She felt like she was being grilled."

"But I was trying so hard to give her my full attention and make her feel comfortable."

"I know. You failed to establish rapport precisely because you were trying so hard to establish it."

"Yeah, I guess I can see that now. I tried so hard that how I went about it undermined my goal. It's kind of ironic, though."

"You also asked some good questions about the abuse, and you were direct and to the point."

"Thanks."

"But your timing was wrong. These questions were leading questions, and should have been asked only after more open-ended questions failed to elicit a productive response."

"But they were good questions?"

"Yes, in the sense that you weren't afraid to ask direct questions about abuse. But, like I said, the timing was all wrong."

"More open-ended questions should have been asked first."

"Not only that. These questions about the abuse should have been asked only after rapport had been adequately established. On top of that, you kept asking questions about new issues when previous questions had been met with silence from Jenny."

"But if she doesn't answer a question, I have to ask another one, don't I? I can't just sit there."

"But you just kept piling on the questions. Piling them on like that only served to teach her to be silent. You helped her to establish a cognitive set to respond negatively, with shrugs and silence instead of words."

"I guess I don't know what I'm doing at all, do I?"

"Well, you know some things. Overall, you attempted to accomplish several important goals in this interview, such as stating the purpose of the interview, establishing rapport, and eliciting information about the abuse."

"Thanks."

"But even though you had these goals in mind, you didn't possess an adequate understanding of how to accomplish these goals, nor in what sequence of stages."

"Stages?"

"Yes, there are a number of goals to accomplish and these can be accomplished in a sequence, in stages."

"What are these stages?"

"That's what this chapter is about."

\* \* \* \* \*

Some of the mistakes we have just examined illustrate the need to conduct the interview in stages, where success at one stage may well depend on how successfully an earlier stage was completed. Sometimes it is hard to view the interview process in terms of stages because each case is so different from other cases, with each seeming to require a different approach. Some cases may concern young adolescent females who have been victimized regularly by their father and brothers. Others may concern isolated incidents of abuse. Some involve young children who cannot yet talk. Since every case is unique in some way, and therefore requires a different body of questions, it is not always clear whether a standard interview format can be applied in a flexible and helpful manner.

While differences do exist in what needs to be known about each case, some of the same questions tend to be asked repeatedly, even across hundreds of interviews representing a diverse range of sexual abuse problems. In addition, these same questions tend to be most usefully applied when certain sets of them are asked in particular sequences. As a result, it can be useful to regard an interview with a child as a somewhat invariant sequence of stages. While these stages may be conceptualized in different ways by different evaluators, I have found it most useful to explicate and sequence them as follows:

1. Establishing the purposes of the interview.
2. Discussing the limits of confidentiality.
3. Teaching the child how to answer questions.
4. Warming up the child and establishing rapport.
5. Assessing mental status, development, and current functioning.
6. Eliciting a description of the abuse.
7. Asking about the effects of the abuse.
8. Exploring possible reasons for making false statements.
9. Patching up the child prior to the end of the interview.

The last four of these stages, which focus on questions specifically related to sexual abuse, are elucidated in the next chapter. The rest of the present chapter will address the first five stages, which concern key considerations for interviews with children in general, whether or not the problem is that of sexual abuse. These considerations are crucial to interviewing children for any kind of court-ordered evaluation, such as for custody and visitation disputes. They are relevant, as well, to intake interviews for many kinds of presenting problems in various counseling contexts. The first four stages can also be blended and interwoven with one another, in idiosyncratic ways that will be dependent on the interviewer's particular style, the child's responses, and the purposes of the interview.

## STAGE ONE: ESTABLISHING THE PURPOSE OF THE INTERVIEW

"Joanie, do you know why you came here today?"
"Yes," said Joanie. "I have to talk."
"Do you know about what?"
"About Jim."
"Okay, good. But you're probably tired of talking about this."
She vigorously shook her head up and down.
"How many people have you talked to about it?"
"The police, and then Steve and that lady [from D.S.S.], and the school guidance counselor, and the nurse, and my mom."
"That's a bunch of times. Five times. You're probably sick and tired of talking about it."

Again, she vigorously nodded her head up and down.

"And I need to ask you to tell it all over again to me, too. I'm sorry about that. I don't mean to make you feel bad, and I'm sorry that you'll feel bad about saying it all again. But my job is to ask you to tell me about it all, again. Do you understand?"

"Yeah."

"That's the job. That's what I'm here for today. That's what you're here for."

"Okay."

"But before we talk about it, I want to ask you some other questions, to find out what kind of a kid you are. Is that okay?"

\* \* \* \* \*

When first questioning the child, it is best to begin by stating the purpose of the interview, so that there is a mutual understanding between the evaluator and the child. Sometimes this can be accomplished very simply, as illustrated above, by asking the child what he has been told about why he is there. In many instances, the child will give an answer that indicates a lack of understanding about the purpose of the interview, which will require, then, that the interviewer state the purpose in language the child can understand.

Although this section of the interview usually takes no more than a few moments, evaluators should try to be sensitive to the significance of what the child is being asked to do. That is, he is being asked to make a statement of some kind that could affect his life and future, as well as that of those persons closest to him. Some children experience this as a heavy burden of responsibility. On the other hand, many children are unaware of this burden at the moment of making a statement but may experience it later, and they may come to feel sorry, and perhaps responsible, for the changes that the statement occasioned.

A burden of this kind has at least two identifiable effects. First, it can cause the child stress and unnecessary pain, that is to say, pain that he would not have experienced if he were not forced to be in this interview. Second, it can inhibit the child from a free disclosure of information.

Therefore, with children who are old enough to appreciate this burden, it can be useful to attempt to mitigate it by pointing out that the statement by itself is not going to cause changes to occur. The evaluator and other professionals involved in the case are very interested in what the child has to say, but they, not the child, are the ones who are responsible for making decisions. The child does not have to figure out what would be best for everyone in the long run. The child only needs to do her best to tell what happened.

The words used to convey this message will depend on the child's cognitive and developmental abilities, and with many younger children it will be pointless to make any statements of this kind at all. This kind of message relieves some children. It frustrates and infuriates others. The latter are those children who want their statements to make a difference and who know exactly how they want things to turn out. For example, the child wants her father put in jail. Or she wants to be out of the house and resents the evaluator's implications that things might be best if the family were reconciled and in therapy. However, even in these cases, it is often useful to give some variation of the above message so that if the child should later change her mind and be sorry about the consequences, she can blame the decision-making adults rather than herself.

## STAGE TWO: DISCUSSING THE LACK OF CONFIDENTIALITY

With children old enough to understand the concept of confidentiality, it is necessary to address this issue at some point early in the interview, before they have disclosed any significant information about themselves or about sexual abuse. This can occur either before or after establishing a mutual understanding of purpose, or during the phase in which the interviewer is warming up the child and establishing rapport. Specifically, children need to be informed about the limits on confidentiality, whether the interview is being taped, and whether there are any observers behind a one-way mirror.

Beginners sometimes tend to rush through this phase, fearful that the child will become upset about the limits on confidentiality, about the presence of an observer, or about the fact that they are being taped. However, with an accumulation of experience in discussing the constraints on confidentiality with children, clinicians gradually realize that, if they themselves are comfortable with these constraints, then they are able to slowly and clearly explain them to children in a way that puts the children at ease as well. In addition, showing the children the taping equipment or introducing them to the observers often serves to enhance their interest, rather than inhibiting their responsiveness.

While this stage of the interview hardly ever takes more than a minute or two, it is wise for clinicians to appreciate the significance of an ethical dilemma in which they may find themselves. The dilemma arises from the fact that children (most of them anyway) are not cognitively competent to give informed consent to the waiving of confidentiality. First of all, many children don't even understand the concept of confidentiality; and it is necessary to understand this concept first before understanding the absence of confidentiality that exists in court-related evaluations. Usually, it is simplest to just explain that what they tell you will not be a secret because you may need to talk about it with a judge or with other people.

However, even after they are fully informed that what they say may be included in your report or testimony, they may inadvertently say things about their parents or about other matters that they wouldn't want their parents to know. This is information that is potentially available to their parents, through access that a parent's attorney may have to your report or by virtue of the parent's presence during your testimony in court.

You will probably even find out things that the child didn't even know he knew. That is, the child will not be aware that he is providing certain kinds of information, or if he is aware of it, he may not have realized fully beforehand that he would be disclosing it. The better you are at the process of sensitive and skillful interviewing, the more likely it is that the child will reveal information that, upon adequate review, the child would probably not want you to reveal to anyone else.

In these kinds of cases, where the interviewer believes that a child may have said things that, if he were an adult, he might have regretted saying, it is possible to review the highlights of the interview with the child in order to identify any statements the child might wish to remain confidential. I sometimes draw a box for the child to see in the bottom corner of a page in my notes, where I make a list of these issues that I will try to keep secret. I tell the child that I will do my best to keep those things secret, but that I can't make any promises because a judge can force me to tell.

The following dialogue with a bright eight-year-old provides a short illustration.

\* \* \* \* \*

"Dawn, you've done a good job and told me a lot of things."

"Thanks," she said, proud of herself and smiling.

"And do you remember how I said that I couldn't keep it secret?"

"Yeah, you have to tell the judge."

"Right, he might want to know some of these things you told me."

"Which things?"

"About you wanting to keep living with your father and some of the reasons why you want to. And about what Ken did to you, about touching you. The judge might want to know some of those things."

"Okay, but you won't tell mom, will you?"

"No, I won't tell her, but she might find out if I have to go to court and tell the judge. She might be sitting right there in the courtroom when I tell the judge, so she would hear. How do you feel about that?"

"It's okay, I guess. You can tell her. I just don't want to do it."

"So, you'd be scared to tell her yourself. But it's okay if I do it for you."

"Right," she said, smiling and looking relieved.

"Good, but let me be sure about some of these other things you told me. I want to know how you'll feel if your mom hears some of this, okay?"

"Okay."

"Well, let's see here," I said, going over my notes. "You told me you loved your mom and wanted to keep seeing her while you're living with your dad."

"Yeah, that's right, but I don't want dad to know that. He'll get mad."

"Good. That's what I want to know, all the things you want to keep secret. You also told me how your mom seems sad all the time. You know, how she cries all the time and tells you she'll kill herself if you stop visiting her. You also told me how she hardly does anything fun and sleeps a lot on the couch. How do you feel about me telling any of that?"

"Do you have to tell everything?"

"Well, which parts would you like me to keep secret? The part about her being sad if you don't visit? Or the part about her sleeping a lot and never doing anything fun?"

"The part about her sleeping and not being fun."

"How come?"

"It'll make her feel bad and she might get mad."

"Okay, so far you've told me that you want me to keep it a secret about you wanting to see your mom, so that your dad won't get mad, and, uh, let's see here, what was the other . . . "

"About her sleeping."

"Right. Okay, then, what about when she cries a lot and tells you she'll kill herself if you stop visiting?"

"That's all true. You can say that."

"It's all true? You mean it's okay for me to say it to the judge in front of her, because it's all true, even though that might make her mad, too?"

"I don't care if she gets mad about that part. It makes me mad, too. She shouldn't kill herself."

"Okay, so there's just these two parts you want me to keep secret, right? I'll write them down here in the corner of the page to help me to remember, and I'll try to keep them secret. But I don't know for sure if I can because if the judge really wants to know, he can make me tell. Do you understand?"

"Yeah, he'll make you do it."

"Right. And there's another thing I want you to know. I might decide later that I better tell about those things if I think they'll help convince the judge to do what I think is best for you. Because my job is to try to tell the judge what I think is best for you."

"What will you tell the judge to do?"

"That you shouldn't see your mom for a while until she goes to a doctor and isn't so sick anymore."

"But I want to see her. Now."

"I know. And I'll tell him that you'd like to see her now."

"But dad will hear you and he'll get mad if he hears that." She shook her head, visibly upset and bewildered by the confusing array of options. "I don't know what you should say. They'll all get mad at me."

"Well, how about if I try not to say that you told me you want to see your mom. Instead, I'll try to say it's my idea. You know, that I think it's best for you to keep visiting your mom, but not right away. First she's got to get better. And then . . . "

"Yeah, that's it, do it that way."

"You mean, so it's like my idea, not yours."

"Yeah, and then I'll stay out of trouble."

"Right, but if the judge makes me, or if they really want to know why I came up with my ideas, well, then, I'll just have to . . . "

"Yeah, you'll have to tell them."

\* \* \* \* \*

As illustrated here, the child is likely to waive confidentiality not only prior to an interview but even after disclosing a great deal of potentially damaging information. This is because the child is not clear in her mind on what it is that has been disclosed and the implications of that disclosure. Because the child is not clear, it is incumbent on the evaluator to make this clear by reminding the child of the issues, clarifying the implications, and helping to discriminate information the child wishes to remain confidential. Further, it is important for the evaluator to avoid giving false promises about confidentiality. Instead, he can describe the conditions and reasons for testifying about information that the child might prefer to remain confidential.

The fact that an evaluator may be legally constrained to reveal anything a child has told him poses a serious ethical dilemma for the evaluator. Keep in mind that confidentiality has been formally waived by parents or by the courts and that children do not have the legal authority to waive confidentiality. The rights of children may be seriously compromised when they have disclosed information that may then be used in such a way that it causes them some damage, such as contaminating a relationship with one of their parents. If an evaluator feels ethically bound to attempt to protect a child's rights, in the absence of legal protection, he or she risks acting in contempt of court.

This kind of situation poses some serious questions. Should the evaluator violate the child's rights by disclosing information he knows the child would not want disclosed? Or should he protect the child and, in doing so, risk the consequences of acting in contempt of court?

While this ethical dilemma is inherent in almost any interview with a child that may later be examined before a court, it more often constitutes a *potential* problem, and usually does not actually become problematic. However, it is a dilemma that is keenly experienced on those rare occasions in which one has given an opinion in court but cannot give the reasons for the opinion because the reasons constitute the very information the child would not want disclosed. One avenue available to the evaluator for negotiating this dilemma involves eliciting the cooperation of the Law Guardian and the judge. This is illustrated in the following dialogue.

* * * * *

"But doctor," said the attorney for the Department of Social Services. "The reasons you have given don't seem to be that compelling. Surely there must be some further basis for your opinion?"

"I've already articulated some of the reasons for my opinion, but there are some additional reasons that I believe the child would prefer to remain confidential if he were capable of competently understanding the notion of confidentiality."

"But, doctor, as I understand it, the child hasn't been given any privilege or confidentiality. These evaluations are never protected by a doctor-patient privilege. Please elaborate all of your reasons for your opinion."

"I'm sorry, but I believe that the child would not want some of his statements disclosed in the presence of his parents. I would prefer to disclose them only in the presence of the judge or, if the court preferred, I could assist the child in an interview with the judge in chambers rather than . . . "

"Objection, your honor," interrupted the attorney for the mother. "The witness is not answering the question. And if he's withholding information that will affect my client's case, then my client certainly has a right to be aware of what it is so that she can answer any charges against her."

"Excuse me, your honor," interrupted the Law Guardian, the attorney for the child. "But I'd like to point out that the doctor is here as the court's witness, not as a witness for either of the parents, and that if he believes the child's rights are being violated, then I would have to argue that he be permitted to remain silent on certain information he gathered with a child who is only six years old and not yet capable of understanding the nature . . . "

As can be seen, the evaluator can be rescued from this ethical dilemma by the Law Guardian, whose job it is to protect the child's rights, and by the judge, who also has a mandate to provide for the child's best interests. The Law Guardian and the judge can be mobilized to provide this kind of protection if they are adequately alerted to the ethical violation of the child's rights. They are likely to remain silent, however, and not even be aware of the dilemma, if the evaluator does not alert them to it. And the evaluator may not adequately alert them to it if he, too, is unaware of it.

While this discussion has strayed from the topic of stages of interviewing children, it has been a necessary tangent. It illustrates that, while confidentiality may be discussed in many instances for only a few moments, there are serious ethical issues inherent in the interview process, with far-reaching consequences. While ethical issues are important, in regard both to confidentiality and to establishing a mutual understanding of the purposes of the interview, and should be on the evaluator's mind while conducting the interview, they need not bog down the flow of the interview. In reality, the stages of the interview that are being discussed here require very little time and can be interwoven with the initial effort to warm up the child and establish rapport.

## STAGE THREE: TEACHING THE CHILD HOW TO ANSWER QUESTIONS

As the evaluator asks initial questions and begins to make attempts to establish rapport with the child, the child may sometimes respond with silence. Even a more voluble child, who chatters away at this stage of the interview, may respond later with silence and shrugs when asked direct questions about the abuse. Silences can frustrate the flow of an interview. They can also be mystifying to the evaluator who has to formulate conclusions. What do these silences and shrugs mean?

Is the child conveying a yes, a no, or a maybe, in the often lengthy and vacillating process of deciding to make a true statement about abuse? Is the child failing to understand the questions you ask? Is it that the child does not know the answer to the question? Does the child, despite understanding the question and knowing the answer, not want to answer? Is the child afraid to answer?

To mitigate against this kind of mystification, it is helpful to teach the child how to answer questions so that a mutual understanding and common language exists between the child and the evaluator.

*   *   *   *   *

"Before I talk to you about what Joe did, I want to ask you some questions about yourself so that I can understand what kind of kid you are. Is that okay?"

"Yeah."

"Okay, then, if you don't know the answer to a question I ask, then just say, 'I don't know.' Can you say that? Go ahead, try saying it. 'I don't know.' Like, if I said, tell me the names of all the oceans in the world, what would you say?"

"I don't know."

"Good. And if you don't want to answer the question, you can just say, 'I don't want to say.' Can you say that for me?"

"I don't want to say."

"And if you're too scared to talk about it, just say, 'I'm too scared to talk about it.' Can you say that?"

"I'm too scared."

"Good. And if you don't understand my questions, you can just say, 'I don't get what you're saying. You're mixing me up.' Can you say that for me?"

"Yeah, I don't get it."

"So, tell me how you will answer this question. How old is your grandmother?"

"I don't know."

"That's good. Try this one now. Who is your mother's sister's daughter?"

"What?"

"Your mother's sister's daughter."

"I don't get it. That's . . . that's crazy."
"Good job in answering. Now, tell me how you'll answer this . . . "

\* \* \* \* \*

As can be seen, the child can be instructed in how to respond to questions, and can later be tested to assure that an understanding has been achieved. The evaluator can vary this process according to the features of the particular case; and she can not only vary it, but alter it as well, as the needs of the situation might suggest.

This stage of the interview will not solve all the problems that arise in the difficult process of determining whether abuse occurred. Children often need to establish a relationship with a clinician in which they can proceed through the difficult process of vacillating about whether the abuse occurred; at some points they need to deny it, at other points to admit it, and at other points to be indefinite about whether it occurred. One meeting, for the purpose of evaluation, may be insufficient to meet this need.

However, you will be in a better position to determine that one meeting is insufficient if you do everything possible to understand what it is that the child is saying, even if what the child is saying is that she doesn't feel like talking about abuse just now. To achieve this understanding, it is essential to establish a common language with the child or a definition of terms and rules for communication. Without that mutual understanding, it is exceedingly difficult to know what to make of what the child has just said to you.

## STAGE FOUR: WARMING UP THE CHILD AND ESTABLISHING RAPPORT

Some clinicians tend to get right down to business and start asking questions about the abuse immediately. This is usually a mistake because the clinician is a stranger to the child, and the child hasn't had an opportunity to orient herself to the situation. On the other hand, some clinicians go to the opposite extreme, because either they are uncomfortable with sexual abuse themselves or they do not wish to push the child to confront painful memories until the child is ready. This, too, is a mistake, because many children readily tolerate the pain of these memories when pushed. The result of a more conservative approach can be a meandering, wasteful, and unproductive interview or series of interviews. Something in between these extremes is generally most useful.

Many children respond well to a short period during which fairly innocuous questions are asked. At this stage, an atmosphere can be created—not only by the particular questions asked, but also by the clinician's behavior and demeanor—that can make or break the interview. Children need an opportunity to orient themselves to the demands of the situation and to the interviewer's personality and style. They need to determine for themselves a particular level of self-confidence, a level that will then dictate how open they will be throughout the next phases of the interview. The success of this stage depends just as much on how the clinician's body is used in space as it does on the particular choice of words.

As was illustrated previously, children do not respond well to immediate questioning, toe to toe, chairs close up with knees touching, and the interviewer's eyes popping out of their sockets in an attempt at good eye contact. All of this intimidates children and distracts them from their need to take in the task demands of the entire situation.

They do much better if the interviewer sits a bit away from them, which permits them to observe and "check out" the interviewer without the interviewer checking them out. They need to figure out for themselves what kind of person this is. There are a number of ways to facilitate this orienting or "checking out" process. Utilizing a notepad for taking notes can be helpful in this process because it keeps the interviewer's attention off the child. In addition to storing information, a notepad helps to provide some distance from the child, permitting the interviewer to disengage from interactions that can contaminate her thinking and planning. For this reason, a notepad can be a useful prop even when there is nothing worth noting. It need not interfere at all with the building of rapport, contrary to the beliefs of many beginning clinicians, who assume that absolute attentiveness is necessary to establish rapport.

Another way of utilizing demeanor and space to set the tone for a comfortable interactional atmosphere is for the clinician to perform custodial functions in the first minute or so. In doing so, the clinician focuses his or her attention on a matter irrelevant to the purposes of the interview, such as adjusting a tape recorder, opening a window, arranging the furniture, or picking up toys. This gives the child an opportunity to check you out as you struggle to get that window open, while your attention is engaged elsewhere and is not focused directly on the child. He gets to figure out what species of animal you are while you are at your most vulnerable, your most human, and not behind the veil of a professional demeanor. It will help even more if you engage in that custodial function in a manner that is not entirely competent. Your incompetence at the task invites their help. When they help you out, they make more of a connection with you and feel less intimidated by your position and by your strangeness.

Aside from the demeanor of the evaluator, the content of the questions asked in the initial period will affect the atmosphere of the entire interview. There are a couple of points that are important to make about the kinds of questions to ask and the sequencing of those questions. First, it is useful to begin with questions that are concrete and easy to answer. That is to say, the questions should be so easy that the child does not need to think more than a split second before knowing the answer. This establishes a cognitive "set" to respond to questions with verbalizations rather than with silences and shrugs. Questions of this kind would include: "What is your name?" "How old are you?" "What grade are you in?" "What is your teacher's name?"

This approach may be unnecessary with a highly verbal and friendly child. However, I have seen numerous interviews die at the outset because a child was initially asked a question requiring some reflection and decision about how to respond, sometimes no more complicated than "What do you want to be when you grow up?" When a child is unsure of how to respond to a more difficult question, a "set" is established to respond negatively, with silence.

In addition to enhancing the child's probability of responding, these "easy" questions provide the child with another nonthreatening opportunity to orient himself to the personality of the interviewer. The child can begin to go through the process of deciding whether this kind of talking is either uncomfortable or an interesting and "fun" thing to do. This is the stage at which initial rapport and trust are either established or not.

After the child has achieved some success with easier questions, a second and subsequent type of questioning consists of asking the child about his strengths and current activities. Talking about his strengths can help the child to feel more confident, and therefore more willing to fully answer questions and to talk more freely. It can also help to render him more willing to give consideration to questions that both require reflection and exposure to painful areas. Examples are: "What are you good at in school?" "What is your best subject?" "Do you like sports?" "What do you like to do when you go home after school?" "What is a typical day like for you?"

Asking about a typical day is sometimes the most illuminating question when the evaluator has enough patience and persistence to obtain answers to the question. It provides an intimate exposure to the context in which the child interacts on a day-to-day basis. The following example illustrates this point.

* * * * *

"What do you do after school on most days? How do you spend your time?"

"Well, after I get home from school I play with my friends next door."

"Like, what? What do you do? Ride bikes? Sit and talk? Or what?"

"We play jump rope. And we talk. We look at comic books sometimes in my room."

"What else?"

"Listen to music. Talk about problems."

"Problems? Like, about what?"

"Like about tests and teachers. And friends. And then she goes home."

"And then? After you finish playing? What happens next?"

"Then we have dinner and watch TV. And then we get ready for bed."

"How do you get ready?"

"We have to pee and brush our teeth and go to sleep."

"Does someone put you to sleep? Does somebody tuck you in and do the same stuff with you every night before sleeping?"

"Mom reads a story and makes us say our prayers and gives me three big hugs and kisses."

"Three hugs and kisses? Every single night?"

"Yeah, I make her do it if she forgets."

"Do you have any trouble getting to sleep?"

"A little. Sometimes I look at books till I fall asleep."

"Do you usually sleep pretty good? Or do you wake up in the middle of the night?"

"Sometimes I wake up in the night to get a drink."

"Or go to the bathroom."

"Yeah."

"And do you have any trouble getting back to sleep?"

"No."

"Do you love to sleep a lot?"

"Yeah, it's hard to get me up in the morning."

"What time do you have to get up?"

"Real early."

"So it's hard to get you up? You want to keep on sleeping?"

"Yeah, mom has to come in about five times to tell me to get dressed."

"So you don't wake right up all ready to go."

"No. When I go to the babysitter's I have to get up at 5:30."

"Why's that? Because your mom has to go to work?"

"Right. At six."

"So how long are you at the babysitter's?"

"Till the bus comes, at 8:30."

"So, when you get up so early, do you dress yourself? Does somebody help you? Do you eat anything?"

"Yeah, mom lays my clothes out, but I get dressed myself. And then I go down and pour the milk in my cereal."

"Who gets the cereal out?"

"Mom does. She puts it in bowls and then goes and takes her shower while we eat."

"What kind of cereal?"

"Cheerios or Frosted Flakes or Cap'n Crunch."

"And what happens when you're done eating?"

"While we're eating, mom comes running in and says, 'Hurry up and get your coats and boots on and jump into the car.' So we do."

\* \* \* \* \*

This kind of questioning requires some patience, and the answers to the questions are often trivial and boring. However, dialogues of this kind provide an intimate look at the everyday life of the child, as if you were a fly on the wall observing her every action. Although you are a stranger she has just met, it enables you to rapidly paint a picture of how the child spends her time and how she functions in her natural context. In addition, it permits the both of you to warm up to one another, to establish rapport, and to develop some degree of mutual trust, which provides a foundation for more difficult questioning at a later stage of the interview.

## Stage Five: Assessing Mental Status, Development, and Current Functioning

Warm-up questions can gradually merge into questions that are intended to more aptly assess how well or how poorly the child is functioning in a number of significant areas of life.

"Do you have friends?" "Do you have a best friend?" "Is your best friend someone you can trust with secrets?" These questions are intended to elicit information that permits an assessment of the child's capacity for peer relationships.

"What do you like best in school?" may elicit information concerning academic and behavioral functioning in the school setting. "What do you hate the most in school?" is a question that almost always results in a smile—when it doesn't, the evaluator should consider whether something has gone wrong in the establishment of rapport, or whether there is something serious to investigate regarding the child's adjustment.

"What do you want to be when you grow up?" In asking this question, the clinician hopes to arrive at some understanding of the child's orientation to the future. The answer to this question may also indicate whether the child is developing a conflict-free interest. Both of these issues are central to the processes of normal development.

Many other kinds of questions can be asked at this stage, and some are suggested in Table 1 in a sample crib sheet. Crib sheets can be useful in reminding us of areas that we have neglected. Sometimes, during interviews, we get caught up in the interaction with the child, or we become enthralled with a line of questioning that is exceptionally interesting, stimulating, or alarming. As a consequence, we forget to ask some important basic questions. It can be very useful to less experienced evaluators to develop crib sheets of their own, with which they feel comfortable and which provide them with structure and guidance compatible with their theoretical orientations.

The crib sheet in Table 1 is not intended to represent all questions or all categories of questions that the evaluator might ask. Nor do I want to try, at this point in the book, to provide the guidance necessary to interpret all of the answers to these kinds of questions. Interpretation can be guided best by the theoretical orientation of the clinician, and many other books are available that will more than adequately guide and inform the clinician.

However, I would like to emphasize that, in order to conduct an adequate assessment of adjustment and development, it is necessary to know something about a number of areas in the child's life. If the clinician limits his questioning to the areas addressed in a typical mental status examination, important areas of family functioning might be overlooked, such as the parentification of a child. Likewise, if the questioning focuses exclusively on the child's role in the functioning of the family system, important areas of individual functioning may be overlooked, such as capacity for peer relations, suicidality, disorders in thinking, or deficiencies in conscience or empathy.

To avoid such limitations when organizing what you need to know to assess a child's functioning, it is useful either to expand one's model or to borrow from various approaches. The areas of functioning about which the evaluator asks questions should represent a set of categories that can help to illuminate each child's unique pattern of functioning.

**Table 1. Sample Crib Sheet for an Interview with a Child**

| ISSUES TO ADDRESS | WITH THE FOLLOWING QUESTIONS |
| --- | --- |
| Purpose | Do you know why you are here? I want to be sure we understand each other. |
| Confidentiality | Do you understand that what we talk about won't be secret? |
| Teaching how to answer | If you don't understand my questions, say, "I don't understand." If you don't know the answer, just say, "I don't know." If you don't want to answer, say, "I don't want to say." |
| Warm-up | What is your name? How old are you? What grade are you in? What is your teacher's name? |
| Preferences | What do you like most in school? |
| Dislikes | What do you hate the most? |
| Strengths | What are you good at? What else are you good at, outside of school? |
| Peer relations | Do you have friends? How many? Do you have a best friend? Do you have problems with making friends? With keeping friends? Do other kids tease you? Are you lonely a lot? |
| Heterosexual interest | Do you have a boyfriend? For how long? How many? |
| Daily context | After school, what do you do? What's a typical day like? |
| Gender identity | What are your favorite toys? Who do you want to be like? |
| Conflict-free interest | Do you have hobbies? A job? What games do you like to play? |
| Future orientation | What do you want to be when you grow up? |
| Affect and mood | Do you know what the word "worry" means? What do you worry about? What makes you sad? Or mad? What do you do about it? Do you ever hate yourself? Are you a happy kid? Or a sad kid? |
| Self-esteem | Do you wish you were somebody else? What are the things you like about yourself? Do you ever hate yourself? |
| Bonding | What person do you love most in the whole world? What person loves you the most? Whom do you feel closest to? How come? |
| Family conflict | When mom and dad argue, what is it about? What do you hate about mom (or dad, sister, brother)? Whose side is she (he) on? |
| Empathy/ conscience | Do you ever feel bad when somebody is hurt? Why? When you hurt somebody, do you ever feel bad about it? How come? |

*(continued)*

**Table 1. (*Continued*)**

| ISSUES TO ADDRESS | WITH THE FOLLOWING QUESTIONS |
| --- | --- |
| Perceptual distortions | Do you ever hear voices when nobody's there? Do you ever think things are crawling on you? Do you see things others don't see? |
| Thought disorder | Do you think somebody is out to get you? Do you think you are really somebody else? Does something make you do things? |
| Anxiety | Do you ever get so scared that you can't get enough air and think you'll die? |
| Fantasy | If you were stuck on a desert island and could only have one person with you, who would that be? If you had three wishes you knew would come true, what would they be? If you were an animal, which one would it be? Tell me about a dream you had. |
| Focal conflict | What is your first memory, from when you were very young? |
| Drug/alcohol use | How often do you get high? With what drugs? How much can you drink without getting drunk? When you're drunk, what kinds of things do you do that you're sorry for later? |
| Suicide | Do you think about killing yourself? Method? Intention? Why? |
| Antisocial behavior | Have you gotten into much trouble for fighting (stealing, etc.)? Have you done these things a lot but not got caught yet? |

The evaluator needs to be able to determine whether dysfunction exists in one or two circumscribed areas or whether dysfunction exists in many areas; where dysfunction exists, it is necessary to be able to determine how mild or serious it is.

This kind of differentiated understanding of a child's functioning is crucial to sexual abuse evaluations, since certain areas of dysfunction may be the direct result of abuse. Areas of family dysfunction can also play a role in causing or predisposing to the abuse. In addition, the absence of dysfunction can raise doubts as to whether abuse actually occurred or, if it did occur, how serious it was.

How the evaluator goes about achieving this kind of understanding of the child will depend on the evaluator's theoretical biases. These biases necessarily dictate the set of categories he believes will be maximally useful, and these categories, in turn, dictate the particular questions that will be asked. At this point, I wish to avoid suggesting that an ideal set of categories exists. A set of categories that I have found useful will be presented later, in Chapter 11, which is devoted exclusively to the topic of formulating conclusions.

The emphasis at this point of the book is not so much on the particular questions to ask but rather on the stage of the interview in which we ask the questions. No matter how meager or extensive our list of questions might be, it is necessary at many points to deviate from the list in order to accomplish the purposes of this stage. The interview is an interaction. It is alive. It is not simply a list of questions to which we require answers. These questions are not asked in a rigid sequence as in a test, but rather, are asked in an interactive dialogue with the child, an example of which is illustrated below. The dialogue chosen for this purpose also illustrates, economically, all five stages of the interview thus far described, proceeding through these stages at a fairly rapid pace.

\* \* \* \* \*

"Come right this way, Cheryl, and have a seat. Yes, right there is fine," I said, rearranging chairs and finding one for myself. "My name is Aaron, and I'm a counselor here, a psychologist. Oh, excuse me for a second," I said, grabbing a microphone from the middle of the table and turning to place it on the floor behind us. "I need to get this out of our way so that we can talk, but I want to make sure it's working so that it hears us. You see, it's a microphone."

"What for?"

"It listens to us. Because I tape everything I do here so I can look at it later. Hello," I said into the microphone. "Knock on the window if your hear me."

There was a knock on the window.

"You see? They heard us. Do you want to talk into the microphone? Tell them to knock if they hear you."

She grabbed the microphone and yelled into it, "Knock on the mirror when you hear me. Knock on the window. Knock on the window."

Immediately, there was a loud knock.

"They're telling you not to yell so loud," I said laughing. "You're hurting their ears."

"Sorry," she said in a whisper, addressing herself to the mirror, and giggling.

"Those people on the other side of the mirror," I said, "are watching and listening because they help me with my job here. And there's a camera on the other side, too. It makes a movie out of us."

"Like a video?"

"Yeah, it's a video. Is that all right with you?"

"Yeah. But how come?"

"So I can look at it later if I want to. And so the judge can see it if he wants to."

"Can I look at it too?"

"If you want to."

"Okay."

"Well, anyway," I said, returning to my seat and arranging my notepad and paper and pencil. "One of my jobs is to talk to girls who have been sexually abused. Do you know what that is?"

Cheryl shrugged, so I went on.

"That's okay, it's a hard question. You see, when a grown-up touches children on their bodies in places where they shouldn't touch them, in private places, it's called sexual abuse."

"I know that."

"Good. Well, then, my job is to talk to the children to find out if it really happened and to find out how the children are feeling about it. Do you understand? What my job is?"

"Yeah. To talk to children. About touching."

"Yeah, and I need to find out if it's on their minds a lot, or if they don't even think about it much. If the kids feel bad about it, what I try to do is to figure out if there's anything that can be done to help. Do you understand?"

Cheryl nodded her head.

"Can you explain to me what I just said so that I know you understand?"

"Well . . . " she started out, then hesitated.

"Hmm-hmm?" I encouraged her, nodding my head.

"You try to help girls who were touched by grown-ups."

"Hmm-hmm?" I nodded, expecting more.

"You want to know if they think about it a lot. And then you'll see if you can help."

"Right, you got it just right. And then after I try to figure it all out, I tell what I think to the judge, and he decides what to do. Do you know about the judge and what a judge does?"

"Yeah, mom and Bill have to go back to the judge next week to find out if Bill can come back home."

"Right, and the things you tell me here are things that the judge wants to know about, so they won't be just a secret between you and me. Do you understand what I'm saying?"

"Yeah, you have to tell the judge what I say."

"Okay, good. Let's see here," I said, shuffling through my papers. "Before I talk to you about Bill, I'd like to ask you some questions about yourself so I can find out what kind of a kid you are. Is that okay?"

She nodded her head.

"If you don't know the answers to something, just tell me you don't know. Can you do that? Say that for me. Say 'I don't know.'"

"I don't know."

"Good job. And if you don't want to answer a question, just say I don't want to answer that. Can you do that? Say that for me. 'I don't want to answer that.'"

"I don't want to answer that," she said with a laugh.

"And if you're too scared to answer a question, just say 'I'm too scared to answer that.' Can you do that?"

"I'm too scared to answer."

"And if you don't understand a question, you can just say . . . "

"I can say I don't get it."

"Right, that's great. So let me ask you some questions, but don't talk too fast because I have to write it all down, okay?"

"Okay."

"How old are you?"

"I just turned nine."

"Nine," I said slowly, writing down this information. "What grade are you in?"

"Fourth."

"What school?"

"St. John's."

"What's your teacher's name?"

"Mrs. Brown."

"What do you like in school the best?"

"Spelling. And recess."

"What do you hate most?"

"That's easy," she said with a laugh. "Social studies."

"What's wrong with it?"

She shrugged.

"Boring?"

"Real boring. You wouldn't believe."

"What about math? Do you hate that, too?"

She laughed. "I'm not crazy about it. I'm not doing too good in math. I can't remember all my multiplication tables."

"They're pretty hard."

"Real hard and I'm so stupid at it."

"What kind of marks do you get?"

"Pretty bad in math. But I get A's and B's in everything else."

"Do you get in trouble in school, too? For talking? For fooling around?"

"Not much."

"What about after school? How do you spend your time?"

"I read my books, my stories that the teacher told me to. And my homework. And then mom lets me watch TV. And I play with my brother and sister."

"In the house or outside?"

"Both. Sometimes I play outside with Carrie and Paul."

"They're kids who live near you?"

"Yeah, but they're younger than me. So mostly I play with my sister and brother."

"So you must be kind of lonely."

"I am a little. But I can play with my brother and sister. I'm used to it."

"Do you have any friends at school?"

"Yeah, lots, but they live too far to come over."

"How many friends?"

"Ten or eleven."

"Is there anybody who doesn't like you?"

"No."

"So you don't get teased."

She shook her head and laughed. "I tease them."

"Any trouble making friends?"

"No."

"How do you go about making friends? Is it hard to do?"

"I ask them if they want to play. And I make friends that way. Or I help them."

"That's a good way to make friends. But do you have any trouble keeping friends?"

"No. Just fighting sometimes."

"What do you do about it?"

"Make up."

"Always?"

"Yeah."

"How about boyfriends? Got any boyfriends?"

"Not yet, but I want one."

"How come?"

She shrugged.

"Got your eyes on somebody?"

"Yeah," she said, blushing and looking down.

"What's his name?"

"Greg."

"How old is he?"

"He's in my grade. He's real popular."

"Do you just have your eyes on him? Or do you talk? Or what?"

"We talk on the phone sometimes."

"He calls you?"

"Yeah, or I call him."

"Do you ever kiss or hold hands or anything like that?"

"No way. My mother would kill me."

"How come?"

"She says I'm too young for a boyfriend. And she wants me to stay out of trouble."

"Did you ever get in any trouble? Like stealing? Or fighting? Or other things like that?"

"No, never. I'm not like those other kids."

"Did you ever steal but not get caught?"

"No, I'm not like them. Because I wouldn't want them to do it to me."

"Okay, so you don't get into any big trouble. But all kids do things that are wrong sometimes. Like when you hurt people's feelings. Do you ever feel bad if you do something wrong? Like if you hurt somebody's feelings?"

"All the time."

"What do you mean?"

"I'm always worrying about if I hurt my friends' feelings. Or my mother's feelings."

"Okay, then, that's good. It's good that you're worried about that kind of thing. It means you're growing up the right way. By the way, what do you want to be when you grow up?"

"I don't know. I didn't decide yet."

"But you must have thought about it a little."

"Well, yeah. Maybe a teacher or a doctor."

"Why a teacher?"

"Because I teach my sister a lot. I'm good at teaching her."

"Why a doctor?"

"I don't know, maybe to help people. I like to help. I help mom with the other kids all the time And with making dinner and cleaning up and sweeping and making beds and vacuuming."

"Okay, good. Can I ask you some more questions about something else?"

"Sure."

"This might be a hard question. Who do you love the most in the whole world?

"That's easy," she laughed. "My mom."

"Who do you think loves you the most?"

There was a long silence.

"Is that a hard question?"

"Well, yeah," said Cheryl. "There's my mom, and my dad, and my grandma, and my uncle, and my sisters and brother. I don't know who loves me most."

"How can you tell when somebody loves you?"

"When they hug you."

"What else do they do when they love you."

"They kiss you a lot. And they buy things for you."

"What else?"

"They don't touch you. Like Bill did. Bill says he loves me the most and that's why he touches me, but I don't believe him anymore."

"Why not?"

"Because he gave me all the attention and it wasn't fair."

"I don't get it."

"He let me get away with everything. Not like the other kids."

"How come?"

"So I would let him touch me."

"So why did you let him?"

"I couldn't help it. He was babysitting. And I thought I had to."

"Okay, how about if we come back to this later. Would it be okay if I keep asking you some more questions about your mom and your sisters and brother and about school?"

\* \* \* \* \*

There were other areas of functioning that needed to be assessed at this particular stage of the interview, so I proceeded with further questions about those areas. However, I have interrupted the interview at this point because its purpose here is not so much to illustrate a complete assessment as to illustrate aspects of this stage, as well as the interactive nature of a stage-wise interview process. From the portion of the interview presented, it is possible to formulate some tentative impressions about Cheryl's capacities to function in a range of areas.

For example, her intellectual and language abilities appear to fall within the broad limits of normal. Impairments are not evident in her capacities for memory, for concentration, or for orientation to time, place, and person. Her thinking is coherent and does not reflect any unexpected kinds of preoccupation. Nothing unusual is noted in her affect and mood, except that she seems to have a good sense of humor. Her judgment is good, as is her impulse control. In fact, she may be somewhat inhibited and overcontrolled, due to a highly developed sense of conscience, fear of disapproval, and empathy for the feelings of others. She stays out of trouble at school, her academic achievement is in the average range, and she appears to be developing a realistic future orientation that may reflect a need to help or to control. There is no reason to think that any problem exists in the development of a female gender identity, and signs exist of a stage-appropriate heterosexual interest. Her capacities for peer and family relationships appear to be strong. She seems to be bonded to her mother and emotionally connected to the rest of her immediate and extended family.

A special relationship seems to have developed between herself and her stepfather, which has blurred family boundaries and roles in a way that confuses her. There are also hints that she may have played a parentified role in the functioning and structure of the stepfamily. She would have liked to tell more about the abuse and its effects, but these areas are to be examined more completely in a subsequent stage of the interview.

In addition to illustrating the assessment of a child's functioning, the interview also shows the interactive flow between the clinician and the child as they proceed from topic to topic. A natural and easy transition is often possible between one area of questioning and the next, but whether this occurs is highly dependent on what the child has to offer. Sometimes the transition from one area of questioning to another is more arbitrary, with the clinician overtly pointing out the next direction to be taken. At other times the interaction in the interview may flow in unforeseen directions, as the child offers comments that need to be pursued. Striking the right balance between rigid adherence to a list of questions and meandering in unforeseen directions is addressed later in the book, where greater attention is given to interview technique and interactional process. For the purposes of the present chapter, it is sufficient to note that the interview is a stage-wise process that is dynamic, interactive, and alive.

\* \* \* \* \*

Once again, I would like to emphasize that the last stage, that of assessing the child's functioning, and the stages prior to it are relevant to many other kinds of interviews with children. Therefore, this chapter may be useful to therapists and evaluators doing work in areas other than sexual abuse. The next stages of the interview are more peculiar to evaluations of sexual abuse.

# CHAPTER 4

# Interviewing the Child as a Stage-wise Process

The previous stages of the interview have provided the child and the clinician with the opportunity to become as comfortable with one another as they are likely to be in one session. This, then, is a good point at which to proceed to stages of the interview that are more specific to topics related to sexual abuse, and that would be more difficult for the child to address without having previously established a certain degree of comfort.

## STAGE 6: ELICITING A DESCRIPTION OF THE ABUSE

"Now that I know a little bit more about you, Cheryl, do you mind if I switch topics?"

"No, go ahead."

"Okay, but this could be tough for you to talk about."

"You mean the reason I'm supposed to be here?"

"Right. Could you tell me what happened?"

Cheryl was silent in response to this question.

"It's hard to just start right out talking about it," I said. "It's kind of hard to know where to begin."

"Yeah," she said, nodding her head vigorously.

"How about starting by telling me when it started happening."

"Around Christmas time."

"Before Christmas or after?"

"Both."

"How much before?"

"I think it was the day before Christmas Eve."

"How do you remember that?"

"Because we went to Mass on Christmas Eve and I know it was the night before, when mom was working."

"About what time was it? I mean, was there a TV show on that would help to figure out what time it was? Or was it right after a meal? Or do you remember anything that would tell me about what time it was?"

"Yeah, it was right after watching "The Grinch That Stole Christmas." The kids had to go to bed right after that and that's when it happened."

"Where were you when it happened?"

"In the living room."

"Where the TV is?"

"Yeah, that's where the TV is."

"What else is in the room? A couch?"

"Yeah, a couch and chairs."

"What else?"

"A rug and a coffee table and a bookshelf and the fireplace."

"Where were you? What were you doing?"

"I was on the couch watching TV."

"Who else was there? Where were they?"

"Bill was sitting in one of the chairs."

"What color was the chair?"

"It's blue."

"And what was he doing?"

"Watching TV, too, and drinking a beer."

"Then what happened?"

"He asked me if I was lonely."

"And what did you say?"

"I said a little bit."

"And what did he say?"

"That he was lonely too."

"Then what happened?"

"He got up and came over and sat down next to me on the couch and then he begun touching me."

"Hold on, now, you're going a little too fast. Let me get this all down in my notes. Be patient with me. You said he got up and came over and sat down next to you, right?"

"Right."

"And what did he say? Or what did he do? What happened next? Go slowly now so I can get it all down."

"He put his arm around me and we just sat there for a minute."

"Did anybody talk?"

"Yeah, he said he liked my company."

"What did you think about that?"

"I just said thanks."

"And then?"

"Then he squeezed me, and then he put his other arm around me and hugged me tight. Real tight."

"Then what happened?"

"Then he started touching me."

"How? With what?"

"With his hand. He started moving his hand around on me."

"Where?"

"Here," she said, pointing with her hand to her chest.

"And then?"

"And then here," she said, pointing with her hand to her genitals.

"And what did you think? How did it feel?"

"I thought it was weird. I was scared."

"What did you say?"

"Nothing. I was too scared."

"What happened next?"

"He unbuttoned my pants and put his hand inside."

"Where did he put his hand first?"

"First he put it on my belly and rubbed around. And then down lower."

"Where?"

"Here," she said, pointing to her genitals. "Where I go to the bathroom."

"You mean where you pee? Or where you poop?"

"Where I pee."

"What did his hand do down there?"

"It moved around."

"How did his hand move around? What did it do exactly?"

"It moved around and then one of his fingers went inside."

"Inside?"

"Yeah, it moved around inside."

"How did that feel?"

"It hurt."

"What did you say?"

"Nothing. I wanted to tell him to stop but I was scared."

"How come?"

"Because he told me not to tell anybody. He said if I told mom, she would get mad and I would be in big trouble."

"When did he tell you that?"

"While he was doing it."

"Doing what?"

"Moving his finger around inside me."

"Then what did he do?"

"He stopped."

"Then what?"

"He buttoned my pants up and went into the kitchen to get a beer."

"Then?"

"He came back and talked for a while."

"About what?"

"About how mean mom is to him. And about how nice I was to him. And that's when he told me that nobody loved me as much as he did."

"And he didn't do anything else to you?"

"No, not till the day after Christmas."

"What did he do that day?"

"He did more that day. He didn't just stick his finger in me. He stuck something else in."

"Okay, hold on, not so fast. Where were you when that happened?"

\* \* \* \* \*

In order to assess the credibility of a child's statement and to assess the effects of abuse on the child, it is first necessary to elicit a detailed description of the abuse. This can be a difficult stage for some interviewers who, for various reasons, may be reluctant to ask direct questions about what happened. Reluctance of this kind may be due to feelings of repugnance, discomfort with issues of sexuality, overidentification with the victim, or fear of causing pain to the child. These kinds of concerns can inhibit the clinician and lead to a vague and ambiguous questioning style, which often results in wasteful and unproductive interviews.

If a detailed description of the abuse is not elicited, for whatever reason, then it will remain unclear what should be done about the effects of the abuse, about protective measures, about possible avenues of litigation, and so on. As a result, nothing helpful will have been done, and only the illusion of help will have been provided. In order to elicit the necessary information, it is essential for the interviewer to feel comfortable with the range of issues involved. Otherwise, he or she will not be able to pose the right questions in a manner so that the child will feel comfortable enough to respond.

What does one need to know about the abuse? First, one needs to know what happened, as specifically as possible. The interviewer should not be satisfied with the statement "I was molested" or "He touched me." What does molested mean? Touched you where? What exactly was done? Was it sexual intercourse? Was it oral sex? If the latter, who did what to whom? Was it fondling? If so, on what part of the body?

Were there threats made or incentives offered? What explanations were given by the offender for what he was doing with the child? And what was the child's response to this? Did the child disclose the abuse immediately afterwards? If not, why?

To adequately examine the issue of credibility, it is important to ask questions about the contextual circumstances surrounding the abuse. That is to say, it is necessary not only to ask what happened, but also to ask when it happened, where it happened, and who else in the family was present or absent (and if absent, where were they?). What was the schedule for the day and where did the abuse fit into that schedule? In which room did the abuse occur, and what did that room look like? Where is the couch located? Where is the television? Where are the end tables and lamps? What clothes did the victim have on? What was the time of day? Was it summer? Winter? During the school year? Near a birthday? Near Mother's Day? Did it occur as an isolated incident? Or as a series of incidents? Was it a chronic occurrence? Did the occurrences conform to a pattern of gradual escalation, beginning with fondling, then frottage, then oral sex, then intercourse? What was the frequency? Daily? Weekly? Monthly? From what age to what age?

In cases of incidental abuse, the one or two incidents will probably be carefully and exhaustively covered in the interview. But in cases of chronic abuse, where the incidents may have occurred weekly or monthly over a number of years, it is tempting to ignore specificity. It is important to resist this temptation and to zero in on at least one incident to get a detailed description of it. Without a certain degree of detail in a statement, it is difficult to make determinations about the child's credibility and the effects of the abuse on the child.

## STAGE 7: ASSESSING THE EFFECTS OF THE ABUSE

"Kathy, you did a good job telling me what he did, but now I want to ask you a different kind of question. Okay?"

"Okay."

"How do you feel about what he did? What are your thoughts about it all?"

"About what? You mean about him fucking me?"

"Yeah," I said. "How did it make you feel?"

"I hated it. That's how I felt."

"What else?"

"Scared."

"Of what?"

"Scared of him. And because I knew it was wrong. It was weird. Like a scary movie."

"Are you still scared?"

"A little, but not so much anymore."

"When you think about it, what are your thoughts?"

"I don't know, but I think about it all the time."

"What do you think about? What goes through your mind? What kinds of pictures do you see in your mind when you think about it?"

"What he was doing. His thing going in me. Putting it in my mouth. All that stuff."

"Does anything else go through your mind?"

"No. Just those things. Everything I just told you about. Isn't that enough?"

"Sure it is. It sounds like there's a lot on your mind. When do you think about all this? All the time or only sometimes?"

"Just sometimes. Like at night."

"When you're in bed?"

"Yeah, it's hard to stop thinking about it when I'm trying to get to sleep."

"When else do you think about it?"

"At school."

"Like when?"

"When I'm supposed to be paying attention. It's hard to pay attention to the blackboard when I'm seeing all that in my mind."

"That probably feels really weird, to have sex in your mind, while you're supposed to be paying attention to what's on the blackboard."

"I know. I can't concentrate at all sometimes. That's why I'm falling behind."

"How often do you think about all this? Every day? Once a month? Once a week? How much do you think about it?"

"It bothers me all the time. Every day."

"Every night and every day in school? In all your classes?"

"Sometimes at school, but not always. Maybe once every day. Not every class, but I think about it every day. Sometimes in math. Sometimes in English. It's always different. But every night for sure."

"Do you think about it other times, too?"

"Only in my dreams. Sometimes I dream about it."

"What happens when you're with your boyfriend?"

"I don't think about it much. It doesn't bother me much when I'm with Danny. Except when he kisses me."

"What happens when he kisses you?"

"I think about dad."

"About . . . ?"

"About him doing it to me."

"Do you get turned on by Danny? Or does it get ruined by thinking about your dad?"

"No, I get turned on. I love Danny. He's so easy to get along with."

"What happens when you're having sex with him?"

"What happens?" she laughed. "We just do it, I guess. Like anybody else does it."

"But do you enjoy it enough? Do you enjoy it as much as he does?"

"I can't get off, like he does, but he doesn't know."

"Why can't you get off?"

"I guess I think about dad. And I keep wondering."

"Wondering what?"

"What Danny would think."

"You mean if he knew?"

"Yeah, like would he think something was wrong with me?"

"Like you weren't like other girls?"

"Yeah, exactly. Like I wasn't as good as other girls."

"Do you mean that you feel second rate? Cheap?"

"Yeah, like a piece of meat. Like a slut. I feel dirty."

"Dirty?"

"Yeah, like a piece of meat being passed around."

"You feel used."

"Yeah, and used up."

"Used up?"

"Yeah, like a used Kleenex that you blew your nose in. Who would want to use that Kleenex again?"

\* \* \* \* \*

Assessing the effects of the abuse is important in both treatment and investigation. In treatment, the therapist needs to know what symptoms exist and how distressing each of those symptoms is, in order to prioritize treatment goals and decide upon therapeutic methods. In addition, initial evaluations—either for treatment or for investigations—initially need to address a more basic question: Do symptoms exist that are typical of sexual abuse? When typical symptoms are absent, there may be reason to question whether abuse has in fact occurred.

Many evaluators stumble around when attempting to address this question. Sometimes they report that a child felt angry or afraid as a result of the sexual abuse, but when asked what other effects the child is experiencing, they report that they neither asked about nor noticed other effects. This paucity of information about effects of abuse in particular cases is often due to the fact that many clinicians are not aware of the range of diverse effects that are typical of abuse.

These effects usually fall into one or more of three syndromes identified in the literature: rape trauma syndrome, post-traumatic stress disorder, and sexual abuse syndrome. While there is overlap between these three identifiable categories, there are also some differences. For example, the violence that is characteristic of rape has certain effects that distinguish rape trauma syndrome from the other syndromes. In post-traumatic stress disorder, it is the unpredictability of the traumatic stress that is the distinguishing feature, even though violence may sometimes have been a part of the precipitating stress.

Those who are suffering from post-traumatic stress disorder often experience a heightened degree of anxiety, a distractibility that can interfere with everyday functioning, an intense preoccupation with the traumatic event, and a reliving of that event in dreams and fantasy. The best-known and most exaggerated examples of this disorder are cases of war veterans who relive their traumatic experiences in hallucinations, as in Jackson Browne's lyric: "veterans who dream of the fight, fast asleep at the traffic light." Other typical causes of this disorder are automobile accidents, muggings, having one's house burgled, and being raped. The common thread is either one or a series of unpredictable and possibly violent stresses.

Many rape victims suffer from post-traumatic stress disorder but also suffer from certain other effects that may be distinct from those who have experienced stresses such as burglaries and automobile accidents. They may experience a heightened sense of personal responsibility for the rape, believing they could have done something to prevent it. They also tend to feel intensely intruded upon, violated, damaged irreparably, and soiled. It is also common for preexisting problems or cognitive styles to become exacerbated or to occur in exaggerated forms. For example, a person who is predisposed to panic disorder and has experienced occasional panic attacks throughout her life might experience panic attacks on a daily basis following a rape. A person with an obsessive-compulsive cognitive style, which was never very problematic, may become noticeably more rigid and compulsive following a rape.

While many sexually abused children experience all of the above effects, particularly in those cases where the abuse occurred with some degree of unpredictability and violence, there are many cases of abuse in which there has been neither violence nor unpredictability. The most commonly experienced symptoms are those of intense emotions at the time of abuse, such as fear, anger, or confusion.

Also common is a moral confusion about how a parent, who is supposed to protect and guide the child, could engage in this kind of act. However, this violation of trust is not always perceived by the child until many years have passed. Due to the trust children have in adults, some children do not even realize there is anything wrong with the sexual acts in which they have been engaged. It is only years later that the moral dilemmas and role confusion are more keenly felt and fully appreciated. Another kind of role confusion can be due to the child's occupying roles inappropriate or incongruent to her age and place in family life, for example, playing the roles of housekeeper and surrogate mother to her siblings and confidante and lover to her father. Feeling like "damaged goods" is also common, referring to the feeling that one is second rate, like a ripped dress or a soiled Kleenex.

Below is a short list of typical effects of abuse that may be helpful to those evaluators preparing to interview a child.

1. A damaged sense of self-worth
2. Anger, guilt, sadness, fear, anxiety, shame, sense of betrayal
3. Loss of control and autonomy over one's body; helplessness
4. Exaggeration of preexisting problems
5. Preoccupation with the abuse
6. Sexualization of nonsexual behaviors and nonsexual needs
7. Confusion about roles and morality
8. Feeling like damaged goods, feeling used up
9. Feeling cheapened, e.g., feeling like a prostitute or whore
10. Role confusion in family relationships
11. Difficulty in trusting adults, especially males
12. Sexual dysfunction
13. Isolating affect, dissociating from the abuse, denial

Probably the most common and most persistent symptom, which may be found in all three of the syndromes identified above, is that of being preoccupied by images of the abusive events. This preoccupation and rumination sometimes occur to the point that they interfere with current functioning, such as concentrating at school or on the job or getting to sleep at night.

Due to variability in persistence and severity of symptoms, it is useful to ask whether each symptom was present at the time of the abusive episodes, immediately following those episodes, and at the present time. In many instances, it will become evident that there were numerous traumatic effects experienced immediately, but that they have diminished to some extent. On the other hand, much of the trauma of sexual abuse is sometimes due not to the abusive experience itself, but to the events following its discovery, that is, to the developing understanding by the child that it is "wrong," the reactions of others to the discovery, involvement in investigatory and court proceedings, and so on. Therefore, the evaluator needs to be sensitive to those instances in which the trauma tends to escalate in the period following the discovery of the abusive event. What has happened to the child both before and after the abuse may be just as important in determining its effects as the abuse itself.

In general, it can be assumed that the greater the severity and chronicity of abuse, the more numerous and more extensive the effects will be. By severity of abuse, I am referring to the extent of sexual involvement, with fondling constituting a less severe act than frottage (i.e., genital contact without penetration), and frottage a less severe act than sexual intercourse. The presence and the degree of violence would also affect a judgment of severity. By chronicity, I refer to the frequency and the length of time the abuse occurred. Was it an isolated act? Or did it occur every few months? Or did it occur on a weekly or even daily basis? Utilizing these concepts together, one would expect that a child whose breast was fondled by a drunk uncle on one occasion would be less traumatized than a child who was raped repeatedly by her father and brothers for years on a weekly basis.

However, there are a great many exceptions to this rule. I have known children who have had sex with adults regularly for years who are less affected than children who have experienced mild abuse in isolated incidents. There may be a number of reasons for this. One factor may be the presence of extraneous issues, such as divorce or alcoholism in the family or a psychotic family member. Such family dysfunction can become attached symbolically to an isolated incident of abuse to render it more important to the child than it would otherwise be. Another factor is the degree to which the abuse is predictable. The more unpredictable and uncontrollable the abuse has been, the greater the traumatic effect is likely to be.

Another factor to consider is the robustness or fragility of the child's personality, capacities, and strengths, the assessment of which was discussed in the previous chapter. A fragile or highly dysfunctional child might be devastated by mild abuse, while a child with many strengths may be capable of accommodating to more severe abuse with little disturbance in his current functioning. Thus, the nature and degree of symptomatology may depend upon a complex interaction between chronicity, severity, ego strength, family dysfunction, unpredictability of the trauma, as well as other relevant variables.

These various considerations point to the need for a very careful inquiry into the effects of abuse. Such an inquiry can be guided by concepts drawn from the three syndromes identified above, as well as from relevant literature on this issue. Overall, the evaluator can maintain a clear focus amidst an array of distracting implications and considerations by keeping a few central questions in mind: Are there effects of abuse present in this case? What are they? And how extensive or debilitating is each effect?

As mentioned earlier, the absence of symptoms typical of abuse can raise questions as to whether abuse occurred. Yet, the presence or absence of symptoms is not sufficient in itself for determining whether abuse occurred. After all, some abused children display no discernible symptoms; in addition, symptoms typical of abuse can occur as a result of other disorders and life circumstances.

There are numerous other factors, in addition to symptoms, that are just as crucial to determining whether abuse occurred. One of these is whether there exist hidden agendas, motives, or other reasons for the child to make false statements. Inquiry into these constitutes the next stage of the interview to be considered.

## STAGE 8: INQUIRING INTO REASONS FOR MAKING FALSE STATEMENTS

"At first you said that he raped you, but now you're saying he didn't. Are you changing your story because you're scared of being put in a foster home?"

This kind of question sometimes stimulates vigorous nods and a breakdown into sobbing, followed by a convincing explanation for why the original allegations were recanted. There are many other kinds of questions that can be equally helpful in discovering whether a child is making a true or false statement, but it is not meaningful to provide a list of them at this point. The specific questions to ask are dictated by the understanding that the evaluator has about why children make false statements. Therefore, it may be more useful here to spend some time discussing types of false statements that are most frequently made.

For example, recantations, that is, reversals of original allegations, indicate that either the original allegation or the recantation is a false statement. These are quite common in cases of sexual abuse. Their occurrence is sometimes due to what is known as a suppression stage in the life of a sexual abuse case—that is to say, a stage in which a great deal of pressure is put on a child to suppress or recant the allegations. This stage occurs after the initial disclosure has been made, but before substantive court proceedings have begun. The stresses and pressures to recant are very intense at this point.

The victim may fear that she and her siblings will be removed from the family and placed in a foster home. The father, who is often the breadwinner, may be in danger of losing his job; therefore, the rent or mortgage may be in jeopardy. He also may be in danger of going to jail, which is a considerable pressure on those children who are attached to their fathers. The marital relationship also may be at a precarious stage, with the mother unsure of whether to believe her husband or her daughter. Talk of divorce may be in the air. The child also may feel unsupported by the mother and by her siblings, all of whom may be angry at the child for making a disclosure that has threatened to disrupt the family. Finally, the child may be in the process of undergoing numerous interviews with police, social service investigators, and psychologists, who ask repetitive and endless questions about the sexual abuse, often causing acute pain and embarrassment, and do so over and over again.

From the child's perspective, the sky is falling and all her hopes and dreams have been dashed. After all, she had screwed her courage to the sticking point in order to make the disclosure, in the fond hope of a happy ending to the sexual abuse. Instead, the pressures of the suppression stage are so powerful that she may soon be sorry that she said anything at all. With the family busting apart at the seams, it is not uncommon for the family members to unconsciously exert subtle efforts to get the child to change her story. Sometimes these efforts are not so unconscious; in fact, often they are quite blatant. It is not surprising that many children tend to recant during this stage. An understanding of this stage, along with an understanding of the particular child, will suggest the kind of question most appropriate for inquiring into reasons for false recantations.

At the beginning of this section, a child was asked whether she was afraid she might be placed in a foster home. She might just as well have been asked any number of other questions. Was she afraid that her father would be put in jail? That her parents would divorce? Or that the family would no longer be able to afford rent, food, and clothes? Any of these fears could constitute sufficient motivation for false recantations of previous allegations of sexual abuse.

Another reason that a child may make false statements about an actual incident of sexual abuse is that she may be going through a difficult time in which she vacillates between assertions and denials of abuse. At times she may say yes, she has been abused; at other times she may say no, she has not; and at other times she may say maybe. This "yes-no-maybe" phenomenon can be frustrating for the evaluator. However, the evaluator needs to be sensitive to the difficulties children have in making disclosures of abuse. It is a hard thing to do for many children. In addition to the influences of the suppression phase, many children do not want to admit, even to themselves, that they have been abused, and even if they are willing to face this themselves, they may not wish to share their shame with others.

Some children may not be able to work through the "yes-no-maybe" stage in one session; they may need numerous sessions in which to establish the necessary degree of trust. While the evaluator probably cannot afford this amount of time, he can at least be alert to this issue and help to identify it where it exists. This course is preferable to inferring that abuse did not occur because of inconsistencies in the child's statements.

Until now, we have spoken only of actual sexual abuse that was initially disclosed and later denied. We need to consider, as well, false allegations of sexual abuse. A decade ago, the lore in the mental health profession suggested that children did not lie about abuse; therefore, recantations were usually considered to be false. However, the last ten years have shown that children sometimes do lie about sexual abuse, and not only due to the suppression phase. Therefore, the possibility always exists that the first story, as well as the recantation, may be a false statement.

False allegations can be due to several reasons, to which the clinician must remain alert. Some general reasons for false allegations are: the child's wish to protect the mother from the father's beatings; the child's desire for revenge against the father figure; the child's poor reality-testing; the child's need for attention; the child's wish to be out of the house; the child's responsiveness to one parent's wishes in a hotly disputed custody or visitation contest; and the child's misunderstanding of a school presentation of the concept of good-touch/bad-touch. It may be helpful at this point to illustrate a few of these reasons with examples.

An example of revenge can be illustrated with Anna, who made allegations of sexual abuse against her stepfather, who she believed was responsible for the death of her natural father. Her father and stepfather had once got into a physical fight, which in her mind meant that her stepfather had somehow caused the death of her father (although he had died from other causes). It was necessary to elicit her exact understanding of these issues in order to determine whether this constituted a reasonable motivation for her to make false allegations. The process of clarifying these issues with her resulted in her admitting that she had made false allegations of abuse as a means to get even with her stepfather.

The desire to protect a parent can be illustrated by the case of Bernadette. Initially she alleged that her stepfather sexually abused her, but then she recanted. She then reversed her recantation, once again claiming that she had been abused. In her first recantation, Bernadette had said that she had made the false allegation because her stepfather had beaten her mother; the purpose of the allegation was to get him out of the house so that her mother would be safe. In this case, it was important to first inquire into why the child had recanted — in other words, why she felt her mother was safe. In addition, now that the child was reversing the recantation and again claiming sexual abuse, it was important to inquire into what had changed to cause the girl to believe the mother was unsafe once again.

Poor reality-testing can be illustrated by the case of Jill, an eight-year-old foster child who alleged that her 15-year-old foster brother had, on one occasion, crept into her bed in the middle of the night, climbed on top of her, and "humped" her. Jill indicated in words and gestures that, while they both remained clothed, he had rhythmically rubbed his hard penis against her stomach. The allegation was described in such vivid detail that it was difficult to imagine how an eight-year-old could have provided such detail if the incident had not actually occurred. However, the foster brother adamantly denied the allegations. He said that Jill was angry at him because he wouldn't spend time with her. The foster father agreed with his son and offered the further observation that Jill's behavior with any male was seductive and inappropriate.

This last observation led to an inquiry into whether Jill had been previously abused, an inquiry that eventually revealed that four years earlier an eight-year-old boy had gotten on top of Jill and "humped" her exactly as she alleged her foster brother had done. My final conclusion in this case was that Jill had fantasized the abuse by the foster brother while in a partial stage of sleep. The fantasy utilized her past experience of sexual abuse in the service of economically meeting two needs: to express her anger at the foster brother for rejecting her and to fulfill her need for emotional contact with him.

Some of the other reasons identified above for making false statements are illustrated in other sections throughout the book. The important point to remember is that the clinician needs to be alert to the child's possible motivations to make false statements. It is prudent to make inquiries of this kind during later rather than earlier stages of the interview because they may alienate the child. The child may feel challenged and doubted, even when questions are carefully phrased, and she may respond by becoming less willing to talk openly. The risk of alienating the child is, however, minimized when rapport has been firmly established in previous stages of the interview. The cost of alienating the child is also minimized when you have already elicited most of the information you need. However, if the child is too upset to continue talking, she is probably too upset to be allowed to exit the interview. The next and final stage of the interview constitutes a debriefing process in which the child is given the opportunity to pull herself together.

## STAGE 9: PATCHING UP THE CHILD AT THE END OF THE INTERVIEW

"What else happened after that?" I asked a 13-year-old child.

"Nothing," she gasped between sobs, shuddering inconsolably, with tears running down her cheeks. She had just finished describing in detail how her father had been having sexual intercourse with her for several months on an almost daily basis. She had also described fully the effects on her of this abuse.

"Is there anything more that you would like to tell me about it?"

"No," she gasped, shaking her head. "I told you everything."

"Well," I said. "I've asked you a lot of questions. Do you have any questions you would like to ask me?"

"Yeah, what will happen in court?"

"I don't know the answer to that for sure. But I don't think your dad will be coming back home right away. Is that what you want to know?"

"Yeah," she gasped again, stifling a sob. "That's all I was really worried about."

"Is there anything else you would like to ask?"

"No."

"Okay, then, is there anything else you think I should know? Anything you want to tell me that I didn't ask you about?"

"No. I think you asked everything."

"Well, I don't have anything else to ask you, so I guess I'm done, but I don't want you to have to go out of here feeling all messed up and crying and feeling so terrible. Maybe we could talk about something that would help to make you feel a little better. When you feel bad like this, what do you usually do to make yourself feel better?"

"I block it all. I try to think about something else."

"Does that work?" I asked.

She laughed at my apparent surprise. "Sometimes."

"Like what?" I asked. "What do you think about?"

"About parades."

"Parades?" I asked in surprise.

"Yeah," she said with a laugh. "I like parades."

"What else do you think about that makes you feel good?"

"Ice cream."

"What flavor?"

"Heath Bar Crunch."

"On a sugar cone or a plain cone?"

"Are you nuts?" she laughed, wiping tears from her eyes with her fingers. "A sugar cone, of course."

"And what's this about parades?" I asked. "When was the last parade you were at?"

"Thanksgiving," she said. "I marched in it with a baton."

"You twirled a baton?"

"I don't know how to twirl. All we had to do was move it up and down."

"But you had a good time."

"The best. With all the floats and all the different kinds of marchers. I loved it."

"Great," I said. "Listen, can I ask you about today? I know you had a tough time this morning with me, but what are you doing this afternoon after you leave? What are your plans for the day?"

\* \* \* \* \*

It is important for the interviewer to keep in mind that the child did not ask to be brought to the interview, yet the interview may cause a great deal of pain. The interviewer is in the position of having to learn about the child's situation and, in the process of doing so, may have to inflict pain on the child by causing him to remember very painful events.

Due to the clinical skill of the interviewer, the child may find himself able to confront and share issues he has not yet decided he wants to confront, much less share with anyone, and may find himself surprised to be disclosing such painful material. Although some children feel extremely relieved and are grateful by the end of the interview for the opportunity to "get it all out," others are a psychological mess. At various points during the interview, they may be in extreme pain, sob uncontrollably, and appear to be inconsolable.

In these cases, the interviewer has effectively ripped the scab off of a wound that has only begun to heal. The interviewer can open up the child and then leave her high and dry. Upon exiting the interview the child may feel defenseless and too disoriented to access usual coping mechanisms.

This may be the case even though the interviewer may have taken extraordinary care to be gentle in the questioning. Just because an interviewer thinks that a question is asked gently, or that a remark is innocuous, does not mean that it will be received or interpreted as such. It is not possible to accurately predict the effect of every question or remark. A remark that causes one child to break down into tears may not even cause another child to blink.

In earlier years, some children were exiting my interviews in the undefended, weepy, disoriented state I just described. The rest of their day was ruined by frequent preoccupation and rumination about the abuse of which I had reminded them. I consoled myself with the theory that the pain of the interview was necessary and inevitable, that the child would heal, and that the subsequent heightened preoccupation for a day or so was itself a part of the healing process, which had been briefly accelerated by the intensity of the interview. I also believed that I handled these children gently and that, if *someone* had to inflict this pain, it was just as well that it had been me.

However, gradually my technique and habits must have evolved, because at some point I realized that the end of the interview became a time for a debriefing process, in which I would attempt to patch up the child or put her back together, psychologically, as best I could. After asking the child all the questions I needed to, I usually asked if she had any questions or anything she wanted to tell me. Then I shifted gears and spent some time asking questions about her strengths, things she liked to do, plans she had for the next week or two that she might be looking forward to, and so on. This was intended to help her put herself back together, to redistribute her attention, and to substitute neutral and positive contents of consciousness for more intensely negative ones.

This debriefing process consists of several important ingredients. First, it requires conveying the message that talking about painful events has come to an end and a new and final stage has begun. One can punctuate the onset of this next stage of the interview process by either shifting into a different type of interviewing process (e.g., asking questions that have nothing to do with the abuse) or making explicit statements about this shift (e.g., saying, "We're done talking about the abuse, and now we can talk about how you're going to get through the rest of the day in a decent mood after just talking about all this.").

Second, it involves reminding the child about what he ordinarily does to try to make himself feel better, and if he can think of nothing, offering suggestions of what other children do to defend against or cope with painful issues. Third, it involves taking the child's attention away from abuse and placing it on everyday, ordinary concerns, such as enjoyable activities and plans for that day. Fourth, this debriefing process may on occasion include an explanation of the debriefing process itself, which can convey some important information about the meaning and utility of the psychological pain that may have been experienced during a session.

This fourth ingredient is useful either with highly articulate children or in a context of ongoing therapy. Specifically, the message is conveyed that memories of the abuse are indeed painful and talking about them may sometimes increase the pain. However, even though it hurts to face what causes the pain, this can sometimes accelerate healing. Yet, it's hard to always be facing painful memories because this interferes with normal functioning. Therefore, it is useful to have certain times and places where one can confront painful events, such as in writing in a special journal, talking about it in therapy sessions, or discussing it with a special person. If one expresses one's feelings in these contained contexts, then one can feel free to let go of these feelings at other times in order to function effectively in everyday life. This explanation helps to contain the pain within the interview and gives the child permission to avoid or deny it outside of the interview, with the reminder that the pain may have a lingering potential for hurting until the child is ready to face it again.

With younger children and with those who lack the verbal facility to fully comprehend the various messages conveyed in this debriefing process, I often just shift the topic away from sexual abuse until we are talking about ice cream, parades, and plans for the week. I terminate only after I am satisfied that the child is dry-eyed, comfortable, reasonably cheerful, and adequately oriented to his surroundings and to the plans for the day. I should point out that I utilize this process in almost any kind of interview that causes pain, such as in a custody evaluation or with an inconsolable suicidal adolescent grieving for her lost love. The process is very much like the trance termination procedures used in hypnosis, where the subject's attention is deliberately drawn away from a highly concentrated focus to those everyday concerns that orient us to reality.

The main point I want to make in closing this chapter is that it is important that we not leave children high and dry after opening them up and asking them to expose the most vulnerable parts of themselves. While it is important during sexual abuse evaluations to confront children on many painful issues, it is also within our area of expertise to provide them with the means to compensate for their pain and to function as optimally as possible in meeting everyday demands. We do not need to accept that our role will inevitably or necessarily debilitate our patients and cause them to be more dysfunctional in their everyday life than they would have been in the absence of our involvement.

*     *     *     *     *

These last chapters have taken a global look at the interview with the child and indicated how that interview can be divided into parts. I hope, also, that the reasons for following the particular sequence of stages outlined here have been clear enough to enable the reader to vary sequence as the need arises. The areas of focus identified here are likely in most cases to yield a maximum of relevant information with a high degree of economy and ease; however, sometimes there may be relevant information that cannot be captured by the particular format presented here. Every case presents circumstances idiosyncratic to the specific allegations, which may be important to identify. Consequently, the evaluator cannot be wedded to a cookie-cutter approach to evaluation, but rather needs to be open, flexible, and alert to unique aspects in every case.

# PART II

# *Interview Technique*

"You're almost ready to begin. With the stages of the interview in mind, at least you have some way of organizing yourself."

"Ready to begin? But I've already begun, and my interviews are a mess, even with the crib sheets and with the rest of your advice. My interviews never work out as well as your examples."

"I didn't say you were ready yet. I said you were almost ready."

"I thought I was ready. I've been trying to do everything you told me, in all my interviews."

"That's not enough, obviously. All I've done is give you a way to organize yourself. I haven't yet spent much time showing you some of the ways in which the interview can be ruined or improved by what you say and do."

"So, everything you said about the stages of the interview isn't enough?"

"No. We need to look at the interview process itself, at the interaction between you and the client. Especially at what you do. At your technique. Then maybe you'll be able to see why your interviews are a mess."

"Good. Because something's not going right. Sometimes I feel really effective, like I'm the best clinician in the world. But other times I feel like I'm at sea. And the worst thing about it is that I don't know why."

"Right. You don't know how to guide yourself because you don't know what is helpful and unhelpful about each of your behaviors."

*"I didn't think about it quite like that. I thought certain behaviors were good and others were just bad. For example, the way you're so directive and matter-of-fact with kids, it gives them a lot of structure and puts them at ease. That's good and I've tried to imitate it."*

*"But it isn't always good to be directive. That's my point. I always need to consider the advantages and disadvantages of being directive. I need to decide in each situation whether it's worth the risks of a directive approach."*

*"Aren't you always directive?"*

*"Not always. I'm sometimes very nondirective. Sometimes it's disastrous to be too directive."*

*"Then why not be nondirective more of the time?"*

*"Sometimes it's a terrible waste of time and the potential for disaster is minimal."*

*"So how do you decide what to do? Which technique is best?"*

*"First, by understanding the potential advantages and disadvantages of each technique. Only then, in a given circumstance, can you make an informed choice."*

*"An informed choice? What do you mean? About what?"*

*"About whether to avoid that particular technique or approach, due to its potential disadvantages, or whether to take the risk of using it when reasons for doing so take priority."*

*"So it's a very difficult balancing act."*

*"That's one way of putting it."*

*"Do you decide before the interview how you will approach it?"*

*"How can you? There's a multitude of techniques and behaviors that you have at your disposal. Your decision about which technique to utilize will change at various points throughout the interview, depending on how the client is responding to what you're doing."*

*"So you're doing this kind of balancing act at every moment during an interview? You're being that deliberate about your choices?"*

*"Yes. You can regard any interview as a series of choice points. At any given moment, if you stopped a videotape and asked me, I could probably tell you what my rationale was for what I had just done or said, no matter how trivial the statement might have appeared to you as you observed it."*

*"But I couldn't do that."*

*"I know. That's why you're not sure why things feel right sometimes and why things feel wrong sometimes."*

*"But if I tried this, I'd be extremely self-conscious, and mostly about my inadequacies."*

*"That can be paralyzing, can't it? But if it doesn't quite paralyze you,*

*it's probably a useful anxiety because it will help you to become increasingly sensitized to all those behaviors of yours that might interfere with your purposes during the interview."*

*"How can I ever learn all this?"*

*"By taking a closer look at what you do during the interview."*

*"And that's what you've been waiting to do with me next?"*

*"Yes. When you were ready for it. That's what the next few chapters are about. The fine-tuning of interview technique."*

# CHAPTER 5

# Common Errors in Interview Technique

"So where do we start?"

"How about starting on some areas of technique that are relevant to any clinical situation, not just sexual abuse."

"But I've got no problem with those other situations. I do evaluations and therapy just fine with other types of problems."

"So you don't think you'll recognize yourself in any examples I might give of errors in technique."

"Maybe, but I kind of doubt it. I'm a good clinician, on the whole. You've told me so yourself many times."

"Yes, but you might be surprised. You might just recognize yourself here. After all, good clinicians tend to bring to their supervisors those difficulties they've recognized. But how do you even know to bring up something that you haven't recognized?"

"What do you mean? I don't get it."

"Like being really friendly with clients. It's something many clinicians pride themselves on, not being aware that it's often problematic."

"What's wrong with being friendly? I'm a real friendly sort of person, especially with kids."

"That's what I mean. I think you'll recognize yourself in this chapter, even though you don't realize it yet. Sometimes, in viewing even one session of a clinician in action, even a session he thought was just great, you can point out a particular way of behaving that is problematic—and problematic not only for that session but for almost any kind of session he might do. It pervades his range of functioning because he is simply unaware that it's a problem."

"But I thought we were talking about sexual abuse interviews."

"We are. The techniques and problems we'll examine here are extremely relevant to sexual abuse interviews, but they're equally relevant to other types of interviews."

"So you think I'll learn a lot that will help in other kinds of work? Are you saying I'm a screw-up in everything I do?"

"Not at all, but often after we learn the basics of interview technique, we move on and don't spend enough time fine-tuning those basics. We take it for granted that we have the basics under our belts, and we falsely believe we do the job well enough. We underestimate how important those basics are to an effective interview and how much an interview can suffer when basic techniques are faulty."

"Like what? What are the basics you want to look at?"

"Well, why don't we start out with something we were just talking about? The effects of being too direct and interrogative. And then, alternatively, the effects of being too indirect and vague. Then the effects of being too complicated in one's use of language, and then the effects of being too polite, and then . . . "

"Too polite? Can you be too polite?"

"Yes, and too friendly . . . "

"That again?"

"Yes, and too patronizing."

"Is that all?"

"It's a beginning."

## THE NEED TO AVOID INTERROGATION

While it is necessary to ask questions in most interviews, the act of questioning has certain predictable effects of which the interviewer should be aware. One such effect was made strikingly clear to me on an occasion in which I spent the entire interview asking numerous questions, one after another, in a relentless effort to discover which of several possible men was the one who abused a child. Only when I was exhausted, gave up, and asked if there was anything else she wanted to tell me did I finally learn what it was that my countless questions had failed to uncover.

"Oh, yeah, there is something else," she told me. "I want to tell you about the time Uncle Frank pulled my pants down in the woods behind the house."

She would have been happy to have told it to me earlier if I had not prevented her with my questions. My questions were evidently not the right ones and therefore had the effect of drawing her attention more to figuring out how to answer those questions than to telling me what was on her mind.

Another effect of questioning is causing the child to be suspicious of your motives. For example, the question, "What were you doing in the woods?" might easily engender a response of silence if the child were suspicious that her answer could get her in trouble. This kind of effect is certainly not restricted to interviews of sexual abuse but is a common, everyday effect in interactions with children.

For example, while I was in the yard wiping from a chair water that I had thought was run-off from the roof, an observing six-year-old expressed the following comment.

"I guess that's what happens when kids stand on chairs."

"Someone was standing on the chair?" I asked.

"Uh, yeah, a kid was."

"Which kid?"

Silence.

"Who did you say?" I asked again.

"Uh, it must of been . . . uh, I think it was one of the other kids. Do kids get punished for that?"

"No, it doesn't matter. It's an outdoor chair that gets wet anyway."

"Then how come you wanted to know who was on it?"

"Because after you told me, I was curious if it was you. Was it?"

"Well, you see, I was standing on it by accident for a while."

\* \* \* \* \*

Whenever you ask a question, you take the risk that the child may feel as if you are trying to get him out on a limb only to saw it off.

Finally, the example of the evaluator in Chapter 3, sitting toe to toe with the child, with eyes glued to the child's in an effort at good eye contact, illustrates the above effects as well as some others. Asking one question after another in this way, or asking the same question repetitively, can feel like an interrogation to the child. The effect is that of intimidating and silencing the child, rather than warming her up so that she can talk freely.

It is important for the evaluator to keep these potential effects in mind during the interview. If he is fully aware of the risks involved when asking questions, then he can do so judiciously, thereby modulating the intensity of the questioning process so that it does not disrupt the flow of interaction.

## VAGUENESS AND INDIRECTION VS. THE NEED TO ASK QUESTIONS

It is also possible to deliberately avoid any questioning at all, instead creating an atmosphere in which the child can talk about whatever she wishes. This approach is certainly nonthreatening, but in almost all cases it is wasteful of the interviewer's time. Asking questions is essential to organizing the focus of attention and the use of available time. Yet, at times, the interviewer may need to sacrifice productivity in order to reduce the child's anxiety and facilitate verbalization.

For example, with a withdrawn, nonverbal three-year-old who has been severely abused, it might be necessary to spend the entire session, or a number of sessions, utilizing an approach of nondirective play therapy, which strictly avoids the use of questions or directions. This same approach, when used with more verbal children and adults, is known as reflective or active listening. While it is sometimes the only approach used throughout entire sessions, such as in client-centered counseling, it is an approach that needs to be available to any clinician for intermittent use in almost any kind of interview situation, even with the more directive therapeutic styles.

This approach consists of reflecting back, in words, the feelings and messages conveyed by what the other person has just said. This reflection is illustrated in the following example. Observe the avoidance of any questioning in this conversation between a mother and her ten-year-old son.

＊　＊　＊　＊　＊

"I don't want to go to dad's on weekends anymore. I hate it when you make me go."

"You're pretty mad about this."

"You're not kidding. I'm real mad."

"About me making you go there on weekends."

"Yeah, but what makes me really mad is it's so boring there, and he's mean, and you guys are here having a fun time."

"You feel like it's not fair."

"Yeah, it's not fair at all. And all he does is yell all the time. About you and going to court and . . . "

＊　＊　＊　＊　＊

This brief example of reflective listening illustrates the listener's ability to avoid intruding her own thoughts and feelings upon the conversation. If she had asked specific questions about why her son hated going to dad's, his attention might have been deflected away from what he really needed to say. If she had said to him that he had to go whether he liked it or not, he would have been angry and felt that she wasn't interested; in addition, there would have been no opportunity for him to discover the sources of his strong feelings and to share these with her. If she had told him that he didn't have to go any longer, she would have cut off the possibility of visiting when perhaps his anger was very temporary and due to a resolvable problem.

When utilizing this approach, it is essential to resist the very strong temptation to express one's own feelings or thoughts, such as stating an opinion, a question, a piece of advice, a criticism, a warning, a threat, a judgment, a lecture, or an argument. Like questions, such statements have predictable effects, which can inhibit a person's responsiveness. For example, advice predictably leaves the other person feeling inferior, as if he could not come up with a good solution himself. Criticism leaves him feeling put down. While each type of statement has unique and predictable effects, all of them tend to leave the person feeling that you are not truly interested in his feelings and in what he has to say. The overall effect is that of shutting down communication rather than facilitating it.

This is not to imply that one should never provide criticism, advice, opinions, lectures, or warnings. These types of statements are important to make at appropriate times. They are unlikely to be very useful, however, when the child is bothered by strong feelings and when your goals are to make him feel understood and to facilitate communication about what is bothering him.

When reflective listening is practiced in its most orthodox form, it has a very powerful set of effects: (1) It helps a person to feel understood, because assiduous attention is paid to each subtle nuance of the person's messages; (2) it enhances self-esteem, because the person learns that his feelings and thoughts really matter to someone; (3) it facilitates problem-solving because the person is encouraged to continue to express feelings and ideas until he arrives at his own solution; (4) it encourages self-acceptance and a fuller use of self, because one is able to express and eventually to accept in oneself negative feelings that have been neither criticized nor approved, but rather accepted by the listener; (5) it enhances communication, because it results in a flow of verbalizations and eventually a readiness to listen nondefensively to any feelings, advice, opinions, criticisms, or questions that the listener may have to offer.

It is worthwhile for beginning clinicians to practice reflective listening in its most orthodox form until they are able to do so without violating its principles; that is, until it is a practiced skill available for use as needed. While this may appear to be an easy task when reading about it in a book, it is not so easy in reality. After a clinician is able to practice it with ease and has a vivid understanding of the potential negative effects of deviating from the approach, it is important for the clinician to go ahead and become more directive during interviews, so that he is not entirely at the mercy of the client's agenda.

It should be obvious that using reflective listening in its most orthodox form would not be a very economical approach to take in an evaluation; the evaluation might never be completed. Yet, it is essential for the interviewer, no matter how directive and interrogative his style may be, to have reflective listening in his repertoire of skills.

Each clinician needs to strike the right balance between questioning and listening. If one is skilled in the use of reflective listening, then one will not repeatedly vacillate between meandering and grilling, which is a common problem for beginners. Yet, it is not easy to find that right balance where one is able to avoid wasteful meandering, get to the point, and at the same time keep the child open to talking. This balance is illustrated at various points of the dialogue in the example that follows.

## THE EFFECT OF GENTLE BUT PERSISTENT QUESTIONING

Sally, age eight, had warmed up to me and was talking a mile a minute. She talked about her interests and hobbies, her anger at her mother for yelling so often, what she wanted to be when she grew up, what her worst fears were, and so on. After I had found out enough to formulate an assessment of her developmental adjustment, it came time to begin to ask her about the sexual abuse. It had not come up naturally, so it had to be deliberately introduced.

"Sally, let me explain something to you, okay? I've spent some time asking you all of these questions so that I can know what kind of a kid you are, but now it's time to talk about why you came here today, which we talked about for a little while when you first came in here."

"Yeah, about getting molested," she responded immediately. The immediacy of this cooperative and quite verbal reaction was probably a result of the rapport that had already been established.

"Okay," I said, "then how about telling me what happened."

There was then a silence on her part, and a shrinking in of her body frame, with her head held down. It looked as if the rapport that had been established was not going to pay off. The trajectory of responsiveness that had been built up was suddenly blocked. She appeared to feel inhibited, but I wasn't sure why—perhaps from shame, or fear, or self-consciousness.

"Sally, listen. I know that this is hard to talk about."

She nodded her head.

"You probably feel embarrassed or scared."

She nodded her head again, more vigorously this time.

"But what I need to know first is where you were when it first happened." This was asked to give her a concrete and easier way to respond and hopefully to restore the response set that had been previously established.

She paused, then said, "In the car."

"When?"

She paused then—it was too long of a pause, about seven seconds. I didn't want her to get used to not answering my questions, so I tried again with a question that might be easier to answer. It was a forced choice question, which provided a framework for the kinds of information I was seeking.

"Was it a long time ago? Like a year ago? Two years ago? Last month? Two months ago? Three months ago?"

"Oh, no, it was just a couple weeks ago."

"In the car? Going where?"

"To the fair," she said as if it was a fact the whole world should know, and why didn't I know it, too?

"And what happened?" This was a probe, an open-ended question. Would she balk or continue with her previous volubility?

Again, she balked, shrunk, and withdrew.

"Okay, so you're in the car, and you're on your way to the fair, is that right? Or did I get it all wrong?" I wanted a verbal response this time, to establish or maintain a psychological set to verbalize, not just to nod or shake the head.

"No, you got it right."

"To have fun at the fair. That's what you wanted to do."

"Right. Have fun."

"So let me get all this down." I paused, writing slowly, though I had been taking notes before as well. I then slowly read from my notes. "To have fun. In the car. Heading for the fair." Do I have that right?"

"Yup," she said, no longer shrunken in upon herself, but attentive and more cheerful.

"Okay, and do you remember what streets you took? Or any stores you passed? So that I can figure out the way you went. Or big signs? Billboards? Or McDonald's? Or . . . "

"Burger King, we passed a Burger King and the K-Mart right across the street from Burger King and . . . "

"Wait, now, you're going too fast for me, I have to get this all down on paper and I'm a little slow. Can you be patient with me?"

"Sure."

"Do you know what the word patient means?"

"Uh, yeah. Like, sitting around. Like, waiting? Yeah, waiting."

"Right. And helping, too. You're helping me when you're being patient with me. Okay, now, so you're driving in the car and you go past Burger King. Do you remember what street that was?"

"No," she said, shaking her head.

"Any of the streets?"

"No."

"Well, that's okay, because we know you went past Burger King, and you were on the way to the fair to have fun and then something happens, but when you tell me what happens, please, go slow, so I can get it all down in my notes. I'm not too quick on the uptake, so help me out and go slow. Okay?"

"Okay."

"So you're in the car on the way to the fair. What happened then?"

"He stopped the car next to some trees, and he told me he was teaching me something."

"He told you he was teaching you something." I said slowly, writing it down. "Okay, I got it down. So, then, you said something? Or did something? Or he did? What happened next?"

"He molested me."

"He molested you," I said slowly, showing by my body posture and concentration that I was more interested in getting the facts written down properly than I was in the fact that she was molested.

"Okay," I said. "I got that down, but I'm confused. I don't understand something. He said he was going to teach you something. What did he mean by that? What was he going to teach you?"

"He said he was teaching me about sex."

"And what did you think about that?"

"I didn't know what he was talking about."

"You didn't know what he was talking about. Okay. So when did you understand what it was he was talking about?"

"When he molested me."

"When was that? What did he do? Like, what did he say? Or what were his hands doing? What happened next?"

"He unzipped my pants and then he molested . . . "

"Wait, you're going too fast." I was trying to stop her from subsuming the entire incident under the term "molestation." I desired a more differentiated description, if that was possible. "He unzipped your pants," I said slowly, "and then what did you do or what did you say?"

"Nothing. I was too scared. I didn't know why he was doing it."

"Did he say anything then? Or did you?"

"He said nobody should know what he was teaching me, and I told him to stop or I'd tell my mother."

"You would tell your mother," I said slowly as I wrote it down. "Do I have that all down right?"

"Yup."

"Okay, you said you would tell your mother. What did he say to that? Or what did he do? What happened next? Tell me what happened so I can see it, you know, so I can see it like in a movie."

"He said he was teaching me and he unzipped my pants and told me he would shoot my mother and me if I told. And then he pulled my pants down."

"Okay, wait, let me get all that down, don't go too fast, okay?"

"Okay," she said, leaning forward and looking over my notes.

"You got all that down the right way?"

"Right, that he would shoot himself and then you . . . "

"No, not shoot himself, shoot me and mom." She was hovering over my notes now as if she was dictating to an incompetent secretary. "And then he stuck his finger in me and pulled out his . . . "

"Wait," I said, "slow down. He said he would shoot you and your mother and then he stuck his finger in you. Do I have that right? And then what did he do with his finger while it was . . . "

"He moved it around a lot."

"Moved it around?"

"Wiggled it around."

"How did that feel?"

"Kind of weird."

"Did you ever feel anything like that before?"

"No, I never had anything stuck up me like that before."

"So it felt weird. How else did it feel?"

"It hurt."

"It hurt."

"A lot."

"So when it hurt like that, did you say something about it?"

\* \* \* \* \*

I will stop at this point because the necessary points have been made. This interview illustrates all those cases in which the client suddenly becomes reluctant to go on, just when you thought she was about to tell you about the abuse. I have found it useful in these cases to exploit, and to point out to the child, some very real limitations of my own, such as my inability to write notes as rapidly as I would like or to fully comprehend all she is trying to convey to me. This serves to shift my position from someone who is questioning or grilling the child to someone needing the child's help.

To provide help to someone who is vulnerable, limited, and incompetent is very often irresistable. When the child responds in a helpful mode she is able to counter the pain of the trauma, as well as the embarrassment occasioned by talking about it. She is often able, as in this case, to go on to describe the abuse in assiduous detail. Assuming a one-down position permits one to question the child at length, because the child is now in a more powerful helping position, which distracts her from her pain. An interview can seldom get better than when the child is scolding you to make sure you get all the information down correctly in your notes because she is sure you are incompetent to do so without her help.

This point is illustrated with a striking clarity by a comment the child made to her mother later. After interviewing the other parties in this case, I met with the mother and child to provide them with some of my conclusions. During that final interview, the mother asked me a question that I did not hear correctly. When I asked her to repeat it, the child looked knowingly at her mother and, in an aside intended for her mother's ears rather than mine, whispered in a forgiving tone: "You got to be patient with him. He don't hear so good and he's a little slow." That comment was precious, in that it showed how masterful and helpful this child felt in a situation that had focused so intensely on painful issues.

## OVERPOLITENESS VS. INTERRUPTING

When clients meander in their telling of events, it is often difficult to manage the interview. After all, we don't want to hurt their feelings and alienate them; yet what they are saying may not be relevant to what we need to know. In addition, they may have a need to feel heard, and though you may not need the information they are providing, you might decide to listen to it for a certain time in order that they will feel that they have had their opportunity to be heard.

Many times, all of the above conditions exist to some extent, but on the whole the client is telling his story in a way that happens to provide you with the information you need to know. In those latter instances, you may deem it prudent to keep quiet until he goes too far off on a tangent for it to be useful.

Whenever a client goes off on a tangent or provides unnecessary details you might interrupt him to get the interview back on track. Usually, it is quite possible to interrupt the client, without any terrible negative effects, by being open, direct, and honest, as well as apologetic. Some examples follow.

"I'm getting lost now. I'm not sure what this has to do with my question. Would it be okay if we got back to my original question?"

Another tack to take, often with adults who control and monopolize the time, is to say: "Excuse me, but we don't have all that much time and there are some other questions I need to ask."

Another, perhaps more polite way of saying the same thing is: "Excuse me, and let me apologize for interrupting you. I know that what you're saying is important to you, but we've only got another 15 minutes and I still have a lot of questions. Would it be okay with you if we went to some of those questions?"

Occasionally you will meet with a serious objection; the client will want his opportunity to be heard in his own way and for as long as it takes, and will feel constrained by your limitations. However, this is rare. Usually, clients are fairly comfortable with these kinds of interruptions and expect them. That is to say, they understand that you are the one in charge of the interview and are supposed to guide them, by asking questions, interrupting, and telling them what to talk about next. Since they view you in this way and depend upon your direction, your interruptions are usually not viewed by them as insults or slights.

## THE EFFECTS OF OVERCOMPLICATED LANGUAGE VS. PUNCTUATING YOUR MESSAGE WITH SIMPLICITY AND REPETITION

While clients sometimes meander, so do therapists, at least from the client's point of view. The clinician may not be technically meandering at all, but may be expressing a complicated and coherent body of information in a very sensible manner. However, it may be so complicated and contain so much information that it is experienced as meandering by the listener, with the consequence that the main messages the clinician intended to send get lost and are not attended to adequately. Here is an example.

"Kathy, what a nice name you have," she said in a high-pitched voice. "And you're so big for a nine-year-old. Do you know why you're here today? You're here today to talk to me about some problems. I'm a doctor who doesn't give needles. I listen to problems and I'm here to help you and to be your friend, but in order to help you I have to ask you a lot of questions so you get to tell me what problems you have. I know there are some things that happened that are very hard to talk about but it's very, very important to tell me the truth or I won't be able to help you. I guess you're a little nervous, and it's natural to be nervous when you come to a strange place and talk to a strange person, but it's very important to tell me the whole truth when I ask questions. It's okay to tell the truth here, because nothing bad will happen to you no matter what you say."

Too much is being said at once. There are a number of important messages here, most of which are poorly phrased and which will receive more attention later. While most of these points should be made, they should not be made all at once. There is also a degree of vagueness and verbal padding, perhaps some positive connotation and reframing, which the clinician uses for the purpose of buffering the pain of the interview process and the pain of the sexual abuse. While the intention is commendable, the result is unhelpful. It distracts the child from the very points the clinician is trying to make and in addition confuses the child. To illustrate, consider how Kathy, from her own point of view, might process the above speech.

"Kathy? A nice name? I hate it. I always hated it. She probably hates it too and is just trying to make me feel good. And what's that got to do with why I'm here? What's she saying now? That I'm big for my age? She has to go and rub it in? Doesn't she know my biggest worry is that I'll be a giant and no boys will like me? Do I know why I'm here today? Of course I know, but I'm too embarrassed to say. But, oh no, here she goes, she's going to say it, I can't believe she's really going to say it out loud. But wait, I think she's saying now that we're here to talk about problems. I don't get it. Problems are in arithmetic. Division and multiplication problems that I have for homework. I don't mind talking about those if she'll help me with them. Or problems with my friends, the ones who tease me sometimes when I have two friends over instead of just one. But wait, what did she just say? She wants to be my friend? I thought she was a doctor, even though she doesn't give needles, which is kind of strange, and which I'm not sure I believe, because you can never trust a doctor. But she's kind of pretty and I wouldn't mind being her friend. Maybe she can come over and play sometime. Maybe tomorrow. But wait, now she's saying she wants to help me, and she keeps saying it. And that I have to tell the truth. And that I'm nervous, which I am. But she keeps talking at me, I can't think straight, my head is spinning.

Is she talking about what dad did to me? I can't tell, because she won't come out and say so. But if that's what she's talking about, maybe she really can help me. Maybe dad won't go to jail and maybe he can come home again if I tell her what he did to me. She said to tell the truth. She said she was my friend and I could trust her, though I don't know how I can trust a lady who likes the name Kathy and acts phony by telling me it's nice to be tall."

This imaginary exercise illustrates how distracting the clinician's monologue could be. It would have been more helpful if the clinician focused on one point at a time and made sure that each was understood. This is illustrated in the following dialogue.

\* \* \* \* \*

"Kathy, you're here because Mrs. Beard, who brought you over here, has been trying to figure out if your father touched you on your private parts. She told me that 'private parts' is what you call them, is that right?"

A nod from Kathy.

"And you know who Mrs. Beard is?"

Another nod.

"Good, well, she wants me to talk to you about it to see if I think it happened. Do you understand what I'm saying?"

Another nod.

"Good. Can you tell me why you're here? Tell me what I just said so I know you understand."

"So you can tell Mrs. Beard what happened to me with my dad."

"Right. That's why you're here. And she wants you to talk to me because I'm a doctor. I talk to kids about things that bother them. Do you understand that?"

"Yeah," she said.

"Lots of kids have things that bother them and they think about it and they wish they could talk about it with someone."

"So do I."

"That's what I'm here for. You can talk about it with me."

"About my dad. He touched me . . . "

"You can tell me all about it, but first I want to make sure you understand everything so far. We can take our time and go slow. Okay?"

"Yeah, okay, but can I tell you everything?"

"Everything that you want to tell me. But if you don't want to tell me something, just say to me that you don't want to talk about it. Okay? Just say, 'I don't want to talk.' That's all. 'I don't want to talk.' You don't have to if you don't want to. Understand? Now, tell me what I just said so I know you understand."

"If I don't want to say, I just say I don't wanna."

"Right."

\* \* \* \* \*

This last example of dialogue illustrates four important points. First, isolate the message you hope to convey and phrase it in language simple enough to be clearly heard. Second, repeat the message when necessary so that it can be differentiated from the surrounding information in which it is embedded. Third, fight against inclinations to protect the client with padded language. Be direct and honest. It will help get the message conveyed in exactly the way you intended it. If you truly care about the person you are talking to, your nonverbal tone and style will communicate that care; excessive verbal reframing, positive connotation, and rambling will be unnecessary. Your innate politeness will suffice to buffer the rudeness of your questions, whereas any sophisticated artistry will be recognized as such and judged as phony. And finally, check with the other person to determine whether she understood you as you intended to be understood; that is, ask the child to repeat back to you the gist of your message.

## MISLEADING THE CHILD BY BEING OVERFRIENDLY

The monologue at the beginning of the previous section contained examples of misleading the child. First, it emphasized helping the child. While helping a child is a hope in the evaluation of abuse, it is often a dubious one. Promising help is a false promise when one knows almost nothing about the case. For those children who might believe this promise, a letdown is probable because often their lives will worsen during and subsequent to the time of the evaluation, sometimes as a result of the interview.

Similarly, to say that nothing bad will happen as a result of the interview is also a mistake. Again, this is misleading. If the child is honest and gives a believable statement, many things could happen that the child might consider bad. The father may lose his job, he might be put in jail, the family might lose its income, and the mother might align with the father and not be sure about whether to support the victim, resulting in foster placement.

Another way to mislead a child is to tell him that you are a friend. The intention of this approach, of course, is to generate in the child a sense of alliance and trust and the assurance that you will understand his problems. But are you really a friend when your job is to evaluate or treat sexual abuse? The child can consider you a friend, perhaps, but that is the child's choice and prerogative. For you to dictate this relationship is presumptuous. What it means to you is very likely quite different from what it means to a child. Can you expect to carry through on the child's expectations of what it means to be a friend? As an evaluator or even a therapist, that is not your job.

Finally, praising the child, by telling her what a good name she has or how beautiful she is, is not the best way to achieve rapport. While it is not exactly misleading, it is often considered a quick way to win over a child. Consequently, it is sometimes recognized by children as a cheap and phony attempt to win their confidence. Praise is often flattering and makes a person feel good, but it can also have some negative effects, which the clinician would be wise to avoid, if possible. The person praised may feel that the praise isn't deserved and may believe the person giving the praise must be stupid. If it isn't deserved, praise can make a person feel like a phony. Even if deserved, it can sometimes cause the recipient to dispute it due to embarrassment.

Praise may have detrimental effects when the phrasing of the words results in praise of the personality or of stable traits, e.g., "You are such a pretty little girl," "You're so intelligent," "You have such good taste," or "You have wonderful poetic ability." While praise is sometimes effective in establishing rapport, this can be as easily established, and with more reliability and integrity, by simply recognizing that the child deserves respect, by affording the child that respect, and by paying careful attention to what the child is saying.

If it is deemed necessary to provide praise, in order to reinforce some desired behavior or even to help establish rapport, it is better to avoid praising personality traits and instead either to praise behaviors and accomplishments or to point out how those behaviors and accomplishments affected you. For example, "That poem almost made me cry," or "I love that shirt. Where did you get it?" or "What a smart thing to say," or "I like your hair done up like that. I wish I had thought to try my hair like that." By commenting on the accomplishment or on how it made you feel, you can avoid many of the negative effects described above and can allow the child to make the inference on her own, if she wishes to make it, that she is wonderful.

## THE NEED TO AVOID PATRONIZING THE CHILD

Unnecessary and conspicuous praise is patronizing and reflects either lack of respect for the child or uncertainty about how to adequately interact with the child. It is a good example of talking down to a child.

Clinicians talk down to children in many ways. One typical means of doing so is using a high-pitched voice that is appropriate for talking to babies, and to which babies evince greater responsiveness than to normal adult pitches and tones. However, four- and five-year-olds and school-aged children are not babies; they do not respond well to such tones and consider them to be condescending.

Another example is that of using language that is so simplified and "kiddified" that it would insult any child with an ounce of intelligence. An illustration that epitomizes this kiddified language comes from a telephone conversation I overhead between a therapist and a father (*not* a child). The therapist was overheard to say, at one point in the conversation, "That's real good daddy-work." While it is possible that this remark was effective and called for, my gut reaction was, "What is she doing in there? Romper Room Therapy?" I felt she was talking down to the father and simultaneously diminishing her own therapeutic role and possible contributions to helping this family. In addition, if she was using this kind of language with the parents, what kind of language was she using with the children?

Children don't respond well to a patronizing patter. They prefer, like all of us, an attitude of respect. Treat them like you would your best friend. Give them the same explanations and rationales, in words they can understand, but not as if they were idiots. Show some care about what is on their minds.

# CHAPTER 6

# Confrontation in Maintaining a Mutual Understanding

One of the best ways to show respect for the client is by establishing and maintaining a mutual understanding with the client. While this is a basic prerequisite to any good interview, it requires skill and is sometimes mishandled. Often, it is mishandled because clinicians consider it too elementary to deserve close attention, presuming that they have established an adequate mutual understanding when, in fact, they have not. This issue is illustrated in the present chapter with content from sexual abuse interviews, but the general points conveyed here are applicable to a variety of problems and situations.

The failure to establish a mutual understanding is usually inadvertent and often seems to be due to intractable politeness, which has been conditioned into most of us. When misunderstandings occur, we have a strong tendency to give people the benefit of the doubt. Even when their talk is rude, tangential, incoherent, or bizarre, we sometimes fail to fully acknowledge this. Instead of confronting them, we politely resolve discrepancies by filling in the gaps, revising their confusing statements with our own imaginings.

This perpetuates a false presumption on our part that shared assumptions exist between ourselves and our clients. Even when we notice that a mutual understanding does not in fact exist, we are often reluctant to confront the client about it, due to good manners. Further, on those occasions in which we do go ahead and confront a client, we often fail to follow up with further confrontation when the client does not satisfactorily resolve the confusion in question. These kinds of problems are illustrated in the present chapter, along with some ways to avoid them.

## ESTABLISHING AND MAINTAINING A MUTUAL UNDERSTANDING

A mutual understanding exists when the client understands exactly what you are saying to him and you understand exactly what he is saying to you. To establish and maintain this understanding, one must take measures to assure that messages are received in the way they are intended. This understanding encompasses vocabulary, grammatical usage, concepts of time, numerical concepts, cultural norms, theories of causality, and any other assumptions or bodies of knowledge that are necessary to share for effective communication to occur. A short dialogue below illustrates what can happen when numerical concepts are not mutually understood.

\* \* \* \* \*

"What did he do?" the interviewer asked four-year-old Casey.
"He put his fingers in my cootie [i.e., vagina]."
"On top of it or inside?"
"Inside."
"How did it feel?"
"It hurt."
"How many times did it happen? Was it more than one time?"
Casey nodded her head up and down.
"How many times?"
Casey shrugged her shoulders.

\* \* \* \* \*

The question about the number of times it happened was not a good one to ask a four-year-old whose cognitive development in numerical concepts is somewhat primitive. In this case, the interviewer was asked by the observer to go back and establish a mutual understanding about those concepts before making a determination on the reliability of Casey's answer.

When asked to distinguish one from many, Casey was able to do so. When asked to count ten coins, she was able to count about six, calling them "One, two, three, six, seven, ten." When asked to count to ten, she replied in the same fashion, substituting six for five. This indicated a particular stage in her development of numerical concepts in which numerical names or labels stood for quantifiable units, although the labels were incorrectly learned. In her case, she was capable of identifying up to approximately six units. This questioning helped to establish the level of Casey's numerical concept formation and provided a basis for more detailed questioning on how many times the abuse occurred.

In a similar case, the interviewer had just found out that the abuse of a six-year-old boy had occurred more than once. As a result, she next asked, "When did it happen again?"

Again, to ask such a question is a very natural reaction in this kind of situation. However, "when" questions are not the best ones to ask when one has not previously established the child's concept of time or internal calendar or frame of reference for anchoring events, such as birthdays, seasons, back-to-school season, the Christmas holidays, Easter holiday, and so on. The child shrugged and gave no further response. The interviewer later consulted with the observer and went back with the following questions.

* * * * *

"Did it happen every day? Or every week?"

A shrug for a response.

"Do you know how many days are in a week?"

"Six."

"What are they? Starting with Sunday."

"Sunday, Monday, Tuesday, Thursday, Wednesday, Friday, Saturday."

"Good. Do you know how many weeks are in a month?"

A shake of the head.

"Do you know any months?"

Another shake of the head.

"How do you know when it's winter?"

"There's snow and you have to wear boots and you go sledding."

"Good. And how do you know when it's summer?"

"You go swimming and don't have to go to school."

"Okay, when he touched you, was it every day? Or once a week? Or every other day? Or just once in a while? How much did it happen?"

"Two times in a week."

"Two times."

"Not always. Sometimes just one time. Sometimes three or four times."

"And when was the last time? You went to live in your foster home a month ago, in July. That's summertime, when you swim and don't have to go to school. The month before that is June, when you're just finishing school and then go on vacation. Did he touch you in the month of June?"

"I think so, but I'm not sure."

"How about the month before that, in May, when you were still in school, did he touch you then?"

"Yeah, that's when he touched me."

"What? About two times every week?"

"Yeah, that's when it was."

"And when did it all start, when you were six years old or when you were five or four or three?"

"Six."

"So it all happened this year?"

"I guess so."

"Well, then, did he do it in April? That's the month before May, you're still in school."

"I think so."

"But you're not sure."

"Yeah, I'm not sure."

"How about the month before that, in March."

"I don't think so."

"So it's probably May and June that he was doing it, and he did it about six times."

"Yeah."

\* \* \* \* \*

There are some problems with how this interview was conducted. It contained overcomplicated statements by the interviewer, a number of unnecessary leading questions, and reflected an assumption that the child would be able to adequately follow all the checks on time frames. These checks required that he learn the months of the year as he sat there being interviewed. To put it mildly, this kind of questioning was beyond his ability to follow. However, the example does illustrate an interviewer's attempt to establish a mutually understood time frame. She attempted to elicit information that would anchor the abuse within that time frame and provide a sense of the frequency of its occurrence.

Misunderstandings can sometimes occur that may or may not be important. Not until they are cleared up is it apparent whether it was worth the effort and time needed to clear them up. The example below illustrates what turned out to be an innocuous misunderstanding. A mutual understanding was pursued only because it was unclear whether the offender regularly ate dinner with the family, and I thought it remotely possible that this issue might have some relevance. The lack of clarity was due to ordinary communication difficulties and occurred while I was asking about a typical day, going through each phase of the day in some detail.

\* \* \* \* \*

"So you usually eat dinner about 5:30? What kinds of food do you usually eat?"

"Steaks, or pizza, or TV dinners. And desserts."

"Desserts? Like what?"

"Pie, cake, ice cream, like that."

"Okay, good, so what happens after dinner? Oh, wait, by the way, who eats with you?"

"My brothers and my little sister. The baby doesn't eat with us."

"How about Jim?"

"What about him?"

"Well, he lives there, right?"

"Right."

"So, when you eat dinner, is it just your brothers and your sister or . . . "

"Sometimes, yeah."

"Sometimes Jim, too?"

"No. Sometimes we all eat together and sometimes we don't."

I couldn't tell whether Jim ate with them or not.

"I don't get it. You mean sometimes Jim is there and sometimes he's not?"

"No. He's always there."

"He always eats with you."

"No."

"No?" Did she mean he was always in the house, but never ate with them? Or that he ate with them when he was in the house, but wasn't always there?

"No, I mean sometimes we eat together. My mom . . . "

"Uh-huh."

" . . . my brothers, and Jim, and my sister, and the baby."

"Right, uh-huh. So sometimes you eat with Jim?"

" . . . and sometimes only me, and my brothers, and my sister eat together."

"You mean without Jim?"

"Without them."

"Them?"

"Mom and Jim."

"Yeah, but Jim is there."

"Yeah, he's there. I already told you."

"Where? You mean somewhere else in the house?"

"Yeah, with mom and the baby."

"Where? In what room?"

"Who?"

"Jim and mom and the baby. Where are they while you're eating?"

"With us sometimes."

"But when you're not with them while you're eating? Where are they?"

"Watching TV."

"What room?"

"The living room."

"And where are you?"

"In the kitchen."

"So, sometimes Jim eats with you and sometimes he doesn't."

"Yeah."

"Uh-huh, okay, so after supper, what happens next?"

* * * * *

Establishing a mutual understanding did not result in anything significant, but it might have. It is interesting to observe that the misunderstanding that occurred was not due to any hidden agenda or desire to mislead. Instead, it was typical of the kinds of misunderstandings that frequently and regularly occur between people in everyday life.

Another example of a failure in mutual understanding is illustrated with an alleged offender who was interviewed as part of a sexual abuse evaluation requested by both D.S.S. and Family Court. His job was in jeopardy due to all the time he had to take off for court appearances and court-ordered evaluations. He had also been removed from his home, which was a trial for him because he loved his family and desperately wanted to return home.

Although he had pled guilty to committing incest with his daughter, his response to every question about the specific allegations suggested that he had nothing much to say because he had not committed any acts remotely resembling the allegations. At first, it appeared as if he was simply denying the allegations. However, his lack of immediate understanding in response to a number of questions prompted the observer (behind a one-way mirror) to point out to the evaluator that the alleged offender might not be comprehending a good deal of what the evaluator had been saying.

For example, the evaluator had employed the phrase "sexual abuse" a number of times throughout the interview; therefore, she was asked to go back and inquire whether the alleged offender understood the meaning of the phrase. It turned out that he had no inkling of the meaning.

The phrase "sexual contact" had also been frequently used in the interview, so she now asked if he understood this phrase as well. Again, he had no idea of its meaning. She also asked about the term "uncommon," as in "it is not uncommon for sexual contact to occur when . . . " Again, he failed to comprehend these terms. Previously, he had been nodding his head knowingly when she had freely used this terminology in the interview process.

At this point, with the observer's guidance, the evaluator proceeded to conduct a mental status examination. This exam revealed that the alleged offender did not know how many days were in a week, nor their proper names, nor the number of months or days in a year, nor the current president of the United States. In addition, he did not understand clearly the charges that had been brought against him nor was he competent to participate in his own defense, despite the fact that he had been allowed to enter a guilty plea.

This case has many implications, some of them ethical ones; but the main point of the illustration is that the evaluator had been talking over this man's head. She had labored under the mistaken assumption that he understood time frames involving the months of the year, as well as numerous common words and phrases such as "sexual contact." Only after conducting a mental status exam was it clear that he was a simple farm worker who was mildly retarded and who had learned to nod knowingly in response to conversation that baffled him.

It is relatively common for clinicians to use language that goes over the heads of their clients. To address this problem, I find it useful to frequently check with clients, especially children, to determine whether they understand my words. If they do not understand the meaning of particular words and phrases, I teach the meaning to them, so that we can communicate on the same wavelength. My preference is to teach them what they don't understand rather than to speak at a level that is beneath their understanding.

While I try to use language that I think they will understand, I do not try too hard, because if I am too successful at it, my language may appear so simplistic that they may experience it as patronizing. After all, they know that I am an adult possessing more education and experience than they do, so they expect that I will use language that is more complicated than their own. Therefore, they are not threatened by frequent explanations of words or concepts that are incomprehensible to them.

To an observer, these kinds of explanations can give the appearance of an adult lecturing at a child. However, to the child, it is an opportunity to be taught something new. It lets the child know that in your effort to communicate you will not hold back information out of fear that it is poorly matched to the child's limited vocabulary. Instead, the child learns that you will help to enhance that vocabulary to accommodate any messages you want to convey. This approach gives the child very clear permission to tell you when she doesn't understand words you are using and to request a definition.

The difference between a child's and an adult's perception of this kind of communication process was made strikingly clear to me while I was engaged in a conversation with two ten-year-old girls. One of them was explaining that she felt uncomfortable with people of a different socioeconomic class, though she was not labeling them as such, and was asking whether there was a way to describe class distinctions. While I was answering her question by explaining the concept of socioeconomic class, another adult walked up to us and interrupted me in a joking tone by saying, "Lecturing these poor girls again? Shame on you!"

"Lecturing?" I asked, surprised at the very idea and wondering if indeed I had been guilty of the crime.

"No, he's not lecturing," said one of the girls, shaking her head vigorously.

"No," said the other one. "He's teaching us."

## CONFRONTATION

To establish mutual understanding, one must confront clients with discrepancies and inconsistencies, and do so with utmost clarity. This need exists not only in sexual abuse evaluations but in the conduct of therapy in general.

To illustrate this need in the context of a sexual abuse evaluation, consider the case of a child who claimed that her father sexually molested her, then recanted the story, and then three years later again alleged that her father sexually molested her. In view of Lucy's history of recanting, the current interviewer had good reason for questioning her credibility. Clearly, she had lied on at least one occasion, either on the occasion of the first allegation, on the occasion of the recantation, or on the occasion of the most recent allegation of abuse. In order to consider her credible, the interviewer had to obtain a mutual understanding with the child about which occasion it was that she lied and why she did so.

\* \* \* \* \*

"Lucy, we've talked a lot about what happened, but I'm confused about something. I have your file here, and I see in here that three years ago you said that your father molested you. Can I ask you about that?"

"Yeah, sure."

"Well, you said he molested you then, a long time ago. And then you changed your story and said he didn't do it. And now three years later you're saying he's molesting you again. Do you remember saying he molested you three years ago?"

"Yeah, in the courthouse, a man in a beard talked to me."

"Okay, and do you remember what you told him?"

"No. I can't remember what I said. But I probably told him that my father molested me."

"And do you remember changing your story and telling him you lied, and that your father didn't touch you?"

She shook her head back and forth. "No, I don't remember."

"Do you remember anything about what you said?"

She shrugged her shoulders. "Just that I was scared."

"And what about now, Lucy? Did it really happen or didn't it?"

"It happened. I'm not lying."

"And you know that your mom wants your dad back in the house. You know that, don't you?"

"Yeah, she doesn't believe me. But it happened."

"How does that make you feel?"

\* \* \* \* \*

This was an important confrontation but it did not go far enough. The fact that the child lied on at least one of three occasions was originally clear to the interviewer. However, it was not made quite as clear to the child, who was able, by virtue of her poor memory, to deflect the interviewer's priorities and management of the interview. The interviewer was asked to go back to focus attention once again on the fact that a lie had occurred and to make clear to the child what the dilemma was for the interviewer.

* * * * *

"Okay, Lucy, you say that you don't remember changing your story. But that leaves me with a problem. I'm stuck here. I'm wondering which time it was that you lied. Do you understand my problem?"

"No."

"Well, I don't know when you told the truth and when you lied. Which one is the lie? Was it three years ago when you first said he molested you? Was it the second time, when you changed your mind and said he didn't do it? Or did you lie this last time?"

"I guess it was the second time."

"Do you remember saying he didn't molest you?"

"No."

"Then if you can't remember, how do you know you lied?"

"I must have. Because he did molest me."

"Then why did you say he didn't molest you?"

"Because my mom changed her mind."

"Changed her mind?"

"Yeah, she stopped fighting with him and wanted him back home again."

"Do you remember that for sure? Or not for sure?"

"I remember it for sure."

"If mom wanted him back, why did you first say that he molested you?"

"Because he was beating up on mom, and because he was molesting me and my sisters."

"Good. But you don't remember saying to the man with the beard that your dad didn't do it."

"No."

"Do you remember telling him that you made the whole story up because your sister told you to tell him he molested you. And if you didn't do it, she would beat you up?"

"I don't remember any of that, but if I said it to him it was because of the reason I just said. Mom wanted dad to come back."

"But your mom wants him back again now."

"I know it. She keeps changing her mind."

"What if she said to you that you better change your story again and tell those people he didn't touch you, or else he might go to jail and you might have to live in a foster home? Would you change your story?"

"No."

"Why not? It's so important to your mother to have him come back and you love her so much."

"Because I don't want to be molested again. I'll live in a foster home instead, if I have to."

"Do you want to live in a foster home? Or do you want to live with your mom?"

"With mom, but only if dad isn't there."

"You don't want your father back in the house?"

"No way."

"Even though your mother wants him back?"

"No, I don't want to see him again. Ever."

\* \* \* \* \*

A confrontation like this must be clear enough so that the child realizes that she must accept and respond to the fact that she lied. The interviewer must be able to make the confrontation in language that permits a mutual understanding, so that it is clear to the child that she has to talk about her lying and do so with specificity and clarity. It must be done so that it is clear to her that she will not get off the hook with vague responses or statements about not remembering.

The disadvantages of confrontations like this are that they can be rough on the child and may require a degree of abstraction of which the child may not yet be capable. There is always the risk that, due to the clinician's frustration, a confrontation will drift into relentless interrogation. In view of these risks, the timing of a confrontation is crucial. One doesn't engage in this kind of questioning when one is attempting to warm up and establish rapport with a child; it should be reserved for a later stage.

Another example of a confrontation is illustrated here with a young mother who claimed that her husband attempted to engage in sexual intercourse with her daughter because, while intoxicated, he mistook her daughter for herself. In the interview she said that it was common for the children to sleep with her and that "sometimes" when her husband came home drunk or drugged up, he would have sex with her in the same bed in which she slept with the children.

\* \* \* \* \*

"Do you think it's a good idea to have sex with your husband when the kids are in bed with you?"

"No, of course not. Do you think I'm crazy? But what I was trying to tell you is that he was so drugged up that I was afraid he might get violent with me if I turned him down. So I went along with it, and that way the kids wouldn't wake up. Isn't that better than waking the kids and him going hyper?"

"Did it happen just that once or other times, too?"

"Um, just that time. Because if I didn't do it, he would have a hyper. And when he does that the kids are really upset by it. He throws things and yells and screams. It's just awful."

"What do the kids do when he has a hyper? How are they affected?"

"They run and hide."

\* \* \* \* \*

The dialogue can be interrupted at this point to look back at what happened. Although the interviewer had discovered earlier that the sex in bed with the children had occurred "sometimes," he accepted the inconsistent statement that it had occurred only once. The client was not effectively confronted, that is, she was confronted merely with a question that permitted her to weasel out of the inconsistent statements she had made. The interviewer did not follow up with questions that would have pinned her down to her earlier statement that sex in bed with the kids had happened not once, but "sometimes," that is, in the plural, not in the singular. Compare the above confrontation with the following one, which occurred after the evaluator consulted with the observer.

\* \* \* \* \*

"You said before that sometimes your husband would have sex with you while the kids were sleeping in your bed, and you said the kids were asleep and you figured it was better to let him do it so that he wouldn't lose his temper and wake the kids. Is that right?"

"Right. I figured he would get hyper or something, so I just went along with it."

"You said it happened 'sometimes.' Not once, but 'sometimes.' About how often did it happen?"

"What do you mean?"

It is clear at this point that she is somewhat wary about the question.

"Well, what I mean is, did it happen every night? A couple times a week? Once a week?"

"You mean how many times did we have sex? Well, I guess it was about three or four times a week."

At this point she appeared to be trying to deflect the question and to answer a different one, shifting from having sex with kids in the bed to the general frequency of having sex with her husband.

"No, that's not what I mean. I mean, how many times did you have sex while the kids were in bed with you?"

"Just that one time."

Instead of giving her the benefit of the doubt as we have all been conditioned to do in polite conversation, it is essential at this point to confront the person with the contradictory statements she has made.

"Wait a second, now, you're contradicting yourself, so I'm getting a bit confused. You said before that it happened 'sometimes.' You did use the word 'sometimes.' I remember you using that word. You said sometimes he came home drunk and would have sex with you while the kids were sleeping in your bed, and you said that the kids often slept with you. You gave me the impression that it happened more than once."

"Just once. That night. That's all I remember, anyway."

Now she pleads loss of memory, and it is very tempting to let her get away with it, because, after all, we are all very polite and don't want to embarrass and hurt the people we interact with. However, if we don't cling to the need to resolve the contradictory statements, we will get nowhere.

"So you are saying it only happened once. That's a problem for me. Because you first said one thing, that it happened sometimes, and then you said another thing, that it happened just once. How am I supposed to know which one is true? Do you understand my problem here? I don't know when to believe you and when not to believe you. How can I tell?"

"Maybe it happened more than once, I don't know for sure."

When she is able to say that it might have happened more than once, she is responding to the confrontation positively. Yet, she is not being definite about it, still trying to leave herself a way out, if she needs it.

"That sounds like you're trying to put one over on me. Why don't you know for sure?"

"I guess it probably happened more than once."

"You're not sure?"

"Maybe two or three times."

"Okay, two or three times. That's very different from one time. Why did you say such different things?"

"Because I don't want you to take my kids away."

"That's what you're afraid of?"

"Yeah, that's what I don't want to happen. I love my kids. I do the best I can for them. No foster mother is going to do better. What do you want me to say?"

"Just the truth. You see, it's important that we understand each other. We both know that you lied to me here. You said it was just once you had sex in bed with the kids when you knew it was more than once. Let's be honest here. How many times was it?"

"Two or three times."

"Two or three times doesn't make sense to me either. I mean, you said that the kids sleep with you a lot. What, maybe every night? Six nights a week? Five nights a week?"

"A couple nights a week."

"What would the kids say, if I asked them?"

A long hesitation. Then, "I guess they would say every night?"

"And is it every night? Or are the kids wrong about that?"

"Not every night."

"How many nights?"

"Six maybe. Five."

"So then, it's not every night, according to you, but almost every night that the kids sleep with you, is that right?"

"Right."

"And when do you usually have sex with your husband? In the mornings, in the afternoons, or at night when he comes home drunk and high? Didn't you say before that it was usually at night?"

"Yes."

"Does it happen at other times of the day, too?"

"Once in a while, but mostly at night."

"So if you're sleeping with the kids almost every night and if your husband is having sex with you four or five nights a week, how often are the kids in bed with you when you're having sex?"

"A lot, I guess. A lot more than three times."

"About how many times a week?"

"I can't remember for sure. About three or four times a week probably. I guess I've been a terrible mother." Tears began to stream down her cheeks.

"If you made some mistakes, well then, you can learn from your mistakes and do better now. Right?"

"Right. What can I do?"

"Well, you tell me. Looking back, what would you do differently? What do you think you did wrong?"

"Staying with him so long, that's what I did wrong."

"And because you stayed with him, you had to let him have sex with you while the kids were sleeping with you, is that what you mean?"

"Yeah, I had to. He would have a hyper if I said no, and it would wake the kids."

"Did that sometimes happen? He had a hyper and the kids would wake up and you and he would fight and . . . "

"Yeah, and he'd hit me and I wouldn't just sit there and take it, that's not the kind of girl I am, I'd throw a clock in his face, or a shoe. And the kids would have to see all of that."

"And the two of you would be naked, without clothes."

"Yeah," she whispered, lowering her head, and crying again.

"Forget for a second what I think about it. Tell me what you think. Was it harmful for the kids to sleep with you while you had sex with your husband?"

"They were sleeping. They didn't know."

"So you didn't think it was harmful."

"No."

"But they would wake up and see two naked people hitting each other and screaming at each other. And who knows how many times they weren't sleeping when you thought they were sleeping."

"I didn't think of all that," she said, sobbing. "You're right. I've been a terrible mother. But they're my kids, they need me, you can't take them away. I'll do better now that he's not around."

\* \* \* \* \*

A short confrontation is illustrated below that is similar to the illustration above in the sense that it focuses on a factual discrepancy committed by the client.

\* \* \* \* \*

"I'd like to hear what you have to say about what your son told me. He said that after he got home from his visit with you on September 12, he decided he didn't want to visit with you anymore because he was very upset and scared when you . . . "

"That's a lie, and I can prove it because there weren't any visits in September. I can bring my mother and my sisters in here, and they'll tell you there weren't any visits in September, so how can what he said be true? His mother's putting those ideas in his head, and I don't know why you people can't see through her. Everything she says is a lie, and I have people who can come in here and tell you things that would make your hair stand up. Do you know about the time that she called social services and told them that . . . "

"Excuse me for interrupting, but we were talking about the visit in September and . . . "

"It never happened, and I can prove it."

"That's confusing, because earlier, you gave me a list of times when you visited with your son. And one of those times was the second week in September."

"I couldn't have said that. You must have made a mistake."

"I have what you said on tape. And you told me then that if I wanted, you would have your mother and sisters come in here and tell me what a good time the kids had on that visit. On that day in September. And one of the things you said happened that day was that you went shopping for school clothes because school just started, in September. So, which is it? A visit in September? Or no visit?"

"Well, if you have it on tape, then I guess I must have said it."

"Did the visit happen in September, or not? Or can't you remember?"

"Uh, I guess it happened."

"You guess? Or you know. Aren't you sure?"

"It happened."

"Then, tell me. How am I supposed to know when you're telling me the truth and when you're not? A minute ago you were sitting in here yelling that the visit never happened and that you had witnesses. Were you telling me the truth then?"

"No, I guess not."

"Why not?"

"Because I didn't do those things to my son that she says I did."

"Then why don't you just say so? Why say that the visit didn't happen in September when you know it did? Why lie to me? How am I supposed to believe anything you say when I can't tell when you're lying?"

"I guess you can't tell when I'm lying, but if I'm lying now and then, it's because she lies all the time. That's why this is all happening, because she's crazy and . . . "

\* \* \* \* \*

In the same interview, this father was confronted about his poor use of the interview time. Every question was an opportunity to go off on tangents that inexorably returned to his preoccupation with his wife. This confrontation, illustrated below, also led to a mutual understanding that his knowledge of his son was no better than a stranger's might be.

\* \* \* \* \*

"Yes, you've already told me that your wife is a liar, but I was asking you about your son. What is he like?"

"I already told you what he looked like."

"But what is his personality like? What kind of a kid is he? What is he good at? What's he like to do?"

"He's a great kid, and we have a great relationship, but he's becoming more like her every day. That's why somebody has to listen and get him away from her before he ends up in a children's home just like she did. He's already lying about me the way she . . . "

"Excuse me, I've got to interrupt again. I don't know what you're talking about again."

"About the way she . . . "

"You keep going off on all these different stories about her, no matter what question I ask. It's hard for me to follow all these stories, and I'm getting confused. I've asked you four times to tell me about your son. Do you know anything at all about him?"

"I know a lot about him, and I've been trying to tell you, but you keep interrupting."

"No, you tell me stories about your wife to keep making the same point, over and over again, that she's a liar, a slut, and a bad influence. But do you know anything at all about your son?"

"Yeah, he's a good kid, and he could do a lot better in school if he was away from her, that's for sure. He wouldn't be doing so bad in school if he lived with me."

"But I have his report card here in my file. It says he's doing fine in school. Did you know he was doing fine?"

"How am I supposed to know that? She never tells me anything. And I only got to see him six times last year. How can you get to know a kid when you've only seen him six times?"

"So you don't really know much about him at all, do you? What he's really like, or how he's doing."

"No, he's a stranger to his own father, and that's the stinking shame of all this."

\* \* \* \* \*

The next confrontation addresses the discrepancy between a parent's description of her behavior and the implausibility of that behavior.

\* \* \* \* \*

"Okay, so for five hours they play and they watch television. But what I keep trying to get you to tell me is what you're doing while they're playing and watching cartoons."

"I told you, I watch them."

"Yes, you said you sit at the kitchen table and watch them while they watch cartoons, and you stand in the doorway and watch them when they're playing outside."

"That's right. I don't get down and play in the mud with them. I'm too old for that. So I watch them from the doorway."

"But you must do something else, too, while you're watching them."

"No, I just watch them."

"That's awfully hard for me to believe. That you just stand in the doorway and watch them for hours at a time. Most parents do something themselves when they're around kids. They either play with them, or watch television themselves, or read, or eat, or drink, or fold clothes, or wash dishes, or fix something. They don't just stand with their arms folded and just watch."

"Well, I do. It's important to watch your kids. I supervise them."

\* \* \* \* \*

This confrontation did not lead to a mutual understanding. The consequence was that this parent's statements could not be regarded as particularly credible. Another kind of confrontation that sometimes fails to lead to a mutual understanding concerns the purposes of the interview. Within the first few minutes of the interview, parents sometimes convey an understanding of the purpose of the interview that is discrepant with the evaluator's understanding of purpose.

\* \* \* \* \*

"Why are you asking me about my fucking age and who I live with? I'm not here to answer any fucking questions about me. All I want to know from you people is when I can see my daughter again. What the fuck's wrong with you people? You got your heads stuck up your asses? Can't you see what you're doing to my daughter? Who's looking out for her?"

"Excuse me, but before we go on, we've got to get a couple of things straight between you and me."

"There ain't a fucking thing between you and me."

"Listen, you can leave right now if you're going to keep talking to me like that. There's the door. Right there. Make up your mind now."

"I'm sorry. It's just that I keep getting the runaround from everybody, and I'm tired of it. I shouldn't take it out on you. But I ain't here to talk about me. I want to know when I'll see my daughter again."

"Well, I'm not the one who said you had to be here. The court ordered that you come here for an evaluation, and if you don't want to answer questions about yourself, we may as well stop right now. I'll let the court know, and you can take it up with the judge."

"Then I'll really be in hot water. Go ahead and ask your questions. I'll try not to fly off the handle."

\* \* \* \* \*

Confrontation is useful in diverse situations. To punctuate the general applicability of this technique, the last illustration will concern a counseling situation, rather than an evaluation.

The patient, a 35-year-old woman, had originally asked for some concrete help with her perfectionism in regard to routine tasks of daily living. Therefore, I provided her with concrete help, utilizing strategic, cognitive, and behavioral interventions.

She responded with only limited progress, and it soon became apparent that, for various reasons, further progress was not probable. She continued to ask for advice, and I continued to provide it in the form of revisions and refinements of previous treatment plans. However, she spent most of the time in the sessions talking about other matters. Very little time was spent on treatment planning and following up on previous plans. In addition, she spent very little time outside of sessions attempting to follow the treatment plans.

I felt uncomfortable about this situation, because my patient and I did not appear to have a mutual understanding about what was happening in the therapy. My patient appeared to be happy to continue making appointments with me, but I didn't feel that I was providing the help, nor that she was achieving the progress, that she originally requested. Therefore, I told her this, in these exact words, elaborating where necessary to make my points clear. Confronted with the discrepancy between her original request and the status of the current therapy, she responded by saying that she had changed her mind and no longer desired concrete help for her problems.

Instead, she asked if it would be acceptable for her to talk about her life and attempt to understand herself better. Thus, we were able to achieve a mutual understanding that altered the direction that treatment would take. With this difference in direction clearly in mind, I was able, finally, to be helpful in various appropriate ways, rather than to inappropriately provide her with advice she ignored.

## CONCLUDING REMARKS

Confrontations can be difficult to make because we have been raised to be polite individuals who are willing to give others the benefit of the doubt and to take people at their word. Yet many occasions arise during interviews in which we feel confused because there is a particular lack of clarity or an inconsistency that we would like to address. In most instances we should go ahead and attempt to address this feeling of discomfort. Even when we are not clear about the exact nature of the dilemma, a readiness to identify a feeling of discomfort or confusion is a helpful first step in articulating the dilemma. This process is enhanced when one can be ruthlessly honest about one's thoughts, even when this process occurs in the presence of clients. This advice applies to treatment situations as well as evaluations.

# CHAPTER 7

# Techniques for Eliciting Descriptions of Abuse

"These interview skills you've been describing, they're all very interesting, but they seem relevant for any kind of clinical work. Not just sexual abuse."

"Do you still think it's beneath you to read about them?"

"That's not what I'm saying at all. I can really see now that I need to fine-tune my skills in a number of areas. But I can also see that these are skills that any good clinician should have."

"That's right."

"But does that mean that any good clinician can do a sexual abuse evaluation? Aren't there any special areas of interview technique that you need to know about for sexual abuse evaluations?"

"Yes, there are some areas, but keep in mind that these, too, are only special applications of general clinical technique—just with more of a focus on sexual abuse."

"Well, like what?"

"To begin with, it could be useful if you knew how to elicit a description of the abuse so that you could obtain a maximum amount of information with a minimal amount of stress to the child."

"But I thought you already talked about that. Isn't that one of the stages of the interview?"

"Yes, but there are different techniques you can use to help you to go through that stage. Techniques that can help you to get more information from kids who have difficulty in giving it."

"Now that you mention it, I have been wondering about some of those techniques I've seen you use. Like when you ask the child to tell you what happened as if it was a movie you were watching. I've wondered why you do that."

"Good, then. Let's start with that one."

## SCRIPT FOR A MOVIE

When asking a child for descriptions of the abuse, interviewers often ask what happened, the child then gives a meager response, and the interviewer then formulates another question that is based on the child's meager response. The child's next answer is again somewhat laconic, and the cycle continues in an unproductive fashion.

\* \* \* \* \*

"Tell me what happened?"

"It's embarrassing."

"Try to tell me. Do the best you can."

"He took my pants down."

"Then what?"

"He touched me."

"Where?"

"On my privates."

"Do you have a name for your privates? What do you call it?"

"My privates."

"That's what you call it."

"Yeah."

"Can you show me where your privates are on this picture of yourself that you drew?" The child pointed and the evaluator continued. "Okay, good. And what happened next?"

"I said stop, so he stopped."

"And then?"

"That's all."

"He didn't do anything else?"

"No."

"Did anything like this ever happen before?"

"No."

"Okay, then, can you remember how you felt when this was happening?"

"Scared."

* * * * *

The interview went on, at this point, to assess the effects of abuse, whether these effects were persistent or severe, and whether threats or inducements were used. While it was a straightforward interview, the portion of it illustrated here is not sufficient for the clinician to make a confident assessment of the child's credibility or of the likelihood that the event occurred. The data disclosed here are simply too meager, and possibly unreliable.

For the clinician to be able to have some confidence in what the child is saying or, alternatively, some confidence that the child is lying, the interviewer needs to know whether the child's data are coherent, sequenced in time, consistent, and redundant in their details. These and other variables are examined further in later chapters. It is enough to say at this point that the clinician needs to get a good sense for whether the event happened the way that the child says that it did.

Therefore, the clinician's questions need to be oriented towards the goal of enabling him to see the event, vicariously, as in a novel or a movie, or as a fly on the wall observing the abuse. When the questioning is dictated by this kind of orientation, many more details can be elicited than were obtained in the dialogue illustrated above.

These ideas can be operationalized by providing for the child a particular format for describing the abuse. You can tell the child that you are a stranger, and because of that you need to quickly understand a great deal of information, and that it helps if you can see in your mind exactly what happened, as if you were watching a movie. If it is not too complicated for the child to understand, you can ask the child not only to help you to see what happened, but also to hear, smell, and feel what was happening. Compare the following dialogue with the earlier one.

* * * * *

"Can you tell me what happened?"

"It's embarrassing."

"Try to tell me. Do the best you can, that'll be fine."

"He took my pants down."

"Then what?"

"He touched me."

"Okay, slow down here, I've got to get this all down, everything that happened, so you have to go slow with me so I have time to write it. Is that okay?"

"Yeah."

"You said he touched you, and before that you said he took your pants down. Do I have that right?"

"Yeah, you got that right, I think."

"Okay," I said, "Before he touched you and before he took down your pants, where were you in the house?"

"The living room."

"Can you tell me what it looks like, and where everybody was, and everything you can remember?"

"Sure."

"Good, because I need to see it all in my mind like I was watching it in a movie. Do you know what I mean?"

"To tell it like it's a movie?"

"Right. Tell me everything you can remember so I can see it in my mind. So, let's start over, before anybody touched you. Who else was there in the house?"

"My brother."

"Where was your mother?"

"She went to work."

"And your brother? Where was he?"

"Upstairs in his room."

"Doing what?"

"Sleeping. He was home sick that day."

"And you said you were in the living room when this happened, right? Where were you just before that?"

"The kitchen. I was eating breakfast."

"Where were you sitting? Or standing?"

"At the kitchen table."

"How did you feel that day?"

"Cold."

"Cold? How come?"

"It's cold in the house in the morning."

"What was for breakfast?"

"Cereal."

"Do you remember any smells in the kitchen that day?"

"No." She hesitated. "Yeah. Coffee. The smell of coffee on the stove. And cigarettes. I hate that smell."

"And what were you thinking about that day when you woke up and got dressed and had breakfast?"

"About my test that day."

"A test in what?"

"Multiplication."

"So what were you thinking about the test?"

"About which times tables I didn't know."

"Which ones?"

"My 7's and my 8's. I'm real bad at my times tables."

"So you were thinking about your test while you ate your cereal."

"That I was going to do bad on it."

"What did you do next after eating?"

"Went into the living room."

"What did you do with your cereal bowl?"

"Left it on the table."

"You didn't put it in the sink?"

"I'm supposed to, but I didn't."

"So when you finished your cereal, you went into the living room. How come?"

"To get my book bag."

"When you walked into the living room, do remember any smells? Close your eyes a second and try to remember."

"Yeah, smoke."

"Smoke?"

"From cigarettes."

"Good. So you were going into the living room to get your book bag. What color was it?"

"It's yellow."

"Where was it?"

"In the living room."

"Where in the living room?"

"In the corner by the TV."

"Is it cold in there, too?"

"Yeah. Even colder than the kitchen."

"And when you stepped into the living room, was anybody there? Or was it empty?"

"Yeah, dad was there."

"What was he doing?"

"Smoking a cigarette and drinking coffee and watching TV."

"Where was the ashtray?"

"On the coffee table in front of him."

"And the coffee cup was . . . "

"On the table next to the ashtray, and sometimes in his hand when he was drinking from it."

"So he was sitting on . . . "

"On the couch."

"What was he wearing?"

"His bathrobe."

"Anything else?"

"His pajamas underneath. And slippers."

"Do you remember the color of his pajamas?"

"Yeah, green and black checkers."

"And then what happened?"

"He said to come over to him."

"And then?"

"So I did. And that's when he touched me."

"Wait, slow down. When he said to come over to him, how far away were you from him? Here, let's draw a map of the living room so I can see it. You're here, okay? Now, where is your father on the couch? Okay, I can see that. And then he said come here, and you went over, and then what happened?"

"He touched me."

"Well, yeah, I know, but first he said, 'Come here.' He was watching TV, right? Do you remember what he was watching?"

"The *Today Show*."

"Do you remember anything from the show? The things they talked about?"

"Something about breast cancer in women."

"Do you know what breast cancer is?"

"Not really, but they said that you had to touch your chest to see if you got it."

"So that's what he was watching. What did he do then? Or what did he say? Go slow now. I want to close my eyes and try to see this happen like I was watching a movie. Tell me what happened next."

"He said sit down for a minute and watch TV with him."

"And what did you do?"

"I sat down and he touched me."

"When he said to sit down, did you say anything to him? Or did he say anything to you?"

"Yeah, I said I had to go to school because I was late and I didn't have time to sit down but he grabbed me and pulled me down."

"What did he grab?"

"My arm."

"Which part of your arm. Your wrist? Your elbow? What?"

"My hand, he grabbed my hand while I was walking by and he yanked me onto the couch."

"So when he said to come over to him, did you go right over? Or did you not listen to him and try to walk by when he grabbed you? I'm not sure I see it the way it happened."

"I said I didn't have time and I was walking by, but he grabbed me when I was walking by and pulled me onto the couch with him."

"What did he do with his cigarette? Was it still in his hand?"

"No, it was in his mouth. He was biting it with his teeth."

"So he yanked you onto the couch. What happened next?"

"He told me he loved me very much, and that mom didn't understand him, and that I was the only one who cared about him."

"So you loved him a lot."

"Yeah. A lot."

"What did you think about what he said to you? I mean about loving you and that mom didn't understand him and that you were the only one who cared about him?"

"I didn't think about it much because he says it all the time."

"And then what happened?"

"He put his arm around me. He always does that when he says stuff like that."

"You were sitting where?"

"Right next to him."

"And he said?"

"'Honey, I need you,' that's what he said. Then he touched me."

"Before he touched you, he said he needed you. Then what did he say? Or do?"

"He said nobody was going to fuck me before he did. And then he started taking down my pants and then he . . . "

"Wait, when he said that and started taking down your pants, what did you do? What was going through your mind?"

"I tried to stop him."

"How?"

"I told him to stop. And I tried to stand up."

"Why?"

"Because I knew it was wrong."

"Did he stop?"

"No, he went on. He pulled me back onto the couch and told me not to get upset because he loved me so much and would never hurt me."

"And then?"

"Then he unzipped my pants and pulled them down, and then he pulled me down, and then he kissed me."

"Wait, what about your underpants?"

"Oh yeah, he pulled them down, too."

"When? Before he kissed you or after?"

"Before."

"So what you're saying is that he unzipped your pants, pulled them down, then pulled your underpants down, and then kissed . . . "

"No, my underpants got pulled down with my pants."

"At the same time."

"Right."

"And then he pulled you down and kissed you."

"Right."

"And then?"

"Then he put his hand on my privates."

"And did what?"

"Touched me."

"How did he touch you? What did he do exactly?"

"He put his finger inside me."

"How did it feel?"

"It hurt."

"Did you say anything?"

"No, I was scared."

"And what did he do with his finger inside you? Show me with your own fingers so I can see what he did."

She held up her middle finger and started moving it around and then stopped. "I don't know how to do it right."

"Here, you can use this doll. You can show me how he did it by doing it to this doll. You see? There's an opening here and you can put your finger inside if you need to."

She promptly put her middle finger inside the vaginal opening of the doll and moved her finger around, stroking it in and out. After a few moments, she stopped. "That's what he did."

"Was the same show on TV when he stopped doing that?"

"Yeah, it was still on."

"What was the show?"

"It was still the *Today Show*."

"Do you know how to tell time?"

"Yeah, pretty good."

"Do you think it was for a minute that he had his finger in you, or an hour, or two hours, or what?"

"Maybe a minute, or five minutes maybe."

"Ten minutes?"

"No, not that long."

"How many minutes do you think you've been here with me?"

"A lot. Maybe 30 minutes? Or more? Maybe an hour? I'm not sure."

"Good, and while he was moving his finger around inside you, what else was going on? What else was he doing?"

"What do you mean?"

"Where was his face?"

"On top of mine. He was kissing me."

"So while his finger was in you, he was kissing you. Did he keep kissing you the whole time his finger was in you or did he stop kissing?"

"He stopped kissing sometimes."

"And did what?"

"He said he loved me and needed me."

"And what did you say?"

"Nothing. I was too scared. It was so weird, you know?"

"Weird? Why?"

"Because it was my own father doing it. I couldn't think straight."

"I guess you felt pretty mixed up."

She nodded. "Really mixed up. I was hoping it was just a bad dream."

"And when he took his finger out or you, what happened then?"

"He got on top of me."

"What did he do on top of you and what did you do?"

"I just lied there."

"And him?"

"He moved around and squished me a lot."

"Wait a second, let's make sure I can see exactly what happened. Take these two dolls and show me."

She put the male doll on top of the female one and moved it around so that pelvis ground against pelvis.

"How long did that go on?"

"I don't know."

"One minute? Five minutes? Fifteen minutes? A half-hour? An hour?"

"Not an hour."

"What then? Take a guess."

"Five minutes."

"Not one minute. Could it have been just one minute?"

"No, it was longer than that."

"Ten minutes? Couldn't it have gone on for ten minutes?"

"No, not that long."

"When he was squishing around on you, where was his penis?"

"On my privates."

"On top of them, or inside them, or what?"

"He tried to put it inside, but he couldn't, so he just put it on top."

"What did his penis look like?"

"Kind of like a hot dog."

"Did you ever see a penis before?"

"No."

"So what happened next?"

"Something gooey came out, and it didn't look like pee. It was white. I had to wipe it off my belly."

"How did he act when that happened?"

"He breathed real hard, like huffing and puffing. I thought he was having a heart attack or something and I thought it was all my fault if he died. I didn't know what was going on."

"Now, listen, you said this all happened on the couch, that the two of you were sitting there after he pulled you onto the couch. Where were you sitting on the couch? On this side, or in the middle, or on this other side?"

"Right here."

"And when he pulled you down, was he standing, or sitting, or lying down?"

"He was sitting. But he was sort of lying down too, kind of slumping."

\* \* \* \* \*

The interview went on for a while longer, but we have heard enough for the purposes of the present chapter. The main point is that, to get the details of an abusive event, it can be useful to ask for a video play-back. This technique may be unnecessary when open-ended questions result in a gush of detailed information from the child. It is most useful with children who require ongoing questioning in order to make a full and detailed statement.

When the child says, "I sat down on the couch and he touched me," the clinician doesn't have to leave it at that. This technique helps to uncover all those things that were said and done and observed by the child between the moment she sat down and the moment he touched her. These details and the way they are rendered by the child can then be used to evaluate the credibility of the allegations, an issue to be addressed extensively in subsequent chapters.

## DISCUSSING A STATEMENT PREVIOUSLY AND REPETITIVELY MADE

Frequently, prior to their interview with the mental health evaluator, children have made statements about an abusive event to numerous other individuals: perhaps a teacher, a school nurse, a police officer, a rape crisis counselor, a physician, and a D.S.S. worker. When this has occurred, it is difficult to get a fresh statement from a child, who is growing increasingly weary of talking about the abuse and who may, at this point, be reciting the story by rote. Yet, the evaluator is stuck with the problem of having to ask the child once again what has happened and to attempt to elicit as much fresh information as possible. This kind of situation occurs frequently enough that the evaluator should have available a comfortable way of dealing with it. One way of doing so is by utilizing a previously made statement as a vehicle for communication during the interview. This is illustrated below.

\* \* \* \* \*

"Do you know why you're here today?"

"Yes. I have to talk."

"Do you know about what?"

"About Joe."

"Okay, good. I guess you're probably tired of talking about it."

She nodded her head vigorously.

"How many people have you talked to about it?"

"The police, and Mr. Jones, and the school nurse, and my teacher."

"That's four times. You're probably really sick and tired of it."

She nodded her head again.

"And I need to have you talk to me about it again. I'm sorry about it. I don't mean to make you feel bad, but that's what we're supposed to do today. The job today is to talk about it."

"It's okay," she said. "I guess I'm getting used to it. But will this be the last time?"

"I don't know for sure, but I hope so. It's tough to have to keep on saying it over and over again."

"You're not kidding."

"But before we talk about it, first let me ask you some questions about yourself, so I can get to know what kind of a kid you are, okay?"

I then proceeded through the next three stages of the interview, teaching the child how to answer questions, establishing rapport, and assessing the child's adjustment. At the conclusion of these stages, it came time to elicit a description of the abuse.

"Okay, now it's time for me to ask you some questions about what happened."

"Okay."

"I have a paper here, where a policeman wrote down what you said happened. I've already read it, but sometimes when I'm reading what a kid said I'm not sure if it's what the kid said or if it's what the policeman said. Do you know what I mean?"

"You mean he lied?"

"No, I just don't know if these are your own words. So I need to ask you about it again."

"Oh, okay."

"Do you remember what you told the policeman?"

"No."

"Well, it says here that you told him that Joe touched you on your boobies . . . "

"Uh-huh."

" . . . and put his finger in your butt . . . "

"Oh yeah."

" . . . and that he had you touch his dick and rub it back and forth, and he would make you sit on his lap and wiggle around."

"Uh-huh."

"Could you tell me how much of all that he did? Which ones are the things he really did?"

"He didn't do nothing except for that one. But mom didn't believe me about that."

"Which one did he do?"

"He did this one," she said, pointing to her vaginal area. "He touched my butt."

"You call that your butt?"

"Uh-huh."

"Where you go pee? Or poop?"

"Pee."

"What did he do there?"

"He put his finger in and squeezed."

"Now what about these other things in the paper here? Tell me what parts you really said and what parts you want to change. Okay?"

"Okay."

"It says here that he made you touch his dick and rub it back and forth."

"I didn't do that. He did it."

"He did it? What do you mean?"

"He rubbed it back and forth."

"He rubbed his dick?"

"Yeah."

"Show me how. Pretend this pencil is his dick. Show me what he did."

She wrapped her fist around the pencil and slid it rhythmically up and down the pencil in an imitation of masturbation.

"Did you ever see anybody do that before?"

"No."

"Did you touch his dick at all?"

"No. I told you already. He did."

"Did he touch your boobies? Like it says here?"

"No."

"Then why did you say he did it? The policeman wrote it down."

"I don't know. Maybe because it happened a long time ago."

"You mean he touched your boobies a long time ago?"

"Yeah. The time that he wiggled around when I was sitting on his lap."

"But not the time he touched your butt?"

"No, he just touched my butt that time."

"And your butt is the place where you go pee."

"Yeah."

"And what do you call the place where you poop?"

"That's my butt, too."

"Oh, okay."

\* \* \* \* \*

It was useful first to empathize with the child, that is, with the pain of having to repeat the story again. Next I used her signed statement as a tool to clarify the description of the abuse. Another option would have been to ask an open-ended question intended to elicit her own current description of what had happened. Exercising this option is encouraged, but it can also risk ignoring the potential biasing effect of the previous statements she had made. In most cases, both options can be exercised. While I like to hear what an open-ended question might reveal, I also like to utilize, rather than to ignore, any previous statements.

I almost always discover inconsistencies between the written statement and the one given to me in the interview, and I prefer to address those inconsistencies directly and matter-of-factly rather than regard them as indications of lying. In the illustration above, the events the child conveyed to me were quite different from those depicted in the official police statement. Sometimes inconsistencies of this kind are due simply to misunderstandings between the child and the person who took the statement. The technique of utilizing a previous statement to elicit a description of abuse can certainly be described as "leading." However, as can be seen by this child's responses, the child does not necessarily follow leading questions with obedient responses. There is something fresh and new in what she has to say.

## TOOLS FOR COMMUNICATION:
## DOLLS, DRAWINGS, WRITING, TOYS

Communication can be enhanced in a number of other ways, particularly with children whose language skills may not be as well developed as those of adults. The most common vehicles are toys, drawings, writing, use of the child's or the therapist's body, and, more specifically in regard to sexual abuse, toy telephones, bathtubs, and anatomically correct dolls.

These various tools can be useful under several conditions. One condition occurs when a child's language abilities are not sufficient to enable her adequately to describe her experiences. For example, she may be able to show with dolls or drawings that a bigger male got on top of her and moved up and down on her, pressing his genitals against hers. It might be impossible for her to describe this degree of detail with words.

At other times, a child may have the requisite language development to describe the experience, but embarrassment about it inhibits her from utilizing spoken language to do so. Sometimes this embarrassment can be bypassed by enabling the child to achieve some distance. For example, the child can be asked to write the answers to your questions, or to show you with dolls what happened, or to communicate about it with someone on a toy telephone, or to write a letter describing the abuse.

Drawings can also be useful. They can be used with open-ended purposes, as is done by many therapists, to understand something about the child's view of himself and his world. For example, in routine therapy sessions, children are often asked to draw pictures of themselves and their families. This kind of exercise can be useful in sexual abuse evaluations to determine whether the child can identify parts of the body and to learn the child's names for different family members. The specific purpose here is to establish a framework for a mutual understanding, so that a common language is used for discussion of body parts and family members.

Drawings can also be used to introduce questions about sexual abuse or to provide clarification at various points in an interview. For example, it is often useful to draw a map of a neighborhood, a backyard, or the rooms in a house in order to better understand the context in which the abuse occurred. The drawing can then be used as a concrete point of reference during the interview, with the child and the interviewer frequently pointing to rooms, furniture, buildings, or other objects under discussion.

In addition, drawings can be used to help a client, as well as the

interviewer, to understand the nature and the content of the symptomatology. For example, after speaking with an adolescent who felt over-
whelmed by anxiety that she was not able to define for herself, I drew
for her a picture of her current problematic situation.

On each side of her, I drew her parents, grabbing her arms and each
pulling in a different direction. Above her head on the left side, I drew a
bubble, indicating a thought, in which I drew a man raping her. On the
other side of her head I drew another bubble in which she was sitting at
a desk and taking a test with a drop of sweat dripping from her forehead.
In the foreground on the left, I drew a young man kneeling with flowers
proffered and a balloon over his head in which he was asking her to
marry him. In the foreground on the right, I drew a picture of her car
with a flat tire, to represent the numerous crises and stresses that this
particular automobile had caused. Closer in the foreground, right next
to her, I drew three little children clinging to her legs to represent her
parentification in the family and the weight of responsibility in caring
for her siblings.

While I drew the picture, she watched in fascination. When I was
done, I asked, "Have I left anything out?"

"No, it's all there. Everything."

"On one page," I said. "You can see it all at a glance."

"No wonder I'm so upset. I guess it's not just being raped that bothers
me so much."

"With all of this happening, you're probably feeling pretty confused."

"I sure am," she said, and then corrected herself. "I mean, I was. I
guess it's not so confusing now, is it?"

This technique served to identify each of the multiple stresses causing
her anxiety and helped to block the generalization of anxiety to neutral
areas. The intention was to bind the anxiety to the circumscribed issues
that were causing it. It enabled the young woman to understand her
problem, to feel justified in feeling symptomatic, to experience a reduc-
tion in anxiety that would improve her ability to function, and to formulate a plan to address each of the stresses one at a time.

It also enabled her to put the issue of sexual abuse in perspective.
While the effects of the abuse were stressful, she was able to see that
other issues weighed at least as heavily on her. While this intervention
was helpful in treating her, it also enabled me, as the evaluator, to
pinpoint the significance of the effects of abuse relative to other problems
in her life.

Each therapist or evaluator tends to develop a greater degree of comfort with certain tools and techniques rather than others, whether these
be drawings or writings, telephones or bathtubs, or anatomically correct

dolls. The more familiar and comfortable the clinician becomes with a particular tool, the better he will be at recognizing its limitations and exploiting its strengths. It is not the tool itself that makes for a powerful interviewing technique, but rather the skill with which the clinician uses it.

It is a wise clinician who remains cautious about particular methods or tools that have been popularized as essential to sexual abuse evaluations. The use of toys and drawings in sexual abuse evaluations has sometimes been severely criticized, because of the possibility that they might stimulate fantasy rather than depictions of reality. The best-known example is the use of anatomically correct dolls. While these dolls can be useful, as was illustrated in the first dialogue in this chapter, it is also important to recognize their limitations and the ways they can hurt rather than help.

There is something disturbing about the notion of child protective workers carrying a bag of anatomically correct dolls to each investigation, like a doctor carrying a stethoscope in his black bag or a psychologist carrying intelligence tests in his briefcase. What is disturbing is that some of those who carry these dolls in gym bags, and who utilize them religiously, regard them as vital to a good interview of sexual abuse. They proclaim this belief to the courts, to the media, to other clinicians, and to the general public.

When a novice clinician uses these dolls in an interview and observes that a child engages in sexual play with the doll, it is not uncommon for the clinician to jump to the conclusion that the child was abused. It is also not uncommon for the clinician to jump to the same conclusion when the child exhibits a stoic response upon observing the doll's genitalia. Conclusions like these are unwarranted. At best, anatomically correct dolls are informal tools, like any others mentioned here, which may be useful at times but which also possess a serious potential for misuse.

For example, it is important to be aware that with young preschool children, any questioning via doll play can go over the child's head. That is to say, some of these children are unable to abstract to a sufficient degree to see the correspondence between their own experiences and those of the dolls. Many clinicians assume incorrectly that all children understand that of the two dolls talking about a problem, one of them represents the child. When a child is unable to identify with the doll that, in the clinician's mind, is supposed to represent the child, the result can be the kind of dialogue illustrated below.

\* \* \* \* \*

"Here honey, look," said the clinician, showing the child a doll. "Here's your mommy, she's saying, 'Hi, how are you doing today?'"

The child stared back blankly.

"'Oh, I'm okay,' says Katie," the clinician went on to say, holding up the little girl doll. "'I went to school today and learned about colors.' And now the mommy doll says, 'Okay, that's good, it's time for lunch. Now what does Katie say?'"

The child again stared back with a blank expression on her face.

\* \* \* \* \*

When using dolls, it is necessary to establish a mutual understanding about who the dolls represent. This is illustrated in the following example.

\* \* \* \* \*

"Katie, look, here's a doll that can be your mommy. You see?" The clinician handed her a doll for her to examine. "And here's another doll that can be Katie. And here's another one that can be daddy. Now which one is mommy?"

"This one."

"And which one is Katie?"

"Here."

"Okay, good, now mommy goes and says to you, 'What did you do bad today, Katie?' Now what does Katie say?"

"Nothing, mommy. I didn't do anything bad."

"Good girl. Did anybody do anything bad?"

"Daddy did."

"Which doll is the daddy?"

"This one."

"And which doll is Katie?"

"This one here."

"What did daddy do? Show me."

She manipulated the dolls in a manner that conveyed no coherent message and then said, "He touched me."

"Where did he touch you?"

"Here," she said, pointing to her genitalia instead of the doll's.

"And what did he do when he touched you?"

On the doll, she stroked the vaginal area and inserted her finger into the vaginal opening. "Is this the right answer?"

"There's no right answer. Anything you say is okay."

"But mommy says he did this," she said, inserting her finger into the vaginal opening and stroking her finger in and out.

\* \* \* \* \*

This interview was highly economical, direct, and to the point, deriving the most information from the least number of questions. The child's limitations were recognized throughout the doll play, and the interviewer remained sensitive to the potential for leading the child to make false statements. In this instance, it is clear that it was not the dolls that stimulated a fantasy or a false allegation; instead, the doll play was useful in identifying the source of a false allegation.

Before ending this section, I would like to point out one additional risk. When using drawings or dolls or other toys, these objects can come to represent the people and the issues that the child most fears. In the case of one four-year-old, the interview questions that were asked by means of dolls scared her. She began to silence herself whenever the dolls were reintroduced. By the end of the interview, it was apparent that the dolls, which the interviewer had told her represented her father and uncle, actually represented those figures to her, to the point that she did not feel comfortable in their presence. When this child was able to confront the abuse that had occurred to her, and she was at one point able to do so, she wailed and shuddered inconsolably. As a result, the therapist who would subsequently be assigned to help her with her problem would probably not be able to make use of similar dolls in her therapy and would have to be cautioned to be wary of severe reactions if he did so.

## CONCLUDING REMARKS

Asking for a video playback, discussing with the child a sworn statement, and utilizing toys are all techniques that have serious potential for leading the child. In fact, they are deliberately intended, to some extent, to lead the child. As mentioned earlier, these techniques are less needed with a child who readily provides a great deal of detail in response to open-ended questions. However, many children are unwilling or unable to provide an adequate amount of detail without help. The techniques presented in this chapter provide this kind of help, prodding or stimulating the child to continue to elaborate as much information as possible. To this extent, they result in leading the child, but they lead the child to elaborate, not to make false statements.

The problem with leading questions is not that they stimulate a child to elaborate but rather that they might encourage a child to elaborate in a direction desired by the interviewer in order to confirm the interviewer's preconceived hypothesis. If the interviewer has no hypothesis, or no vested interest in whether abuse did or did not occur, then the leading questions will help just as much to unveil false statements as they will to elicit support for true ones. This point has been illustrated by the examples and dialogues of the chapter.

Leading a child who has made false allegations can result in an abundance of inconsistent and disputable statements. Leading a child who is describing a true experience results, instead, in an abundance of confirmable and consistent statements that are redundant with one another. Thus, the strengths and weaknesses of a child's statement can be amplified by leading questions. These strengths and weaknesses are examined in some detail in the next two chapters. They constitute a system of checks and balances that mitigate against the risks of asking "leading questions."

*     *     *     *     *

"This chapter wasn't really all that different from the others."

"What do you mean? Wasn't there enough about sexual abuse for your taste? I thought this chapter dealt more with sexual abuse than the previous chapters."

"Well, it did. What I mean is that you keep repeating certain interview techniques from previous chapters."

"Too much repetition? Did it bore you?"

"No, I like the repetition. I like the resonance it creates. It really gives me a feel for things. I think that someone who never did any interviews might be able to do one just from reading your examples."

"Why's that? Because I repeat myself over and over again?"

"Not just that. The book doesn't just teach what to do in a sex abuse interview. It gives me a feel for it. It makes me feel like I'm right there, not just reading about it."

"Like a fly on the wall?"

"Sort of. It makes me feel like I'm getting experience at doing it, and internalizing what you're trying to teach. And it's not just sexual abuse interviews. I really see that now. You can use these techniques with any problem. I guess that's the point I was trying to make. That's why the chapter isn't that much different from the previous chapters."

"But I've presented some ideas here that can help you to elicit a more differentiated description about the abusive events. These ideas are specific to sexual abuse."

"Don't get me wrong. I think these ideas are great. The stuff about doll play, telephone conversations, drawings, a script for a movie, all of it. But I think you could use any of these techniques for other kinds of problems as well. Couldn't you?"

"Well, yes, but I specifically focused them on sexual abuse. And in sexual abuse evaluations, these particular techniques are especially useful. You were asking for a more specific focus on sexual abuse, and I was hoping that this would help to answer what you were asking for."

"It does. I'm not complaining."

"Oh, I didn't realize. I thought you were complaining again. I'm glad you're finally satisfied."

"But now that you mention it, I do have a question about your focus on sex. I do kind of wonder whether you're addressing it enough."

"What do you mean? Whether I'm focusing enough on sexual abuse?"

"No, that's not it exactly. It's the examples of sexual abuse that you use. Some of the examples are of serious abuse, but most of them are kind of, I don't know, kind of mild, not so serious."

"Not a lot of sexual intercourse, you mean."

"Well, yeah, I guess."

"You expected to hear about more explicit sex. And maybe in more detail?"

"I guess I did."

"So the examples bore you."

"Not exactly. The techniques are really interesting, but the examples, well, yeah, I guess they are kind of boring. I've seen a lot more juicy cases myself, and I'm not even an expert at this."

"So you're wondering why I'm not using more juicy examples if I'm such a hotshot expert?"

"Yeah. Isn't it kind of odd? I mean, if you're such an expert at this, how come most of your examples consist of mild molestation? Where maybe some uncle touched his niece's nipple one time."

"And to make it worse, sometimes it's not even clear whether the nipple was actually touched at all."

"Exactly. I expected to hear a lot of stuff that would blow me away. Stuff that would knock my socks off. Stuff that would keep me up nights."

"So you're wondering whether I have experience with more severe cases, where the sexual activity and the violence are more graphic, more complicated, with anal and oral sex five times a week with various family members and household pets and maybe even some whips and chains from time to time."

"Well, yeah. I was kind of wondering. Don't you have any of those kinds of examples that you could write about?"

"Yes, I do have some, but I don't see much point in emphasizing them."

"But why not?"

"For a few reasons. To begin with, most sexual abuse that's been reported is somewhat mild in nature. Most of the cases don't involve intercourse. If I used the more severe cases as examples most of the time, it wouldn't be representative of reality."

"Oh. I didn't know that. I thought most abuse involved intercourse."

"No, most of it involves touching. Petting. Inappropriate behavior. That sort of thing."

"I didn't realize."

"And suppose I chose to use a lot of graphic examples. Where do you suppose your attention would be focused? On the gory details? Or on the technique that I'm trying to illustrate?"

"On the gory details, I guess."

"So, it might be a more entertaining piece of work, or more horrifying, depending on where you sit and how prurient your interest is. But it wouldn't be as instructive."

"That's kind of insulting. To say that I'd like it better if it had more gory details."

"You're the one who said it. Not me."

"So that's why you use examples of less severe sex abuse."

"There's a third reason, too. More severe cases are much easier to evaluate. There's not much to figure out. Especially when medical evidence strongly supports the hypothesis. On the other hand, mild abuse and molestation are extremely difficult to evaluate."

"Hmm. I never thought of that."

"Yes. With less severe abuse, it's very difficult to figure out how harmful the effect is. It's even difficult to figure out whether it happened or not."

"So that's another reason you've emphasized examples of mild abuse."

"They're more challenging. You need to utilize all the clinical expertise you have. They bring out the best technique available to you."

"So if you can handle yourself with one of these milder cases, a more severe case should be a piece of cake."

"Exactly. In mild cases, you may not even get much description of any abuse, so even the techniques described in this chapter here might not yield you very much in your effort to figure out what happened, or even whether it did actually happen."

"So what do you do then?"

"You have to be able to interview the child in such a way that you can analyze the statement itself."

"What do you mean?"

"You don't just analyze what she tells you, but how she tells you. And your interview technique needs to maximize aspects of the interview process that will permit this kind of analysis later on."

"Have you talked about these techniques yet? Did I miss it somehow?"

"No. That's next."

# CHAPTER 8

# Techniques to Amplify a Story's Strengths and Weaknesses

"I keep thinking about that sworn statement you discussed with the child in the last chapter. Obviously you didn't take that affidavit at face value."

"No, I didn't. Because affidavits aren't usually sufficient to enable you to determine whether the allegations are true or false. It's never clear whether the child intended to say everything that's in a written statement."

"Even though it's filled with details? Vivid details? I mean, those details might have convinced me."

"Vivid detail does lend a statement some credibility, but that's only one of many variables that can help you to determine how believable the child is."

"You mean what she says isn't that important?"

"No. What she states is certainly important. But even more important is how she goes about stating it."

"How she goes about stating it? I guess that might be hard to figure out from an affidavit."

"That's exactly my point. It's virtually impossible to determine the veracity of an allegation when reading an affidavit."

"Because you can't tell how the statement was made? Like whether she wouldn't look you in the eye, or if she hesitated a lot, or maybe she talked too fast?"

"Yes, exactly. And you need to examine some other strengths and weaknesses of the statement that aren't likely to be apparent in a written affidavit."

"Why couldn't they be included in a written statement? Couldn't the person who took the statement take precautions to include the kinds of information you're talking about?"

"I suppose it's possible. But most people who take sworn statements tend not to do so. I doubt if they're even aware of the variables that permit this kind of qualitative analysis."

"Why not?"

"Because everybody does it his own way. The field is too new. Even as we speak, research projects are attempting to address these very questions. Maybe someday useful and uniform procedures will be available for eliciting statements about sexual abuse. But they're not available now."

"Is the situation that bad? Won't some people who take statements do it in a way to ensure that the statement's strengths and weaknesses are evident?"

"Some might. But most won't. Right now, you can expect, in general, that they won't utilize techniques that will magnify those strengths and weaknesses enough to make them apparent to a third person reading the written statement. So there's no way of getting a sense for how the statement was made."

"So, are you saying that it's essential for people who take statements to know how to do this?"

"No, but it's important for you to know how to do it."

"When will you get around to explaining some techniques for doing this?"

"Right now. That's what this chapter is about."

## ELICITING CONFIRMABLE AND UNCONFIRMABLE STATEMENTS

One relatively easy technique for amplifying strengths and weaknesses consists of keeping track of confirmable and unconfirmable statements. This is useful because the confirmability of the statements in stories helps to discriminate between true and false stories. True stories tend to be characterized by an abundance of potentially confirmable statements, whereas confabulations and lies tend to be characterized by a noticeable abundance of unconfirmable statements. To illustrate this point, an example of confabulation is provided below.

\* \* \* \* \*

"Okay, so after you fell off your bike, you say he dragged you into his house?"

"Right, him and his friends."

"Did you know who he was?"

"No, I never seen any of them before."

"Where was the house? What street was it on?"

"I don't remember. I think I was lost."

"Could you find the house again, do you think?"

"I wouldn't want to."

"But could you if someone helped you?"

"I don't know, maybe. But I doubt it."

"When you fell off your bike, did you get hurt?"

"Yeah, I hurt my knee. It was bleeding all over the place."

"Can I see the cut?"

"Uh, it didn't cut, it just got banged and it's better now."

"Did you tell anyone about your banged knee, so they could fix it?"

"No. It just got better by itself."

"Did anybody else look at it?"

"No, it got better too fast."

"Do you have a scar there? Or a bruise? A black and blue mark?"

"No. Well, yeah, I did, but it's gone now."

"How long ago did this happen?"

"About a week ago."

"Okay, tell me, did this guy just come up and drag you away, or did he talk to you first, or what? You were sitting there on the ground, right?"

"Right."

"In the street? On the sidewalk? On the grass? Where were you?"

"On the street."

"And how come you fell off?"

"I hit a bump."

"And so you fell off and banged your knee and then this guy and his friends came over and what did they say?"

"They asked if I was hurt and they were nice at first and told me to come with them. But I didn't want to, so they dragged me in."

"And this happened right out there on the street?"

"Yeah."

"There must have been some people around or cars going by. There must have been someone else who saw you fall."

"Uh, well, maybe there was. Yeah, there was this car that drove up behind me real fast, that's why I hit the curb and fell off, and a guy got out and asked me if I was okay and I said yes. God, you wouldn't believe how drunk he was."

"And then what did he do?"

"He got back in his car and left."

"Did he see the boys who dragged you?"

"No, they were just walking over then."

\* \* \* \* \*

In addition to inconsistencies and other indications of lying, this story contained a number of unconfirmable statements. For example, her statements about her injury contained qualifications that ruled out the possibility of confirming that it actually occurred. Similarly, she ruled out the possibilities of locating the house where the alleged rape occurred and of finding witnesses to any aspect of the episode. While true statements cannot always be confirmed, they tend to be made in a manner that offers the potential for confirmation. When unconfirmable statements begin to pile up, the story becomes increasingly suspect. In this example, there are very few, if any, confirmable statements that could help to support this adolescent's story. In contrast, consider this exchange with a different child, who made a number of confirmable statements.

\* \* \* \* \*

"Okay, so you saw him go in the garage and your friend was in there with him. Is that what you're saying?"

"Right, they were both in the garage."

"And later she told you he molested her."

"Right, she said he raped her."

"He raped her. Okay. And is that how you know what happened? From her telling you?"

"Yeah, and I saw it through the window."

"The window? What window?"

"The window of the garage. I climbed up."

"And what did you see?"

"They were just talking."

"Did he do anything besides talk?"

"No, just talk."

"No rape?"

"No, just talking."

"No touching or kissing or hugging?"

"No."

"Then how do you know he raped her?"

"She told me."

"But you didn't see it happen?"

"No, I already told you that."

"Why were you looking in the window?"

"To see what they were doing."

"How come you wanted to see what they were doing? What made you want to look?"

"They were alone in there. I wondered what they were doing."

"Where was the window?"

"On the side."

"The window was on the side of the garage?"

"Yeah."

"How high was it?"

"High up. Up to your head. Real high up."

"High up? About this high?"

"Yeah, about that."

"Well, you're not that tall. How did you see them through the window."

"I told you. I climbed up."

"Climbed up on what?"

"The fence."

"So you were standing on a fence?"

"Yeah, that's what I already told you."

"Okay, try to be patient with me. Could you draw me a picture of this garage, and where the window is, and the fence?"

\* \* \* \* \*

In this example, the height of the window and the height and proximity of the fence were facts that were realistically confirmable. The child protective worker was able to find out that a fence did exist alongside the garage, that a window existed about six feet off the ground, and that a four-foot tall child standing on the fence could look through that window. By itself, this confirmation did not mean that the child's statement about what she saw was true, but a disconfirmation would have suggested that the statement was untrue.

Actual confirmation of a statement is a bonus; it is not possible or feasible for every one of the dozens of statements that are made during the course of a single interview. However, when a statement is made in such a way that it is at least potentially confirmable, it has the ring of truth. Therefore, it is useful for the questioning to be conducted in a manner that maximizes the opportunities for the child to make either confirmable or uncomfirmable statements. To do so, the clinician needs to do three things. First, she needs to elicit a great many details, which should concern the wider context in which the abusive event occurred, not just the event itself. Second, as the clinician listens to every single statement made, she needs to determine whether it is potentially confirmable or not. Finally, when the clinician can't tell whether a statement is confirmable, the clinician needs to follow up with further questions, seeking answers that will help to make this differentiation. The clinician will then be in a position, at the end of the interview, to describe the extent to which the story was characterized by confirmable or unconfirmable statements.

## ASKING THE CHILD TO REPEAT THE STORY

"Would it be okay if I go back now and ask some questions about your brother?"

"What about him?"

"Well, you said he was sick that morning. I think you said he was sleeping upstairs when your father pulled you onto the couch."

"Right, he was upstairs sleeping."

"How did you know he was up there?"

"Because dad told me he was."

"When did he tell you that?"

"When he had me on the couch and was kissing me. I told him that Bobby might come in, but he said don't worry because Bobby was still sick and was sleeping and wasn't going to school that day."

"Did he tell you that while he was kissing you? Or while he was on top of you?"

"It was in the middle, I think."

"In the middle?"

"After he kissed me. But before he got on top. It was when he was pulling down my pants. That's when I said that Bobby might walk in."

\* \* \* \* \*

Another technique for amplifying the strengths and weaknesses of a child's story is to ask the child to repeat it. However, telling the entire story again can be stressful for the child. Usually it is unnecessary because, throughout an interview, certain portions of the story often beg for clarification or further elaboration, as was illustrated above. As these portions are retold by the child to meet these other needs, strengths and weaknesses of the child's story are amplified and the reliability of the child's statements is tested in several ways. For children who are lying, repetition of the story provides opportunities for them to contradict themselves, while for those who are telling the truth, the consistency of the story can be enhanced. Repetition can result in redundancies that confirm a previous telling, as well as fresh, newly remembered details that are consonant with and supplement previous details. Repetition also enables the evaluator to determine whether various people and objects continue to be positioned in the same relationship to one another and whether sequences of events are invariant.

Despite these advantages to hearing a story more than once, the evaluator needs to decide whether the advantages are worth the risks. One risk is that the child may feel you are asking the same question repeatedly because she hasn't provided the "right" answer. As a result, the child may respond with false statements due to either a desire to please or fear of disapproval. The risk also exists of conveying a message that you have a bias against believing the child. These risks are serious ones if the evaluator's questioning reflects a biased stance, oriented solely in one direction, toward determining either the falseness of a statement or, alternatively, its truth.

However, these risks are minimized when the evaluator does not in fact have a bias toward either believing or disbelieving the child. From such a neutral stance he can remain alert to any inconsistencies between the tellings of the story, as well as any redundancies that will help to enhance its credibility.

## TESTING CONSISTENCY WITH LEADING QUESTIONS

Another technique for magnifying the strengths and weaknesses of a story is to encourage inconsistencies with questions that are intended to lead the child to make statements inconsistent with previous statements. The outcome is either an increase in inconsistencies or an increase in consistent statements. The intention is to amplify the client's potential, during the interview, for making either consistent or inconsistent statements.

Some readers may view this technique as a method for tricking abused children into making false statements, which will damage their credibility. That is not the intention. I prefer to view it as a method that can help to determine the child's vulnerability to leading questions. A child who responds with false statements to leading questions may be lying, but she may also be doing so due to confusion, cognitive limitations, a desire to please, or a fear of disapproval. It is acknowledged that a technique like this can stimulate false statements in a child who was truly abused. Fortunately, inconsistency is not the only indication of lying, so other variables can be used to help identify such children. However, the child's degree of vulnerability to leading questions is useful to know, and it can be assessed with this technique.

Tests frequently accomplish the same purposes by asking the same basic question several times using different words and requiring a different form of response each time. These purposes are often accomplished accidentally in interviews when the clinician makes a mistake in restating to the child what the child has already told him. At those moments, the child either goes along with the evaluator's mistake, by making inconsistent statements, or corrects the mistake.

Since these kinds of mistakes on the part of the evaluator tend to occur anyway on a routine basis, it is not difficult to unobtrusively include similar mistakes with deliberation and purpose. It is tempting to do this when the interviewer suspects that the child is lying, fantasizing, or confabulating. However, the evaluator may feel as if there is something unethical about it when there is the ring of truth in the statement and the child seems to be genuinely sincere. It is in these latter cases that an evaluator may feel most uncomfortable, as if he is trying to trick a child into making false statements. While it might be entirely unnecessary to utilize this technique in such cases, it does provide a chance to assess the child's vulnerability to being led; moreover, a child's failure to respond to leading questions can be used later to buttress an opinion of her credibility.

The example of Lucy, illustrated below, shows that when this technique is used with a child making a true allegation it can enhance her credibility rather than damage it. Lucy had told the interviewer that she had been sitting in a pickup truck with her father and a friend of her father's, on the way home from a circus where she and her father had spent the day. She had been sitting in the middle of the front seat; her father's friend, Dan, had been driving; and her father had been sitting next to the right-hand window. When they stopped at a store, Dan had got out of the pickup and gone into the store. While he was gone, Lucy's father had attempted to put his penis in her mouth. Upon Dan's return, Lucy's father had slid over to drive, and Dan had taken the window seat, with Lucy in the middle. Many other details about previous and subsequent events were also elicited. The purpose of stating the above history is to permit a comparison to the questioning that subsequently occurred.

\* \* \* \* \*

"Okay, let me get this straight. I know I asked you about this before, but let me make sure I have it right. Okay?"

"Okay."

"You and your father and Dan were driving back from the circus and your father was driving and Dan was sitting . . . "

"No, Dan was driving."

"Okay, sorry, I got that. Okay, Dan was driving and you were sitting against the window and your father was in the . . . "

"No, wrong. I was in the middle."

"Okay, let me make sure I write that down so it's right. Okay, then, after Dan came back to the truck and got behind the wheel, were you sitting in the middle, or at the window? The window I think."

"No, you got it all wrong. My dad drove after the store, and Dan was at the window and I was still in the middle."

"Okay, I think I've got it now."

\* \* \* \* \*

This child sticks to her story despite leading questions to the contrary. By way of contrast, recall the young adolescent who claimed she had been dragged from her bike to a house and then raped (p. 153). In the earlier dialogue, she contradicted herself at least twice: about her injury, saying that it bled and then saying that it didn't; and about what caused her to fall off her bike, first saying that she hit a bump and later saying that she hit a curb due to the reckless driving of a drunk who then stopped his car. In addition, she readily contradicted herself when encouraged to do so with leading questions. Here is a later portion of the interview.

\* \* \* \* \*

"What did he look like?"

"I couldn't tell. He had a ski mask on."

"What else did he have on?"

"Bandanas."

"Bandanas? How many?"

"Two, on his head and on his leg."

"Both legs?"

"Yeah both legs."

"On his arms?"

"No. He didn't have any on his arms."

"What color were they?"

"Red."

"Both of them?"

"Well, no. The one on his head was red. He had a yellow one on his leg."

"What was the color on the other leg?"

"Blue on the other leg."

"What about his arms?"

"He had a black one on his right arm and a white one on his left arm."

\* \* \* \* \*

The child was confronted at this point with the discrepancies she had just made: first saying that there were only two bandanas and then gradually increasing the number; also, saying that they were not on the assailant's arms and then saying that they were. She was also told bluntly that much of her statement, prior to the dialogue in this illustration, did not sound true. She was asked at this point whether her assailant had really worn a ski mask or not. She broke down and cried and admitted that she had lied, that he had not worn a ski mask. When asked why she had lied about it, she said it was due to fear, but would not specify what she feared. Below we pick up the interview at this point. Keep in mind that the purpose of the example is to illustrate how leading questions can result in contradictions.

\* \* \* \* \*

"So, then, what did happen? Did someone sexually abuse you?"

"Yeah, that same guy with the ski mask, only he didn't have a ski mask."

"The same one who helped you when you fell off your bike?"

"Right. He's the one."

"It wasn't anybody else?"

"No, it was him."

"You said he got on top of you and moved around a lot, and you said that all your clothes were still on, is that right?"

"Right, he just moved around on top of me with my clothes still on."

"So your underwear was still on, but did you say that he had already pulled your pants off?"

"Yeah, he pulled my pants off before he got on top."

"Your underwear, your panties, did you have them on?"

"Yeah."

"You're sure?"

"They were on. He only took off my pants."

"Okay, so what happened then?"

"He forced me down and got on top of me and put his finger in me and then he moved around on me and . . . "

"Okay, stop, wait a second. Let me get this right. He forced you down and got on top of you and pulled your pants down, and then pulled down your panties, and put his finger in you. Do I have that right? Any mistakes so far?"

"No, it sounds right to me."

"So he had already taken down your panties?"

"Yup."

"You're sure of that."

"Yup."

"You know, you told me about a minute ago that he didn't take down your panties. What am I supposed to believe? First you tell me that he didn't take down your panties, and then you tell me he did. I'm kind of confused. Do you understand my confusion?"

\* \* \* \* \*

It seems fairly clear that the child is responding falsely to leading questions in order to try to convince people that she was sexually abused. Therefore, it is somewhat doubtful that she was abused by this teenager in a ski mask and bandanas. Although other indications existed to suggest that she may have been abused, it probably did not occur as she originally described it.

Another example of encouraging inconsistencies is illustrated in the case of 15-year-old Babette. She was living in a residential facility because she had been first abandoned by her mother and then surrendered by her aging aunt and uncle, who could no longer effectively parent her due to their own physical disabilities. She was referred for a sexual abuse evaluation because she had made several serious allegations of abuse. While on visits to her mother's home, she alleged that her mother encouraged her to have sex with a dog, that her brothers and cousins had sexually abused her, and that her father may also have abused her on one occasion. The D.S.S. investigator wondered whether the child was a pathological liar or whether the case merited the kind of investigation that would petition the parents to court. Samples from this interview follow.

* * * * *

"After a birthday party, I went to my grandparents' house, and my brother tried to fix my bike in the basement. While he was doing it, he pulled me down on the ground and had sex with me."

"Did he threaten you?"

"No."

"Did he threaten you with weapons?"

This question was intended not only to encourage an inconsistency, but to provide a leading question regarding actual weapons, which are rarely used in instances of sexual abuse.

"No, just with his fist, and . . . uh, with nunchucks."

"What did he do with the nunchucks?"

"Nothing."

"Wait now, try to remember, did he hold them in his hands and spin them around like this and tell you he would hit you in the face with them?"

"Yeah, he said he would knock my block off."

* * * * *

The key quote here is "No, just with his fist and with nunchucks." First she agrees that she wasn't threatened, which is very common, and then she immediately responds to the suggestion that she was threatened with weapons, which is highly uncommon. Then she elaborates further when encouraged, even after denying that anything further happened.

* * * * *

"When he pushed you on the floor and made you have sex with him, were any of your clothes on? Or did he take them all off?"

"All my clothes were off. He took them off. Everything."

"Then what did he do."

"He fucked me."

"But what did he do first, the very first thing after he took your clothes off?"

"He kissed me and then grinded himself on me."

"Okay, so he moved around on you for a while. Did he take your panties off next?"

"Yeah," she said, oblivious to the contradiction she had just made.

"What color?" I asked, seeking to verify whether she was sure she wanted to commit herself to the contradiction.

"Red."

"How is it that you can remember the color of your panties?"

"I remember what I put on that day."

\* \* \* \* \*

Before leaving this section, I would like to emphasize a particular point. While the last few illustrations have demonstrated a vulnerability to leading questions that is highly suggestive of lying, it is not possible to determine from this vulnerability that these girls were not abused in some way by someone. The girls in these examples may have made their numerous false statements as a result of confusion, a desire to please, or for other reasons. Inconsistency is only one of the many factors that the clinician takes into consideration when analyzing the qualitative characteristics of a child's story.

## EPISTEMOLOGICAL QUESTIONS

We are so often preoccupied with figuring out what actually occurred that we focus exclusively on the content of what people tell us, trying to put together for ourselves a coherent ontological picture of a possible reality. While ontology concerns what one thinks one knows about reality, epistemology concerns how one goes about the process of knowing it. In other words, how does the informant know what he says he knows?

The question of how the informant gained the information he is reporting is often forgotten by the interviewer when his primary concern is trying to develop a coherent picture out of bits and pieces of a story conveyed by numerous informants. As he listens to child protective investigators, parents, relatives, and victim, the evaluator's first task is to try to arrive at some overall impression of what happened and to get the story straight. He must not forget, however, to ask each of the informants whether what he says is based on his own observations and experience or whether it is second- or even third-hand information.

Children often incorporate into their own statements information that they have heard from others or information that they believe others want them to offer as the truth. To establish how they obtained their knowledge, it is necessary frequently to ask how the child knows this or that fact to be so. Other useful questions are: Who told you? What does that word mean? How can you tell when mommy is drunk (or crazy, or acting like a whore, etc.)? The following dialogues illustrate the use of these questions, starting with, "How do you know?" and "Who told you?"

\* \* \* \* \*

"Does he ever hit you?" asked the evaluator of a four-year-old.
"No, we don't spank in our house."
"How do you know there's no spanking in your house? Who told you?"
"Mommy did."

\* \* \* \* \*

The phrase "We don't spank in our house" tipped off the evaluator because this use of language is atypical for a four-year-old. Yet, it is not uncommon for a four-year-old to repeat this kind of adult statement.

\* \* \* \* \*

"Yeah, daddy was drunk as a skunk," reported another child.
"How do you know that?" asked the evaluator.
"I just know."
"Who told you he was drunk?"
"My brother."
"How can you tell when somebody's drunk?"
"I can tell."
"How can you tell? How do they act?"
"They walk funny and bump into things."
"What else do they do when they're drunk?"
"They talk funny, so it's hard to get what they say."
"Was your daddy walking funny and talking funny when he took you for pizza?"
"No. But my brother said he was drunk as a skunk."

\* \* \* \* \*

In this example it was possible to differentiate the child's own observation from his brother's. Sometimes children utilize phrases they have heard others use in such a way that they appear to be mouthing another person's opinion when in fact they are formulating their own opinions.

\* \* \* \* \*

"My daddy is blinded by the devil," said one six-year-old girl.

"Blinded by the devil? What's that mean?"

"He's blinded by the devil. It means he's bad. The devil tells him what to do. So he must be blind. And bad."

"Where did you learn to say that? Who said 'blinded by the devil'?"

"My Sunday School teacher. He teached me."

\* \* \* \* \*

Her Sunday School teacher didn't teach her that her father was blinded by the devil. He only taught her the phrase. She incorporated this vocabulary while formulating her own opinion about her father. While at first blush it appeared that she was mouthing an expression of her mother's, further questioning revealed that she was stating her own opinion.

It is natural for people to incorporate second-hand information into their report of experiences. It is not usually done with ulterior motives. However, when children utilize second-hand information that does not appear to constitute their own opinions and yet they insist strongly on its veracity, one can suspect that they have been either coached or influenced by others. This kind of situation is the subject of the next section.

## COURTING TRUTHFUL INCONSISTENCIES

"Hello, Tommy," said the evaluator. "You're here today to talk to me about . . . "

"I'm here to say mommy put my wee-wee in her mouth and I want to live with my daddy."

\* \* \* \* \*

When a child makes a statement like this, which he obviously wants the evaluator to believe, the evaluator needs to remain alert for any further statements that may be inconsistent with the first one. Unless an inconsistent statement is made, the evaluator cannot know for certain, and can only suspect, that the first statement is false. Unfortunately, in this kind of situation, the evaluator cannot encourage the utterance of an inconsistency with leading questions, as was suggested in a previous section. After all, the child is motivated to convince the evaluator that the first statement is true and therefore would immediately deny any leading questions that suggested the contrary.

It is more prudent to practice patience and reflective listening, lending an empathic ear to the story the child wishes to tell you, gaining rapport, and waiting to see where the interview progresses. What sometimes happens is that the child spontaneously and innocently makes a remark that casts doubt upon, or even directly contradicts, his opening remarks. If this kind of inconsistency does occur, the evaluator shouldn't pounce on it with a confrontation, because this would alert the child to the significance of what he has just said and would inhibit further statements in the same vein. Instead, the evaluator again needs to practice patience and reflective listening by gently courting further elaborations on the statements that are inconsistent with the first one made. The following example of eight-year-old Debbie illustrates these various points.

Debbie had made very specific allegations against her uncle, with whom she lived, saying that he had given her and her friend some candy and then touched them in their vaginal areas and asked them to touch his penis. Her aunt, who had raised her, and her mother, who visited her occasionally, were present when the police took a statement; they became quite hysterical at what they heard from Debbie in the police station. They were then alone with Debbie for a short time before the D.S.S. investigators took a separate statement from her in which she recanted the allegations.

In her recantation, she said that her uncle did not abuse her but rather had only touched her like uncles and parents are supposed to touch children, that is to say, by hugging, tickling, and kissing. The D.S.S. investigators strongly suspected that Debbie was making a false recantation, due to the pressure put on her by her mother and aunt, but Debbie was sticking to her story.

When she was brought into our offices for an evaluation, she immediately announced that she had been misunderstood.

\* \* \* \* \*

"Debbie, you're here today because . . . "

"Because I got all mixed up, that's why. They thought I said that my uncle molested me, but he didn't. He would never do that. He touched me, but he didn't touch me in a bad way. He touched me like uncles are supposed to. You know, hugging, and tickling, and kissing. They got me to say things that weren't true."

"You mean, they got you all mixed up and made you say he molested you."

"Right."

\* \* \* \* \*

Normally, children are not sure why they are in the interview situation, they are not sure of what the clinician's role is, and they need to be coaxed to answer even innocuous questions. It is highly unusual for a child to interrupt the clinician's introductory explanation by blurting out her own agenda. It does happen enough not to be a rarity, but it is not common. When a child tries immediately to take control of the situation by providing a statement that resolves the question of concern, one should suspect that there is somebody whispering in the child's ear or that the child is fearful enough of some anticipated consequence that she will do her best to deliberately persuade the evaluator to believe something that is not true. However, to confront the child at too early a point in the interview would only heighten her defensiveness. Reflective listening and gentle questioning are best at this point.

\* \* \* \* \*

"You mean, they got you all mixed up and made you say he molested you?"

"Right."

"Okay, Debbie, listen for a second. There aren't any right answers or wrong answers here. If you know the answer, give the answer to my questions. If you don't know, then say you don't know. If you don't want to tell me, then say you don't want to tell me. Do you think you can do that?"

"Sure."

"Okay, good. Now Debbie, you said a word before. 'Molest.' What does that word mean? Molest."

Debbie was silent and didn't answer the question.

"When you're quiet like that, I don't know what you mean. Does it mean that you know the word, or you don't know what it means, or that you don't want to tell me?"

"I guess I don't know what it means."

"Do you have any idea?"

"No. But maybe it's something bad."

"Well, yes, it is. It means that a grown-up touches a child on her chest or between her legs where she goes to the bathroom. Is that what you thought it meant? Or did you think it meant something else?"

"I didn't know."

"That's okay, it doesn't matter right now. Right now, I guess, you want to be sure that I know that your uncle is a nice guy and that he didn't do anything bad to you."

"Yeah, he didn't do any of those nasty things they said he did."

\* \* \* \* \*

In addition to Debbie's blurting out her agenda at the outset, other indications existed here to suggest that her statements might be second-hand rather than first-hand. Phrases and words were used that one would not expect a child to use naturally, such as "he would never do that, he touched me like uncles are supposed to." She also used the word "molest," the meaning of which she did not know.

The interview went on in the same vein, with the interviewer accepting her statements without confronting them. Debbie then explained that she was living temporarily with her mother, as a result of her original disclosure of abuse, but that she wanted to return to her aunt, who had raised her from infancy. In addition, she gradually indicated that she was terrified of the possibility of being placed in a foster home, which was what her mother and aunt threatened would happen if her uncle was believed to have abused her. It also emerged that she was frightened of her uncle and had nightmares about him, dreaming that he sneaked through her window at night and "kissed on me." The interviewer continued to accept her statements and to draw her out until she finally made a slip and stated that her uncle did indeed touch her. He seized on this by encouraging her to elaborate.

\* \* \* \* \*

"Okay, he scared you, but he didn't do all those nasty things that they said he did, he just scared you, is that what you're saying?"

"Right, he didn't do all that nasty stuff but he scared me all right."

"How?"

"When he said to kiss it."

"Kiss what?"

"His thing."

"You mean something on his body? Or something else?"

"Yeah, his wee-wee."

"What's a wee-wee?"

"You know, the thing you go to the bathroom with."

\* \* \* \* \*

At this point, the interviewer wondered about contextual details of the event. For example, he would have liked to ask her whether she had clothes on, and if not, where her clothes were; what room they were in; the positioning of the furniture, and so on. However, to ask her any of these questions at this point would have seriously risked alerting her to the significance of what she was saying. He believed it probable that she would become defensive and withhold further verbalization about what happened. Therefore, he remained patient and stayed with what she was saying, with questions that did not push her further than she wished to go.

\* \* \* \* \*

"So he asked you to kiss it."

"No, first he asked my friend."

"And she said?"

"No way."

"And you? What did you say?"

"No way."

"So what happened next?"

"He just tickled us."

"Where?" The interviewer put the dolls in front of her. "Show me."

She pointed to the vaginal area of the female doll.

"Show me how he did it. Use your own fingers."

She used her forefinger to tickle the vaginal opening and then inserted the finger and stroked for a little while.

"What else did he do?"

"That's all."

"What did he do to your friend?"

"Nothing, she wouldn't let him."

"What did she say?"

"She said, 'No way,' and she jumped up and moved away."

"Was that after he put his finger in you or before?"

"Before."

"Okay so after she jumped away, he touched you there." The interviewer pointed to the vaginal area of the doll.

"Tickled me."

"Right, but not your friend."

"He tried but she wouldn't let him."

"So that's when he did it to you."

"Right."

"Okay, so when he did this, when he tickled you there, where were your clothes?" The interviewer at this pointed decided to go after contextual details.

"What do you mean?"

"Did you have your clothes on? Or off?"

"On."

"What were you wearing?"

"Pants and a shirt."

"How did he get his finger in you to tickle you? What about your pants?"

"He pulled them down a little."

"He pulled them down, and then put his finger in there and tickled you."

"No, I got that wrong, he didn't pull my pants down. He just tickled me, like uncles are supposed to. He didn't do anything nasty."

"You know, I'm a little mixed up. You told me before that he didn't touch you at all. That he just hugged and kissed you. Then you said that he put his finger in you. And now you say he didn't."

"He didn't, he just hugged me and tickled me like uncles are supposed to," she said, on the edge of tears, looking confused and caught.

"You don't know what to say, do you? You're so scared of saying the wrong thing."

Vigorous head nods from Debbie as tears rolled down her cheeks.

"Maybe you're not even sure what really happened because you're all mixed up about what you're supposed to say."

"Yeah, I'm really mixed up. I don't say it right, like I'm supposed to. Maybe I don't remember it right."

"And you're scared about going to a foster home."

"Yeah. Really scared. I don't want to go. I just want to go home."

"I know. And I won't ask you any more questions today because you're feeling so mixed up and upset. I think these questions are really upsetting you, so I'll stop. Okay?"

"Yeah, but don't forget about my uncle. He didn't do anything nasty. He didn't molest me."

"Okay. What you really want to tell me is that your uncle is a nice guy and didn't do anything bad."

"Yeah, he didn't do anything bad."

"Okay, before we stop, is there anything else you want to tell me? Or any questions you want to ask me?"

"Yeah, what should I do if he does it again?"

## CONCLUDING REMARKS

The techniques illustrated in this chapter alter the interview process by amplifying qualitative strengths and weaknesses of the child's story. Such amplification enhances the subsequent process of formulating impressions and drawing conclusions. In addition, the evaluator has had the chance to become familiar with several means by which the differentiation between true and false allegations might be made during the interview itself, prior to formulating final conclusions.

The focus on interview technique is brought to a conclusion with this chapter. We turn next to the stage of the evaluation in which data are analyzed and conclusions are formulated. As we begin, we will once again examine the problem of differentiating between true and false statements.

\* \* \* \* \*

"Wait a second. Not so fast."

"What's wrong? Don't you want to go on?"

"I've got a question or two."

"About?"

"About that technique of encouraging false statements with leading questions. I'm very uncomfortable about it. There still seems to be something unethical about it."

"I thought I addressed that issue."

"You did a lot of reframing to try to prettify it. But when you come right down to it, isn't it kind of deceptive?"

"I don't think of it as deceptive. It's no more deceptive than a lot of things that are done in evaluation and therapy. Psychological testing is full of deception."

"But you are clearly tricking the child. Isn't that deceptive?"

"I can see your point, and I have thought a lot about it. But again, I don't think of it as deceptive. I think of it as one more technique for eliciting information, just a way of talking, of asking questions, of communicating. I don't think it's any more deceptive than reflective listening."

"How can you even compare the two? Reflective listening is such a benevolent, nonintrusive technique."

"Is it? I once watched a professor utilize reflective listening with a student in such an effective manner that within minutes she had broken down in tears and was telling the whole class the intimate details of her troubled marriage. She was very embarrassed and angry afterwards."

"She had a right to be. The professor used extremely poor judgment. It was clearly inappropriate to use reflective listening like that in the context of a classroom. It wasn't a therapeutic context."

"Well, when you utilize reflective listening in a therapeutic context, do you ever first warn your clients that they might end up spilling their guts and telling you far more than they wish you to know? Or that they may be discovering things about themselves that they aren't ready to face?"

"No, I guess not."

"Yet, you know that this commonly occurs. Is it deceptive on your part not to warn them?"

"But to explain to them in advance all the effects of reflective listening would be like teaching them a course in communication skills. Besides, if I thought that the client was saying more than she wished to, I'd probably stop her and talk to her about that. It's a question of using good judgment."

"So you're saying that it's how you use the technique that determines whether it's deceptive or not?"

"Yeah, maybe that's what I am saying."

"Well, that's what I'm saying, too. It's not the technique itself that is deceptive or unethical, but how it might be utilized. Even a technique as benevolent as reflective listening can be used with malevolence."

"How? You mean like with that professor?"

"With an intent to trap or persecute or hurt the other person in some way, or to meet your own needs at the expense of theirs. Trying to find out something that you can then use against them. If your intent is to prove that a child is a liar, reflective listening can be used with just as deadly an effect as the technique of eliciting inconsistencies with leading questions."

"I guess I never thought about it like that."

"But you don't need to feel compelled to use the technique if you're still uncomfortable with it."

"What do you mean? You just finished convincing me that it was okay."

"What I mean is, if you don't think you can utilize the technique in an ethical fashion, I wouldn't want to encourage you to utilize it. When a child uttered an inconsistency, I wouldn't want you to say to yourself, 'Aha, I've got her now' and then pounce on her to prove her a liar. I hope I'm not providing an unethical model for you. Do you see me beating up on kids with these techniques?"

"No, not at all. You do confront them, but you do it gently, and you try to find out why the child was inconsistent."

"Yes, and often it's because the child is confused or has certain cognitive limitations. If the child is too vulnerable to respond consistently to questions that strenuously scrutinize the child's statements, I don't automatically assume she is a liar. I want to know why. And I don't formulate conclusions on the basis of this one variable of consistency. I try to use as many variables as I can to pull everything together."

"Well, how do you do that? This process of filtering information, sifting it, weighing it against other information. How do you actually pull it all together?"

"That's next. It's the subject of the final section of the book."

# PART III

# *Evaluation*

"Now that you've gathered all your data, you're at the stage where you'll be evaluating it and arriving at some conclusions and recommendations."

"What's the main purpose of this evaluation stage? To determine whether the allegations are credible? Whether they're true or false?"

"That's only one purpose. After all, there are many cases where you don't even need to address that question because it's clear from the beginning that sexual abuse occurred."

"Then what else are you trying to do at this stage?"

"Pull everything together in order to arrive at an understanding of the factors that account for the problem. Only then can you make recommendations that address those factors."

"That sounds like what you do in any kind of a case, even treatment cases."

"That's right. It's essential to figure out what factors account for a problem before you try to treat the problem. Before you figure out what needs to be done. This is where treatment often goes wrong from the outset. There's an incomplete evaluation to begin with, so the therapist is off and running with therapeutic interventions that target the wrong problem."

"I guess I've done that, too. How can I get better at preventing it?"

"One thing is to get better at recognizing when the evaluation isn't yet *complete. That's an essential part of this evaluation stage. Figuring out what's missing."*

"Can you proceed any further when something important is missing?"

"Sometimes you can, sometimes you can't. That's something you have to figure out in each case—whether you can still move forward and formulate some useful conclusions and recommendations even when your evaluation is incomplete."

"That sounds awfully difficult. But I guess it's realistic. Lots of times you don't have all the information you would like to have."

"That's right. You have to make do with what you have."

"So, then, the main task isn't always to figure out whether abuse occurred. It's to figure out why it occurred and what to do about it."

"Yes, what remedy to apply."

"You mean what to do to protect the child? Like whether an abusive father should be removed from the home or not?"

"Yes, or even figuring out whether treatment is indicated."

"Why wouldn't treatment be indicated?"

"Well, sometimes the abuse is so mild that forcing a child to undergo treatment is more traumatizing than the abuse was itself."

"You mean you might recommend that nothing be done?"

"Well, yes—in some cases. You've got to look at each possible remedy and decide whether that remedy hurts more than it helps. And you've got to look at each act of alleged abuse and decide whether it's harmful."

"What? You mean figure out whether it happened?"

"No. It might be very clear that it happened, but it might not be clear whether it was abusive or harmful."

"Can you explain what you mean? I don't think I'm following."

"Well, a four-year-old boy says to his preschool teacher, 'My daddy tickles my butt every night.' The D.S.S. worker comes to school and interviews the child, and the child goes on to clarify that, yes, his father does touch his buttocks, not only near his waist, but all the way down to the bottom of his buttocks, near his anus, right down to the top of his thighs. When asked how the father goes about touching the boy's buttocks, the boy shows the D.S.S. worker on a doll that his father's fingers tickle and caress and squeeze the entire area."

"What does the father say? Does he deny it all?"

"No, he admits to it all."

"Then isn't it fairly clear what happened? That the boy was abused by his father?"

"It's not at all clear. The father is outraged at the suggestion that this touching is regarded as abuse."

"What do you mean he's outraged? What's he doing with his hands down his son's pants?"

"He's outraged that you think he's engaging in a sexual act."

"But he is. He's obviously getting something out of it for himself."

"Nothing but his son's pleasure. He's indignant that you're implying that he gets off on it in a sexual way. He's simply scratching and tickling and massaging his son's back and buttocks, in a nightly bedtime ritual that he's been engaging in ever since his son was 18 months old."

"But on his son's butt?"

"The area he tickles and massages extends quite naturally from the boy's back to his butt."

"But his butt isn't his back."

"Isn't it? Where exactly do you draw the line?"

"At the waist."

"What? An imaginary belt line? Why there? Isn't that kind of arbitrary? His son keeps saying, 'Go lower daddy. That feels good, daddy, do it lower.'"

"But he keeps going lower, all the way to the bottom of his son's butt, all the way to his thighs."

"Right. But is there really a reason to draw a line? Keep in mind that he's not inserting his finger in his son's anus or anything of that sort. He's simply massaging and tickling, just like he does on his son's back. And if he forgets to do his son's butt, his son reminds him by saying, 'Daddy, go lower, go lower.' Does this sound sexual to you?"

"But is that a reason to do it? Just because his son is turned on and asks for it isn't any excuse for the adult to go on doing it."

"But he says that his son isn't turned on in any sexual way. He regards massaging his son's buttocks as no different from massaging his son's back. If he stopped now, would his son understand why? What's daddy's reason for not going lower?"

"Because he's moving into a genital area, where a person can become aroused. Even a child."

"Is that what you would tell him?"

"Yes, that it's inappropriate to touch his son there."

"He'll tell you that you're outside the limits of your expertise and that you're imposing your misguided value judgments on his relationship with his son. He'll tell you that he knows his son better than you do and cares more than you do about his son's welfare. He'll insist that his son doesn't think of this massage as sexual. He says his son loves it and depends on this routine each night and would not understand any reasons for discontinuing it."

*"Does he plan to go on doing this when his son is five? Six? Seven? Eight? Nine?"*

*"No, he says that at some point, his son might eventually construe this act as a sexual one."*

*"How does he know that his son doesn't construe it as sexual now?"*

*"He claims his son doesn't. That he's at a developmental stage where having his butt caressed is no more sexual than having his back caressed."*

*"But if an expert tells him that it is indeed sexual and that it is indeed inappropriate . . . "*

*"Then he would challenge your credentials and inform you that his own expertise happens to be in developmental psychology, particularly in the area of sexuality in the preoperational and early latency stages of child development."*

*"Well, I guess that would throw me. But what if he's wrong? How can he know for sure that his son doesn't experience this massage as sexual? How does he know exactly when his son will start experiencing it as sexual?"*

*"I think he would agree that you don't know anything for sure. After all, he's a scientist. And like I said already, he agreed that he can't know exactly when his son is likely to start interpreting a massage like this as sexual and that at some point he'll have to discontinue the practice."*

*"But what if it's happening now? Obviously his son is turned on by it if he keeps begging for it every night."*

*"Yes, but he's not turned on sexually. He's turned on sensually. It's a sensual and emotional experience that they're sharing with one another."*

*"Well, maybe that's my point after all. Maybe it's not appropriate to be so sensual with your child."*

*"You mean you want him to stop rubbing his son's back, too?"*

*"I didn't say that."*

*"Didn't you?"*

*"I don't know what I'm saying anymore."*

*"It's very complicated. Whether an act is harmful is not as simple as determining whether something is black or white. There are many shades of grey here."*

*"You're not kidding."*

*"And it would be even more complicated if the father became frightened of your value judgments and what effects they would have on his son, his family, and his reputation."*

*"You mean he might deny that he even touched his son's butt."*

*"Yes, and then you'd be back to the first issue you raised a few minutes ago."*

*"Figuring out whether it even happened in the first place."*

*"Yes."*

*"This is all very complicated. Will you be going into all the issues we've been talking about here?"*

*"Yes, they're all crucial to the evaluation stage, and the next several chapters will cover them all. But let's begin with the first issue, trying to make clear whether anything happened at all."*

*"You mean when the alleged offender denies the abuse?"*

*"Yes, when your first question is whether the allegations are credible."*

# CHAPTER 9

# Differentiating True Allegations From False Ones

"In your opinion, doctor," asked an attorney during an examination in court, "was this child sexually abused?"

"Yes, I believe she was," answered the psychologist, a therapist with expertise in treating sexually abused children.

"And what is the basis for that opinion?"

"She described what her father did to her in the most vivid of terms. And she's been in treatment with us now for a number of months, and she still has a long way to go before recovery is complete. She may never fully recover."

"So the basis of your opinion that she was abused is that she needs counseling and that she made some vivid allegations. Is there any further basis for your opinion?"

"She experienced a number of symptoms typical of abused children. She was fearful, angry, and sad, her school performance declined, and she has significant trust issues in regard to males."

"Is it possible for those symptoms to be due to any other disorder, doctor?"

"No, they were the effects of her being abused by her father."

"I don't believe you answered my question, doctor. I asked whether it was possible for symptoms such as those you described to be due to any other condition or disorder?"

"But they weren't due to another disorder. They were . . . "

"Doctor, please, perhaps I can state this differently. I understand that you believe this child was abused by her father and as a result experienced those symptoms you described—sadness, anger, academic problems, and so on. I do understand your saying that these symptoms are typical of abused children. But I am asking if these can sometimes also be symptoms of some other conditions and disorders. A yes or no will do, doctor."

"Yes."

"Well, then, doctor, I'd like to ask you further, if this child had not actually been abused and was lying about it, what kinds of data might constitute the basis of your opinion that the child had lied?"

"It's my opinion that she was abused. She was traumatized in a manner that was typical of abuse. She was angry, sad, suffered from low self-esteem. . . . " The testimony went on to describe again the effects of abuse, repeating what had already been said with slight variations in phrasing.

"You have said that in your opinion the child is telling the truth, and you have given the reasons for your opinion. But if she were lying, what would be the kinds of reasons you would point to? How would you arrive at an opinion that she was lying?"

"This child wasn't lying. In my opinion she told the truth about her abuse. The effects of the abuse are evident. They are . . . "

"Doctor, you are not answering the question. How would you know that a child was lying? Any child?"

"Children don't generally lie about abuse."

"Are you saying that no child ever lied?"

"No."

"So you grant that it is possible for a child to lie."

"Yes, of course it is."

"How would you know, or what would be the basis of an opinion, that a child lied about being abused?"

"This child didn't lie. I believe her."

\*　\*　\*　\*　\*

Unless the judge is naive or significantly limited in intelligence, testimony like this does nobody any good. It reduces the credibility of the therapist and thereby reduces the chances that the therapist's testimony will help to protect the child if the child has indeed been abused. Despite this therapist's expertise in treating children who have been abused, he labored under the naive assumption that children never lie about sexual abuse. This therapist and others like him would have a great deal more credibility with attorneys and with the courts if they were able to answer the question put above: How would you know if this child were lying?

The purpose of the present chapter is to identify characteristics that differentiate between true and false allegations. Most of these characteristics have been presented in previous chapters, particularly in the last chapter. However, after all the data have been gathered, it is necessary to consider all of these characteristics once again, comprehensively and at the same time, for the purpose of formulating some overall conclusions.

## REASONS FOR DISCLOSING OR NOT DISCLOSING AT A PARTICULAR TIME

Sometimes there appears to be no rhyme or reason why an allegation was made two years following the onset of abuse rather than in its first few weeks. This may be due to the interviewer's neglecting to inquire into such reasons. But even if the interviewer asks, he may elicit no reason to account for the timing of the disclosure. This absence of a reason for disclosure at a particular time may be due to the child's inability to remember her experience accurately or express her memories or to embarrassment or anxiety about discussing her experiences with a stranger.

However, when these kinds of qualifying conditions do not seem to exist, the absence of a reason suggests that something other than sexual abuse may have motivated the child to make the allegations. On the other hand, an allegation is made more credible when there is a sound and convincing reason for disclosing or not disclosing at a given point in time. For example, in one case in which the D.S.S. investigators suspected the child of making a false allegation for the purpose of keeping her father out of the house, the child was later asked by a psychologist why she decided to disclose the abuse at the time that she did.

\* \* \* \* \*

"But I didn't tell. My best friend did."
"Why did you tell her?"

"It was bothering me. It was hard to keep it in. I had to tell somebody. And I trusted her."

"Did you want her to tell somebody who could make it all stop?"

"No way. I made her promise not to tell anybody. She swore she wouldn't."

"How come you didn't want her to tell?"

"Because dad said if anybody ever found out he would shoot my mom and then shoot himself."

\* \* \* \* \*

It was her friend, not the victim, who made the disclosure to a teacher, doing so against the wishes of the victim. Her very specific reason for not disclosing lends weight to the credibility of her allegations of abuse.

Another child who was introduced to sex at a very young age wasn't sure there was anything wrong with it. "My father told me that all fathers do these things with their little girls," she said, "but he told me it wasn't polite to talk about it with anybody." It took years before it gradually began to dawn on her that something was amiss.

Other children are able to say that initially they were too embarrassed or afraid to disclose the abuse but that, as they became more disturbed by its effects, it became more imperative to do something to put a stop to it. Sometimes a simple comment, such as, "I couldn't stand it, I finally had to tell somebody," is sufficient to account for why the disclosure occurred following a long stretch of silence.

This variable is not always useful in differentiating true from false statements, since it is not difficult for a lying child to conjure up a convincing reason for why she either disclosed or did not disclose at a particular point in time. However, it is not altogether useless either, as the examples above have illustrated. Also, in cases where there is no reason for disclosing or not disclosing, this variable can make a useful contribution when considered alongside the other variables examined in this chapter.

## THE PRESENCE OR ABSENCE OF TYPICAL EFFECTS OF ABUSE

In formulating a conclusion about whether abuse occurred, it is often useful to consider the presence or absence of symptoms that are typical of abuse, rape, or post-traumatic stress disorder, all of which were described in Chapter 4. The presence and the severity of these kinds of symptoms suggest that abuse did occur. The absence of typical symptoms indicates that the allegation may be a false one.

However, these are only indications; they do not constitute proof of any kind. A syndrome, or a set of symptoms, cannot be used to reliably discriminate between abused and nonabused children. A child who has never been abused at all can present with numerous symptoms that are typical not only of abuse but of other disorders as well. Nor does the absence of symptoms indicate with certainty that abuse did not occur. In one case where intercourse and other sexual activity were extensive, it was surprising, initially, to find an absence of symptoms, until this absence was made understandable by a statement that the child made.

"I didn't know it was wrong. Nobody told me."

At a very young age, she had been gently and gradually introduced to sexual activity by a gentle father in whom she had total trust. She appeared to be much more traumatized by the intrusion into her life of investigators than she had been by the sexual activities with her father.

It is extremely important to keep these kinds of exceptions in mind when making final conclusions. Nevertheless, the presence or absence of symptoms is a variable that can play some small role, along with other variables, in differentiating between true and false statements.

## SCENARIOS TYPICAL OF ABUSE VS. SCENARIOS TYPICAL OF OTHER KINDS OF PROBLEMATIC SITUATIONS

Details of a case can create a scenario that resembles sexual abuse problems with which one is familiar. For example, the daughter is parentified, the parents are distanced from one another, the mother works long hours, and the father gets his emotional affirmation from his daughter. On the other hand, the scenario may more closely resemble other kinds of problems. One might discover during an abuse investigation that there is a striking absence of characteristics one would expect to find in view of the particular allegations that have been made. Instead, the various features of the situation may conform more closely to a hotly disputed custody contest in which suspicions of abuse may have been exaggerated to bolster the case of one of the parties.

Resemblance does not indicate proof and cannot be used reliably to discriminate between abusive and nonabusive situations. However, it can help one to make some educated guesses about whether the alleged details of specific situations are realistic or plausible. Resemblance to typical scenarios other than abuse may occur for any problems containing common and predictable characteristics. These include: visitation and custody disputes, adolescent rebellion in which a child is attempting to leave home, revenge against a parent's emotional abuse or strict discipline, a child's desire to remove the stepparent from the home, a child's attempts to remove the father to protect the mother from domestic violence, and misinterpretations by children of good-touch/bad-touch presentations.

In one situation, a father routinely tickled his daughter on her stomach whenever they wrestled and engaged in horseplay. This tickling went below her belt line or her waist, but did not involve the vaginal area. However, following a good-touch/bad-touch presentation in school, his daughter came to believe that bad touch constituted any touching below the belt line. Therefore, she reported to the school nurse that she was "bad-touched," which then stimulated a lengthy investigation by numerous evaluators. She felt "bad" about being bad-touched only because she had learned in the presentation that she was supposed to feel bad, not because the tickling had ever made her feel bad.

Following a similar presentation, a mildly retarded boy reported that his brother had touched him in his genital area. He did not feel particularly bad about this but felt he should report it because this was what he had been told to do in the training. He neglected to mention at the time, and the teacher and nurse neglected to find out, that the genital touching consisted of kicks to the groin, which commonly occurred between the brothers in their routine squabbling and horseplay with one another. He would have been quite happy to explain this had he been asked. It was apparent that these situations lacked common characteristics associated with abuse and instead more closely conformed to typical scenarios in which good-touch/bad-touch presentations are misunderstood.

When the characteristics of the situation more closely resemble a scenario of sexual abuse than some other scenario, it is important to point out the resemblance, and to point out also that this resemblance by itself does not constitute proof of abuse. When the characteristics of the situation more closely resemble some nonabusive scenario, it is just as important to point this out, though this by itself does not constitute proof that the child lied.

Finally, when the characteristics of the situation simultaneously resemble both a sexual abuse scenario and another kind of scenario, it is important to state this. While you may not be giving any kind of clear direction, you are providing a vision of your thinking, which can be illuminating to a judge or other interested party who may have information unavailable to you.

## AN ABUNDANCE OR A DEARTH OF POTENTIALLY CONFIRMABLE STATEMENTS

The value of noting the confirmability of statements was illustrated and discussed in Chapter 8, where confirmable statements were associated with true stories and unconfirmable statements with untrue stories. However, I would like to warn the clinician that true stories can contain unconfirmable statements and that false stories can contain potentially confirmable statements. In other words, there are many exceptions to the rule. I cannot provide a numerical proportion of confirmable to unconfirmable statements that would enable the clinician reliably to identify either a true story or a false one. I can only say, as I have previously, that true stories are often characterized by a noticeable abundance of potentially confirmable statements and that false stories are often characterized by a dearth of such statements.

In the absence of empirical support, the clinician is left to his own judgment in this matter. Like each of the other variables described here, this one cannot be used in isolation to discriminate between true and false stories; rather, it must be used in combination with the other variables.

## CONSISTENCY BETWEEN STATEMENTS VS. INCONSISTENCIES

When a child's various statements about the allegations are consistent with one another, the body of statements is more credible than when the child has contradicted herself. In the previous chapter, Lucy gave a consistent set of statements about the seating in the pickup truck, despite the interviewer's attempts to encourage inconsistencies with leading questions. On the other hand, Babette repeatedly contradicted herself.

While inconsistency suggests the possibility of lying, it does not always reflect lying. It is not at all uncommon for D.S.S. or police investigators to assume that a child is lying on the basis of inconsistent statements, when the child has only been doing her best to tell the truth within the limits of her cognitive abilities. If the child has certain memory limitations and primitive concepts of time and number, due to either developmental limitations or cultural impoverishment, then certain inconsistencies are to be expected.

For example, Mary said in one statement that abuse occurred in November only, and then, during a subsequent interrogation, she said that it occurred throughout the winter and into the beginning of spring. She also said that it happened "a few times" in one statement, and in another statement said that it happened only "a couple of times, one or two." She said in one statement that he made her touch his penis and in another statement that he did not make her touch his penis but, rather, that he touched her vagina. It is apparent that inconsistencies of this kind could lead an investigator to be inclined to believe that the child was lying.

However, differences in interview questions can elicit differences in response. Similarly, the conditions of the interview, the tone of voice and inflection used, implicit suggestions, the personality style of the interviewer, and the sex of the interviewer can all influence variations in the child's statements. In addition, in interviewing a child like Mary, what one sometimes discovers is that the child does not have the capabilities to commit the particular inconsistencies that the investigator has in mind.

For example, Mary was inconsistent about when the abuse occurred, saying it had occurred in the spring and also saying that it had occurred in November. However, this was only an apparent inconsistency because she didn't really know the differences between the months and seasons, nor was she able to name them in their correct sequences, nor was she able to anchor them accurately to holidays or weather conditions. While making her inconsistent statements, Mary was not aware of the significance of her inconsistencies and how they would be interpreted by the interrogator.

She realized she possessed inadequate knowledge to answer the questions accurately but she figured that she would probably conduct herself adequately enough given her good intentions. She didn't realize, from an adult perspective, what her limitations suggested, and therefore could not anticipate how her answers would be interpreted.

When she said that the abuse occurred a few times, meaning three or more times, her intended message was that it occurred more than once. When she contradicted herself in the subsequent statement by saying that it happened one or two times, she still meant that it happened more than once, but was attempting to minimize it because she felt embarrassed that she had allowed it to continue more than once. Therefore, the inconsistency between two vs. three occurrences was resolved.

When she said that he touched her vagina in one statement and in the other statement that he made her touch his penis, she had been telling the truth in both instances. The statements had appeared to be inconsistent because the investigator had assumed in his questions that he and Mary had a mutual understanding in which they were both referring to one occasion; he had been trying to pin her down as to time and location, but due to her ignorance of the exact location and her primitive framework for time, she provided inaccurate information. What she was trying to say was that both of these things occurred, but on separate occasions. She was able to articulate the sequence, and further, was able to anchor these events in time when given ample opportunity to relate the events to other events occurring in her life at the time. These other life events were later confirmed by her mother.

In this particular case, it was possible to conclude that the child's overt statements were inconsistent due to developmental limitations, but that the intended contents of her messages were consistent with one another. This kind of a conclusion is a very important message to convey to the investigators and to the court. In other situations, blatant inconsistencies like these might be more indicative of lying when supported by data from other variables.

## INVARIANT SEQUENCING AND POSITIONING OF DETAILS

Credibility is enhanced when there is an invariant sequencing of events in time and an invariant positioning of objects in space. That is, the listener sees the same sequence of action each time the story is heard and sees the same people and objects positioned in the same way. The listener is able to see the same moving picture on each telling of the story, such that details added or taken away do not constitute contradictions.

Credibility is diminished when positioning of objects in space is random. For example, in one rendition of a story the victim sits on the couch while being abused, and in another rendition she sits on the floor. Credibility is also threatened when there is variation in the sequencing of events. For example, in one rendition of the story the victim sits on the couch after going to the bathroom, but in another rendition she gets up to go to the bathroom after sitting on the couch.

This variable overlaps a great deal with the previous one, that of consistency. The value in considering it separately is that it focuses the evaluator's attention on the visual scenario as it unfolds in the dimension of time, on how things stay the same as they seem to change.

## CONGRUENCE BETWEEN TIME REQUIRED AND TIME REPORTED

The daily activities that clients describe each require a certain amount of time to complete. For example, eating breakfast may require anywhere from a few moments to a couple of hours, but it probably would not require six hours. If a client reported that this activity took six hours,

then the time period reported would have to be considered seriously
incongruent with the time required for the activity.

An incongruence like this suggests that the statements are false in
some way, perhaps due to lying or exaggeration, but perhaps due to an
inability to tell time or to a distorted sense of time. Usually, the time
period reported is roughly congruent with the time required for the activities in question. However, sometimes too much activity is crammed into
too small a time period to be feasible, and sometimes, as in the six-hour
breakfast, there is too little activity to be believable. The latter is illustrated first. This example is a continuation of a dialogue begun in Chapter 6.

* * * * *

"So you supervised them by watching from the doorway."

"Right. I just stood there and watched the kids while they played
outside."

"Are you sure you didn't play with them or do something else while
they played?"

"No. I already told you. I just stood there and watched them."

"For three hours? You just stood there in the doorway?"

"Yeah, the whole time."

"But why?"

"That's what a good parent should do."

* * * * *

The incongruence in this example between time required and time
reported could not be accounted for by a poor sense of time or an
inability to tell time. Aside from this incongruence, there were other
variables that also suggested that she was making false statements. My
overall conclusion was that she was exaggerating certain facts so that
they would conform to what she thought was my conception of a good
parent. The next example illustrates the opposite phenomenon, jamming
too much into too short a space of time.

* * * * *

"Are you sure you only left her home alone for 45 minutes? Do you
really want to stick to that?"

"Are you calling me a liar? I already told you, I left the house a couple
minutes before 12:30, because Donald has to be to school at 12:30, and

I was back by 1:30 when my favorite soap comes on. So she couldn't have been there alone for more than 45 minutes."

"You said that, after you dropped Donald off at 12:30, you went to the bank to cash your check, make a deposit, transfer money from one account into another, and do some other things there for your husband. That had to take you at least five minutes."

"Yeah, maybe more. Probably about ten minutes at the bank."

"And getting to the bank from the school had to take you ten minutes. I mean, I know where it is, and I know how long it takes to drive there."

"Yeah, it's about ten minutes, I guess."

"And then it had to take you another ten minutes to get to your doctor's appointment."

"But I didn't have to wait long."

"About how long?"

"Five minutes maybe."

"And how long did the doctor spend with you?"

"About five to ten minutes. No more than that. Really, I was in and out of there in a jiffy."

"Okay, and then you raced to the market, and that might have taken you only a couple of minutes, so getting there and parking and walking from your car to the door might have taken only about five minutes. But you said that you bought between $50 and $60 worth of groceries. Were there any really big expensive items?"

"No, just the usual small things. Just a few things we needed. Eggs, milk, juice, detergent, cereal for the kids, butter, bread, that sort of thing."

"To buy $50–60 worth of small groceries can't be done in less than 15 minutes, can it? Unless you're some kind of wizard at it."

"Well, I am kind of good at shopping."

"But counting in the time needed for the checkout line too?"

"Okay, it probably took at least 15 minutes, probably almost a half-hour, but probably not more than that."

"And then you raced across town to the mall to pick up the blinds. No matter how fast you went, it had to take you at least ten minutes to get there."

"But I probably wasn't inside there more than five to ten minutes."

"And then you stopped at McDonald's so that your three-year-old could have a Happy Meal. And you said that you sat there while he ate it all. Maybe your child doesn't dawdle like other kids do, but . . . "

"Oh, he dawdles with the best of them."

"So how long do you think that took?"

"Maybe ten minutes."

"And then another ten minutes to get home, in time for your soap."

"Right."

"Let's see here, let me add these numbers up. By your own reckoning, these add up to anywhere between a minimum of an hour and a half to a maximum of over two hours."

"Okay, okay, maybe it was longer then 45 minutes."

"So you didn't get to see your soap that day?"

"I just didn't want you to think I neglected my daughter. She was safe enough in her playpen, wasn't she? What's the big deal if I do a few errands?"

\* \* \* \* \*

As the reader has probably surmised, the congruence between time reported and time required for an activity is not particularly useful for examining the stories of young children whose framework for time is quite different than an adult's. It can sometimes be useful, though, in examining the stories of older children, adolescents, and adults.

## COHERENCE AND REDUNDANCY OF DETAIL VS. CONFABULATION

Coherence has something to do with consistency, but is not exactly the same. Consistency refers to whether details support or logically contradict one another. While coherence shares this meaning as well, also referring to the way things support one another, it refers more to the way in which things belong with one another—that is, to the way things stick together and make sense with one another and ring true for us.

The details provided by the child must cohere in this way in order to be credible. This coherence is often created when there is a redundancy or repetition in the details provided by the child. That is to say, with each fresh detail added to a story, there may be accompanying details that are repetitious with details that have been mentioned before.

First the child says, "He didn't have clothes on when he came out of the bathroom." This statement could possibly suggest a threatening picture of events.

Later she says about the same event, "He stood in the doorway and told me to come over." This may sound even more threatening. Yet, there is redundancy (i.e., he is standing in the doorway), and there is the elaboration of further details that have not contradicted previous details.

Next she says, "He had a towel around his waist." This statement reduces the picture of a threat; possibly, the man had innocent intentions. Again, what is redundant is that he is still in the doorway.

Even later, "He had shaving lotion on his face." Now he appears to have other business on his mind than sexual abuse.

And later still, "He had a razor in his hand."

And finally, "He asked if I would find him some razors in the kitchen drawer."

As long as the different or new information is consistent with old information, the resulting overlap and layering of repetitive details generate a resonance that enables the various objects and events in the story to cohere with one another. It is this redundancy and richness of detail, this resonance, that makes the story ring true for us, because it matches our own everyday notions of real events.

On the other hand, credibility is diminished when details do not cohere or stick with other details. That is, when they have the appearance of not belonging to one another, of seeming discrete from one another, unanchored to a larger reality, and made up on the spot. Statements containing these kinds of discrete details are referred to as confabulations. Compare the illustration below with the preceding illustration of coherence.

"He didn't have clothes on when he came out of the bathroom, just a towel."

"I don't get it. What are you trying to tell me?"

"Well, that's why I know he was about to jump on my bones. Because he was standing in the doorway with no clothes. Naked as a jaybird."

"What was he doing in the bathroom?"

"I don't know, probably jerking off thinking about me. Yeah, that's it, that's what he was doing, jerking off."

"How long was he in there doing that?"

"I don't know, a little while, no, maybe an hour. Wait, let me think, maybe two hours, yeah, that's it, it was about two hours."

"And I bet you had to pee and couldn't get in there."

"You better believe it. He was in there so long I almost peed in my pants. That's why I had to barge right in there, and when I got in there, guess what? I caught him jerking off and that's when he raped me."

"I thought he came out and stood in the doorway."

"Oh, uh, did I say that? Well, maybe he did, I think maybe it was after he was done fucking me. Yeah, that's when it was."

When a person confabulates in this way, she tends to add elaborations to her original statement that appear arbitrary and unanchored to the surrounding reality. There is a noticeable lack of resonance and redundancy.

A more realistic example of confabulation in sexual abuse interviews was provided in the interview with Babette in Chapter 8. In another part of that interview, the interviewer was asking her about her allegation that her mother had had sex with her own brothers.

"You said that your mother had sex with your uncles."

"With two of them. She's like a whore. With Bob and Steve. I was watching."

"How many times did you see this?"

"Just once."

"With which one, Bob or Steve?"

"Bob."

"Then how do you know she had sex with Steve?"

"Oh, yeah, I saw that, too. That was another time."

"When did you see her have sex with Steve?"

"I hardly remember it. It was a long time ago when I was little."

"How about with Bob? When was that?"

"Not too long ago. I think in June. She shouldn't have done that. It was abnormal."

"What does abnormal mean?"

"It means it's sick, not normal. She shouldn't have done it with him."

"So she did this abnormal thing in June, you said. June is the last month of school, just before summer vacation. Are you pretty sure it was in June?"

"Yeah, it was just before vacation. And then she got pregnant."

"How did you know she was pregnant?" This was a total surprise to me.

"She told me. And the baby was born, but it died."

"It died? I didn't know about a baby." This was also a surprise.

"Yeah, well, that's because it was born and then it only lived a couple of days and then it died."

"When did this happen?"

"In July."

"What? It was born in July? You mean it happened one month later? One month after she had sex with her brother?"

"Yeah, it was an abnormal baby."

"You know that July comes after June? Do you know the months of the year?"

"Sure, January, February, March, April, May, June, July, August, September, October, November. Is that right?"

"Perfect. Do you know if it was actually born alive, with arms and legs, breathing, crying, or if maybe it was a miscarriage? Do you know what a miscarriage is?"

"No, but it looked like a baby to me, with arms and legs and crying."

"But do you know what you're saying? That your mother had sex with her brother in June and got pregnant from that and then had the baby in July and it lived a few days and then died?"

"That's what happened all right."

"That's not possible, to get pregnant and have a baby all in a month."

"Well, that's why it was an abnormal baby. Because she shouldn't have sex with her own brother. It was abnormal and she shouldn't have done it."

When a client is confabulating, one never knows what is going to come out of her mouth next. There is an element of the fantastical, of suspense in waiting to hear what she will come up with next. On the other hand, when a client's statements cohere, are redundant, and create the resonance of remembered living, there is a predictability in the child's next response, a ring of truth as she adds a further intimate layer of detail onto a scenario that the interviewer can see as in a movie.

## MESSY REALITY VS. TIDY FICTION

As mentioned in the last section, a made-up story is less likely than a true one to be anchored to real details connected to and surrounded by other details. That is, it is not tied to the constraints of reality in the same way that a real story must be. A real story is messy with details, potential tangents, and incomprehensible allusions, all of which will be compatible with one another and resonate with redundancy. On the other hand, fiction can be very tidy, especially when it is cleansed of the kinds of inconsistency found in confabulations. This tidiness has its source in the same factor that accounts for the inconsistencies of confabulation; that is, a fantastical confabulation and an internally consistent piece of fiction are similar in that each lacks anchorage in a redundancy of detail. However, it is sometimes difficult to identify a statement as a piece of fiction when it is internally consistent, i.e., when the clinician cannot be aided, or tipped off by, contradictions and fantastical statements. That is why it is worthwhile to look at the difference between the tidiness of fiction and the messiness of reality.

Like a confabulated statement, a set of consistent fictionalized statements may not be tied to the constraints of reality in the same ways that a true story tends to be. As a result, it can sometimes look like an abstract summary of an event, a summary in which closure has been achieved on each of its constituent statements. That is, it may appear as if there is nothing more to say about it. There is always more to say about real events because closure is almost never achieved. There is always one more uncertainty or ambiguity, always more details connected to other details. That is why a true story doesn't look like a complete story. There are usually dangling ends, potential tangents, and allusions to other details not fully presented, which all require a fuller hearing before the story can be completely understood. It is messy with dangling detail, whereas a piece of fiction tends to be tidy.

That is why a person telling a true story can go on endlessly when asked to elaborate, whereas the creator of fiction is done. His elaborations are limited by the world he has created, by the assumptions on which his piece of fiction rests. Consider the statement below, made by an adolescent who was brutally raped. Although she later admitted that the perpetrator was her boyfriend, she initially attempted to protect his identity due to a combination of fear, shame, dependence, and loyalty.

* * * * *

"I had an argument with my boyfriend, so I left his house and went for a walk about 10 o'clock. It was my own fault. I should have known better than to go walking in the park after dark. I was walking through the playground when this big black man came up behind me and threw me down on the ground. I tried to fight back, so he beat me up pretty bad. After he did this to me," she said, pointing to her bruised and puffy face, "I guess I just gave up. So he lifted my skirt and pulled down my panties and raped me."

"Did he take off any other clothes? Besides your panties?"

"No, he just lifted my skirt."

"What were you wearing?"

"A skirt and shirt and sweater."

"It was cold that night. Did you have a coat on?"

"Yeah."

"Was it a warm coat? What color?"

"Yeah, it's pretty warm. It's a white ski coat."

"Was it zipped up or unzipped?"

"It was zipped up. It was cold."

"Did this black guy unzip it?"

"What are you trying to find out? No, he didn't unzipper it. I already told you that. He just lifted my dress. Are you trying to mix me up?"

"No, but I'm confused. You see, the police said that your coat didn't have any dirt on it. How could that be?"

"I don't know. Maybe he threw me on the grass."

"But the playground is dirt. There isn't any grass on the playground."

"Maybe it wasn't the playground. Maybe it was on the ballfield. I can't remember everything."

"If your coat was zipped up, how did you get the bite marks on your back and on your left breast that the medical report talked about."

"It must have come through the coat."

"But your coat is thick and the police say that there aren't any tears in it or bite marks."

\* \* \* \* \*

She had difficulty elaborating consistently beyond a certain point because the assumptions upon which her story rested did not adequately take into account the surrounding reality in which her story was encapsulated. Compare her summary statement of fiction with the one she later gave.

\* \* \* \* \*

"We were waiting for my boyfriend's parents to get home so they could give us a ride and he started yelling about how I was standing too close to Danny at the basketball game and then he just went nuts and his face turned all red and it was like he changed into another person. I can't remember everything that happened next because it was like I was getting pounded in the face even before I saw him punching me."

\* \* \* \* \*

Unlike the previous rendition, this one is pregnant with details waiting to be discovered. Get a ride to where? Where were his parents? Who is Danny? And why was she standing close to this Danny? It is a messy story, replete with statements lacking closure and with multiple pathways to the larger context in which the story is encapsulated. It is a much more incomplete story than the tidy piece of fiction she first presented.

As with the other variables described here, a caveat is in order on this variable as well. The utility of this variable is dependent on a liar's lack of skill in lying. A highly skilled liar may be quite able to render a story with the messiness that gives it the ring of truth. A person suffering from an encapsulated delusion might also be able to do the same. An encapsulated delusion is one that is highly compatible with the surrounding reality.

For example, there might be nothing abnormal in the appearance or functioning of a man who labored under the false belief that he was the only true human on earth and was being trained by an earth population of androids for a special mission on another planet. There is a high degree of linkage between this story and the surrounding reality, which is so replete with redundant detail that he could go on for years acting as normally as the next fellow. That is, inconsistencies between his delusion and the real world would not necessarily be apparent to either himself or to those who observed his behavior.

The kinds of false stories we are examining here are encapsulated by reality in the same way as is a delusion. We need to remain keenly alert to those areas where a story might lack a connectedness to the reality encapsulating it. The less connected, the more tidy the story.

## SECOND-HAND VS. FIRST-HAND INFORMATION

Statements that appear to consist of second-hand information are more suspect and less credible than statements containing first-hand information. One type of first-hand information is readily identifiable as such because it appears to be privileged information, that is, data that a person could not know if he or she had not been in the situation alleged to have occurred. For example, if the alleged rape occurred in a police car, then the victim should be able to describe characteristics of the car much more accurately than someone who had never been in a police car. Similarly, someone lying about a rape in a police car would probably not be able to describe the inside of the car unless he or she had, for some other reason, been in one on another occasion.

Another example of privileged information is knowledge of sexual matters inappropriate to one's age. A five-year-old who describes a penis as looking like a "hot dog" and dripping "white stuff from the end of it" is not likely to have learned about this matter in the ordinary course of five-year-old existence. Children often learn about sexual matters inappropriate to their age from either experiencing or witnessing sexual interaction. However, other options are also possible and need to be explored, such as learning about sex from X-rated videotapes, pornographic magazines, classroom lectures, network television shows, or sexual play with other children.

The primary question is whether there is knowledge about sexual interaction which could only have been obtained in a sexual abuse situation. Or, is the knowledge about sex so common that the child could have obtained it in some routine and nontraumatic context?

The symptoms of post-traumatic stress disorder and of rape and sexual abuse also fall into this category of knowledge that the client is unlikely to otherwise possess. Some of these symptoms and effects are so esoteric that one could not expect a person to conjure them up in a lie or to hear about them second-hand. Again, this is not an absolute rule. There are exceptions. There have been cases evaluated in which the clients had previously read articles I had written on this topic; they were prepared and ready to provide exactly the kinds of details I needed to convince me that abuse had occurred. If I had not become aware that these clients had been prepared in this way, I would have mistaken second-hand information for what I believed to be privileged, first-hand information.

To examine the presence of both first- and second-hand information in the same interview, the reader can recall Debbie (from Chapter 8) who tried valiantly to vindicate her uncle, claiming he was a nice guy who would only touch her "the way uncles are supposed to." An unsolicited announcement like this, given at the beginning of the interview, is fairly suspect. It has all the earmarks of second-hand information. That is, it appears to be a statement that has been contaminated by the influence of the adults in her life.

Despite her sustained attempt to vindicate this man, she repeatedly broke down and indicated that he had abused her. The most poignant example of this is, when she responded, having been asked at the end whether she had any questions, "What should I do if he does it again?"

This response sounds like a first-hand inquiry, like she's really wondering for herself and is seeking advice. It doesn't sound as if someone could have put her up to asking that question. Other statements made earlier, such as "he scared me" and "he said to kiss it" sound first-hand, especially in light of the contrast between these statements and her vigorous insistence on her uncle's innocence throughout the interview.

## CONGRUENCE VS. INCONGRUENCE OF MESSAGES

"He didn't do it to me, but what should I do if he does it again?"

Hardly any child will convey incongruous messages this succinctly, as Debbie did in the last chapter, but they will convey them nevertheless. Such messages are paradoxical, conveying on the one hand that sexual abuse occurred, and on the other hand that it did not.

Incongruence between these primary, overall messages is a more global kind of inconsistency than the kinds previously described, where the focus was on contradictions between particular statements and details. The inconsistency between stating that an offender wore a blue bandana and that he wore a red one might reflect lying, but it might also reflect a victim's difficulties in conveying her message or her heightened responsivity to leading questions.

An examination of the congruence or incongruence of messages goes beyond the consistency and inconsistency of details to look at the larger picture of what the child is trying to convey. Is there a single congruent message underlying the various statements made? Or do the child's statements reflect a struggle to reconcile the two primary and incongruous messages that something happened and that something didn't happen?

## CONCLUDING REMARKS

The issue of credibility has been raised repeatedly throughout the book but especially in this and the previous chapter. The emphasis on the credibility of a person or of his statements may have conveyed the impression that an assessment of credibility is a commonly accepted purpose of evaluation. It is not.

I wish to point out, with clarity, that some courts do not admit testimony on credibility. Many people in the legal and mental health fields argue that determinations of credibility are in the court's domain and fall outside the limits of expertise possessed by the mental health professional. If that is the case, the reader may ask why this issue has been addressed in such assiduous detail.

There are three reasons for doing so. First, while some courts do not admit testimony on credibility, other courts not only admit it but request it in some form or other. It is also a common request from D.S.S. investigators. Second, while a court must make the ultimate decision about credibility, the formulation of that decision is dependent on the availability of relevant data. The set of variables presented in this chapter can help to provide data of this kind.

Third, formulating impressions — of credibility or anything else — is an inescapable human act; if it is to be done, let it be done as ably as possible. Even if there were a consensus in both the legal and mental health fields that determinations of credibility were outside the limits of a mental health professional's expertise, clinicians would still be making their own informal determinations of credibility while doing initial assessments. After all, the clinician needs to get a sense of what happened in order to know how to plan the treatment.

In regard to this last point, an objection can be raised that leads us to a separate but related topic: the relationship between reality and credibility. The objection is that figuring out what happened (i.e., whether sexual abuse occurred) is not the province of the therapist. In other words, the therapist's job is not to determine truth, but rather to determine whether his or her skills can help to improve the client's functioning in some way. To do so, the therapist needs to work with what the client presents, that is, the client's beliefs about reality. Due to the fact that each of us has a point of view that cannot possibly be exactly shared by any other individual, it is inevitable that, to varying extents, we will each see things differently than others.

In other words, because we each are limited by our own unique positions in time and space (i.e., by our points of view), we all distort to some extent, some more, some less. We each construct our own realities. I have alluded to this earlier in Chapter 2, when I cautioned a student to be less hasty in condemning parents for trying to show themselves in their best light. They were simply describing themselves as they saw themselves, or as they wanted to see themselves, and perhaps exaggerating a bit to assure that the interviewer would see what they saw.

This is what most people do, and we should expect no less from clients. That is, we should expect that, to some extent, the stories our clients present to us are distortions, and that, as clinicians, our job is to work with these distortions as best we can.

If I am in agreement with these ideas, the reader may ask, why do I bother to even initiate the difficult process of differentiating between true and false statements? Isn't this endeavor fated for failure if everything presented by the client is to some extent a distortion? Shouldn't we simply take what is presented at face value and work with it as best we can? If an abused child has convinced herself that she was not abused, shouldn't we simply accept her statement, rather than challenge it with our skills and constructs? If a nonabused child has convinced herself that she was abused, shouldn't we just treat her for the effects of the fantasized abuse?

The answer, for me, is no. An abused child who has convinced herself that nothing happened to her is not the same as a child who was never abused. Debbie, if given enough time, may convince herself that her uncle did not abuse her, especially with a lot of help from her mother and aunt. However, the resulting cognitive confusion, as well as other effects, would make her a very different child from one who hadn't been abused. I am convinced that the variables that have been consolidated in this chapter can help us to identify such children, even those whose beliefs are contrary to what most of us consider to be reality.

Even the child who falsely believed herself to be abused could be identified. She may be seen to be suffering from some effects typical of abuse (perhaps even convincingly), but her statements would probably not be supported by a freshness and redundancy of detail, an abundance of confirmable statements, and other characteristics that have been elaborated here. In her case, it might be important to address in treatment not only the symptoms of a fantasized episode of abuse, but also the reasons for the fantasy. A case like this was illustrated previously, in which a foster child believed herself to have been abused by her foster brother.

I am not saying that we have the market on truth or reality. I accept that truth or reality is relative or subjective. But this doesn't mean that we have to throw up our hands and go home. We can, I think, be of some use. We can try to figure out what happened, whether it is for the court or whether it is for ourselves in treatment planning for our clients.

The variables presented in this chapter, as well as some others, can help us in our formulations of these clinical judgments. This chapter has been an attempt to explicate some of the more important variables that are implicit in the reasoning process that precedes a final clinical judgment. When we give that judgment, in an opinion to the court or to anyone else, we are articulating what we think. We are explicating what is implicit in our thinking, not necessarily giving a statement of scientific fact.

Empirical evidence is not available to enable us to utilize a single variable, or even a combination of variables, to differentiate between true and false allegations. In fact, a theme that has emerged in the discussions of each of these variables is that none can be used as an infallible determinant. Rather, while indicating how each creates a rule for differentiating true from false statements, I have tried to show the exceptions to each rule. These exceptions are essential to keep in mind when formulating clinical judgments. And it is a clinical judgment that we will be making, not a statement of scientific fact. It would be wonderful if we could formulate statements about which we were certain, but we can't.

However, as I said earlier, formulating impressions and judgments is an inescapable human act, so it is in our interest to do it with as much skill as possible. We can enhance that skill by utilizing a set of variables that will grasp as aptly as possible the multiple distinguishing features of truth and fiction. Our intention must be to cast a net that is sufficiently dense, through which it is exceedingly difficult for lies to pass undetected, yet one that is wide enough to capture truth where it exists. In pursuing this goal, it is necessary to examine the variables presented here simultaneously, so that each can be weighed against the others. For this reason, and to provide a convenient summary, the variables in question are listed here:

1. The presence or absence of a reason for disclosing the abuse
2. The presence or absence of symptoms
3. Scenarios typical of abuse vs. scenarios typical of other problems

4. An abundance of confirmable vs. unconfirmable statements
5. Consistency vs. inconsistency between statements
6. Invariant sequencing in time and invariant positioning in space
7. Congruence or incongruence between time reported and time required
8. Coherence and redundancy of detail vs. confabulation
9. Tidy fiction vs. messy reality
10. First-hand vs. second-hand information
11. Congruence vs. incongruence of messages

It is not necessary that each of the variables be invoked in the process of formulating conclusions. As each of them is examined, one or more may be deemed useless in differentiating between true and false statements. For example, symptoms of abuse may exist to some extent, but not extensively enough to be convincing. Or a situation may resemble a hotly disputed custody contest just as much as it does a sexual abuse scenario. Sometimes it is important to indicate the reasons why the variable is not useful so that you can help to educate a judge or attorney or child protective worker who may have information unavailable to you. It is possible that the combination of their own information and the rationales you provide may enable them to arrive at a conclusion more valid than yours.

It would be presumptuous to think that you have to make the final decision. You can state only what you think you know and why you think it. That is to say, you can state how confident you are about the opinion you have formulated, giving reasons for why you are confident or not so confident about it. Your reasoning processes, if you are clear about them, can often be more helpful than a strong recommendation one way or another. Explication of your implicit reasoning might not enable you to state an opinion with the inflated degree of confidence and certitude displayed by the expert witness illustrated at the outset of the chapter, but it does help you to articulate a more differentiated, realistic, useful, and understandable opinion.

\* \* \* \* \*

"Doctor, do you have an opinion as to whether this child was abused."

"I do have an impression."

"Doctor, I'm not interested in impressions. Can you state a professional opinion with an acceptable degree of scientific certitude?"

"No, I cannot. I can only give you my impressions or opinions."

"Well, since you're my witness, I suppose I'll have to go ahead with this, unless there are any objections to the doctor's testimony."

"Objection, your honor," stated the attorney for the accused. "The doctor has implied that an expert opinion is outside of his limits of expertise."

"Objection overruled," stated the judge. "The doctor is here as a friend of the court, as the court's witness, in the interests of the child. He's not here as a witness for the Department of Social Services nor as a witness for the accused. The doctor is instructed to go ahead and give his impressions or opinions, if that is all he says he is able to do. The court has been quite satisfied with the opinions he has provided for us in the past."

"But, your honor . . . "

"I am quite capable of using my own discretion in deciding whether the doctor's opinions are outside the limits of his expertise."

"Shall I go on, your honor?" asked the attorney for the Department of Social Services.

"Please do," instructed the judge.

"Doctor, as you know, the child stated that her father had anal intercourse with her and later stated that her mother fondled her. And then she reversed her story. What is your opinion as to what really happened?"

"I think that she was abused by her father, but I'm not as sure that she was abused by her mother. She seemed to suffer a number of symptoms typical of abuse, and these all related to the story about her father. Her recantation was in regard to the abuse by the mother, not the father. She had grown accustomed to going for walks for ice cream cones with the D.S.S. investigator after the interviews were over, and I think she concocted the story about her mother just to get some extra time with the caseworker, as well as an ice cream cone."

"Doctor, are you serious? She lied for an ice cream?"

"Yes. A chocolate one with sprinkles on a sugar cone. When I confronted her about a number of inconsistencies in her story, she confessed that she had lied in order to try to get some extra time with the caseworker, who usually took her to Friendly's after interrogating her about her father."

"Excuse me, doctor," interrupted the Law Guardian. "I'm fascinated by this notion that children lie about being abused. Do you know how many children lie? Do you have an accurate number?"

"No, I don't. Not even an estimate that would be reliable."

"Would you say that the vast majority tell the truth? Or that the vast majority lie?"

"I can only say that lying isn't a rare event. After all, most of the cases that D.S.S. or the court refers to me are those cases in which there is uncertainty as to whether the child is telling the truth."

"Well, then, how do you distinguish between children who were truly abused and those who are making false allegations?"

"As I said before, children who have been abused usually suffer from a number of effects that are typical of abuse. They also possess knowledge about the sexual acts that they would not otherwise possess. When they're telling the truth, they're often able to describe the clothes they were wearing, where they were sitting, what was on television, and other items in their surrounding environment. And they do so in such a vivid and real way that the listener can see it in detail. These are details that would be difficult for a lying person to invent."

"Doctor, is this different from a person who is lying?"

"Yes. A person who is lying tends to add items, on the spot, in response to specific questions. A liar will be more responsive to leading questions. For example, you can more easily get her to make inconsistent statements in response to those leading questions."

"Can you elaborate on that? Give an example of what you mean?"

"After saying that her underpants were taken off, you might suggest with a leading statement that the offender next fondled her by sticking his hand down between her jeans and her underpants, and she would then agree and elaborate on it."

"I'm not sure I understand," interrupted the judge.

"Well, let me use another example. I might ask her if she had any clothes on and she would say she didn't. Then I would say, 'But you still did have your panties on, didn't you?' And she would then say, 'Oh, yeah, I did and that's when he jumped on top of me.'"

"I see," said the judge.

"That's clear, doctor," said the Law Guardian. "Are there other signs of lying that you could describe to us?"

"Yes. Ulterior motives that become apparent in the interview. For example, a need for attention, revenge against a stepfather, fear of threats by a sibling who wants the alleged offender out of the house, or a desire to protect the mother from beatings. These are just a few of the more common motives for making false statements."

"Doctor, in your experience, how many other children have said that they lied in order to get more time with a caseworker?"

"A few. And that's a good question. It may suggest something about the amount of attention the child ordinarily gets at home. And it might say something about . . . "

"Objection, your honor," shouted the attorney for the mother.

\* \* \* \* \*

As can be seen here, the variables consolidated in this chapter can help to make explicit what may be implicit in the process of formulating clinical judgments. Such judgments do not yet have the status of expert opinions that can be supported by an acceptable body of empirical data, and the evaluator should be prepared to say so. If we can be clear about what we think, why we think it, and why we might doubt what we think, then the epistemological strengths and weaknesses of our statements will be clear enough for the court to choose what is admissible and what is not. Our opinions or lines of thinking may or may not be admissible in court, but they are all that can be offered at this time. We can feel comfortable in providing these opinions insofar as they are the same kinds of opinions that we use to construct treatment plans or to formulate recommendations about what remedies will best address particular problems.

The dialogue above was cut off shortly before the attorneys began to ask me questions concerning my recommendations in this case. In the next chapter we will leave behind the question of whether abuse occurred and move on to this other important component of the evaluation process: figuring out which of several remedies is best suited to particular acts of abuse. This part of the job, formulating recommendations, can be a heavy burden and can rarely be exercised with extreme confidence. It is fraught with uncertainty, ambiguity, and value judgments that can contaminate the clinical judgment of the clearest of thinkers.

# CHAPTER 10

# Transcending Value Judgments in Evaluation: Ensuring That You Help More Than Hurt

Paul Ulansky violently raped his 14-year-old daughter while he was drunk. He admits to the violent rape, and his daughter suffers a number of severe symptoms as a result of it.

Jack Wilson began fondling his stepdaughter when she was five years old, and over the next few years progressed to oral and genital intercourse. He taught her that this was what fathers normally do. His daughter is confused in a number of ways about her father, her own relationships in the family, and her attitude about boys, but is not fearful of her father or otherwise symptomatic.

Sara Houseman is a 30-year-old teacher who has fallen in love with a 15-year-old male student in her social studies class, whom she has seduced and with whom she engages in sexual intercourse every chance she gets. She is not sure that what she has done is wrong and is grappling with that very question. Her student is delighted with the turn of events in his life. His mother is livid.

David Katz felt an overwhelming desire to caress the breast of his 13-year-old daughter, Andrea, while watching television on the sofa with his arm around her. He acted on this desire by fondling her, on just that one occasion. Mr. Katz felt embarrassed, apologized to his daughter, and it never happened again. Andrea felt a little bit confused and embarrassed, but these feelings soon dissipated, and she experienced no other negative effects. She told her best friend about it while she was still confused, and her friend disclosed it to others. The overall result was that her father had to move out of the house. Andrea doesn't understand why and wants him back.

Peter Helmsly accidentally rubbed against the genital area of his 15-year-old stepdaughter while wrestling with her, stimulating her sexually. This pleasured her, but confused her. As a result, she is drawn to wrestling with him any chance she gets. He is unaware of her heightened sexual arousal during these encounters until a child protective worker knocks on the door to inform him that he is under investigation for allegedly sexually abusing his stepdaughter.

Leona Dodd walks around the house without any clothes when her five- and seven-year-old boys visit with her on weekends. Her ex-husband thinks this is bad for the boys; she disagrees. This issue becomes the basis for a visitation dispute in court.

Joseph Wilson has been kissing his daughter on the lips to say good night to her ever since he can remember, when she was three years old, four years old, and so on. She is now 14 years old, and he feels uncomfortable about kissing her on the lips. His wife tells him it is inappropriate and he should have stopped years ago. While he is still debating the question, he is shocked one day to find a child protective worker at his door asking him why he still kisses his daughter on the lips.

\* \* \* \* \*

Do all of these illustrations comprise instances of sexual abuse? Do they all cause the same degree of harm? These questions must be addressed at the point of formulating conclusions. However, determinations of this kind are complex, because it is not always clear what constitutes abuse or how it should be defined. A great deal of thought and research has gone into this question, but the question has been avoided in this book until now for the very reason that it is incredibly complex. To address it earlier could easily have impeded the flow of the narrative. Until now, the phrase "sexual abuse" has been used to refer to any act in question, for the sake of convenience in communication. However, these examples make it clear that this phrase is an oversimplification of a range of diverse possibilities.

In the final stages of an evaluation, when the evaluator is attempting to formulate a determination of the seriousness of the alleged act and what should be done about it, one must ask what specifically it is that is harmful about the act. To say that the act is either right or wrong, to say that some acts are more wrong than others, or to ask what is specifically wrong about particular acts requires moral judgments that almost at once go outside the limits of our expertise and into other arenas. Asking what is harmful about an act is a more manageable question.

This is the question we try to answer in evaluations of individual situations like those illustrated above. Since it is evident that some of these acts are more harmful than others, it is necessary to use language that communicates something about the distinguishing features of each act. Therefore, the phrases "inappropriate behavior," "sexual exploitation," "sexual abuse," and "rape" will be used here to communicate a scale on which these various illustrations can be located. This kind of classificatory scheme is by no means superior to other ways of thinking about this issue and, in fact, is somewhat simplistic in certain respects.

However, from a clinical standpoint, it is a sensible and practical scale, enabling the evaluator to get on with his business without endless rumination about moral, societal, and psychological issues. A scale in which inappropriate behavior is at one end and rape is at the other is at least sufficient to prevent the evaluator from lumping together all acts of sexual abuse. This differentiation is crucial when trying to determine what, specifically, is harmful about a given sexual act, and whether it is more or less harmful than another particular act. Variables useful in making determinations of this kind are clarified when one examines in what ways the examples illustrated above are different and in what ways they are the same.

To begin this exploration, it is useful to recall the effects of rape and abuse discussed in Chapter 4. In that chapter, some differentiation was made between rape and abuse. While both were considered to be acts in which force is inflicted, violence and the infliction of physical pain tend to characterize rape and more extreme forms of abuse. When the presence of violence, force, or pain is not clear, as in many of the illustrations above, it is more difficult to make differentiations among sexual acts and to assess the relative degree of harm occasioned by each of them. Therefore, it is useful to ask whether in the absence of pain and violence there is anything inherently harmful about sexual acts between children and adults who love one another, between brothers and sisters, between consenting adults who happen to be teachers and students, or between employers and employees.

The secretary vehemently denies that she has been sexually exploited by her boss or that she was attracted in any way by his power over her. She insists she is in love and would have fallen in love with him if she had met him in other circumstances. There are also cases of father-daughter incest in which the "victim" insists, even in her adulthood, that there were no negative effects. There are precedents in Egyptian history in which royalty commonly married within the family of origin and were expected to do so.

It is too easy to say that these examples of individuals who are unaffected negatively by their sexual relationships are exceptions to the rule. It is more likely that the sexual act in itself, between two people, even between an adult and a child, may not be inherently harmful. Other factors that come between the two people may be what render that act harmful. The Egyptian princess was expected to marry her brother, father, or uncle; this expectation legitimized the relationship and allowed for little role confusion. However, in a different society, where the norms and expectations do not legitimize such a relationship, there is a great deal of role confusion occasioned by couplings of this kind.

The taboo against this kind of relationship in many societies probably evolved for some very sensible reasons. For example, sexual relationships often do not last very long, and in their termination they can alter a previously existing relationship. This is sometimes evident when a previous friendship is soured or damaged after the friendship has become sexualized. Since a daughter is destined to spend a good portion of her life in the family of her father, and the two of them need to maintain a fairly good relationship, it is simply not very sensible for them to give in to a sexual attraction. Doing so would risk rocking the boat even under the most liberal of family and cultural norms. Another possible reason for the taboo is that a daughter's sexual relationship with her father could create a dependency and excessive attachment that could prevent her from leaving the family to find a nonfamilial mate. This could threaten the survival of the wider society.

This example illustrates only that, when people live with one another in families and communities, they develop specific roles, norms, and expectations which maximize advantages, minimize problems, and enable them to function together with a reasonable degree of economy and civility. Boundaries are established between those roles, creating for individuals some privacy and autonomy as well as particular expectations and responsibilities. When boundaries become blurred or are intruded upon, confusion is one of several stressful results.

Differences in power exist between roles as well, where the person with less power is expected to defer to the person with more power, permitting the more powerful person to show the way, as in a teacher-student relationship or a parent-child relationship. In these complementary role relationships, the subordinate person usually benefits in some way by his or her deference to the other, such as by gaining protection in the case of the child, or gaining wisdom in the case of a student. When superiority ceases to be used to benefit the subordinate person in a complementary relationship and is used only to benefit the superior person at the expense of the subordinate, the subordinate feels misused and exploited.

When a complementary relationship, in which two people are expected to perform different functions (such as teaching and learning), shifts to a symmetrical one, in which they each perform the same function (such as sexual intercourse), the incongruity between these two forms of relationship generates paradoxical expectations that can be intensely confusing. On the one hand, the child is expected by his teacher to learn social studies while sitting in her class; on the other hand, he can't concentrate because he is preoccupied with memories and anticipations of the sexual satisfactions that she provides for him.

From a hypothetical point of view, it is conceivable that a culture could prescribe a ritualistic format for sexual interactions between child and teacher, so that such interactions did not represent an exploitation of power and a blurring of boundaries. To do so, it would be necessary that any sexual preoccupation was contained within the prescribed channels, without spilling over and interfering with other expectations that exist for the child. Without norms and expectations of this kind, the blurred boundaries and the intense stimulation of such a relationship are a burden that children are not cognitively competent to organize and to carry. It is a burden that can play havoc with developmental processes.

Because role expectations and hierarchies of power are different in different cultures, incest may not have been as traumatic to Egyptian royalty as it might be to modern people in Western culture. Differences in cultural norms and expectations also can account for why particular acts, such as Leona Dodd walking around naked in front of her boys, might be traumatic to them in one context but not in another. It might be deemed an inappropriate behavior causing some distress, but in another context, such as a nudist camp, it might be deemed merely an expectable behavior causing no distress.

Sexual acts between individuals are distressing to the degree that particular norms and expectations are violated. It is through this cultural filter that particular acts become abusive, exploitative, or inappropriate. Whether an act is abusive rather than exploitative, or exploitative rather than merely inappropriate, can be determined by an identification of which norms and expectations are violated.

Where a blurring of boundaries is the only violation characterizing an act between individuals, it might be described as an inappropriate behavior, rather than as abuse, exploitation of power, or rape. To illustrate, a first grade student shows his penis to another student while sitting in class. Inappropriate behavior of this kind may consist of an act with sexual overtones occurring in a nonsexual context or an act that intrudes upon the privacy of another individual. While acts of this kind might be distressing, and sometimes intensely so, the degree of distress and harm is often mild to moderate, and usually milder than acts that misuse power or involve violence.

Acts that are characterized not only by a blurring of boundaries but also by a misuse of power are better described as exploitations of power. To use the same example of a penis being exposed to someone, consider for the moment, that it is a boss who shows his penis to his secretary. As a result of this kind of event, she may feel used, soiled, and exploited. She may fear losing her job if she does not comply with his implied or stated wishes. On the other hand, she may not feel victimized at all and may embrace with relish the opportunity provided.

Acts of abuse or molestation can be characterized by a blurring of boundaries, an exploitation of power, and an additional distinguishing feature: coercion by means of moral or physical force. To use our example of an exposed penis once again, this time it is a father who exposes the penis, and it is his daughter to whom the penis is exposed. He might simply expect her to look at it, or he might go further and ask her to touch it or to put it in her mouth. And she may comply with his expectations because she believes he can make her do this, or that it is right to do so. After all, he is the one who knows what is right and wrong. That is to say, she feels forced to do so by virtue of a moral imperative, or because she believes she has no choice due to his greater physical size and strength.

While moral or physical force characterizes an act of this kind, there is still an absence of the violence and physical pain that would characterize a rape. Abuse might be further characterized by an intensification of the intrusion into areas of privacy—that is, a more intense blurring of boundaries, sometimes even without the use of any force. Although it is difficult to determine where abuse leaves off and rape begins, it is still useful to keep some differentiation in mind.

Table 2 may help to crystallize these various considerations. It hierarchically categorizes the various levels of sexual misconduct by the extent to which the variables just examined are implicated in each. Please keep in mind that this categorization is simply a construct, a convenient device that may be used to organize our thinking. It is not the final word on

### Table 2. Categories and Variables in Sexual Misconduct

|  |  | CATEGORIES OF SEXUAL MISCONDUCT | | | |
|  |  | Rape | Abuse | Exploitation | Inappropriate behavior |
|---|---|---|---|---|---|
| VARIABLES | Blurred boundaries | X | X | X | X |
|  | Exploitation of power | X | X | X |  |
|  | Physical/moral force | X | X |  |  |
|  | Infliction of pain | X |  |  |  |

categorizing particular acts. It can easily be argued that many particular acts of "abuse" involve pain or, on the other hand, that many acts of abuse involve neither pain nor force of any kind. It can be argued that moral and physical force is not separate from, but rather a further example of, exploitation of power. It can also be argued that the perceived intention of the offender, the cognitive competence of the victim to give consent, and other such variables not yet examined can be utilized to construct a more useful model.

A model of this kind can help us to address the differences of opinion that exist concerning the appropriateness of particular behaviors. Results of questionnaire data can be frightening when one views the differences of opinion people have about the appropriateness of a father kissing his daughter on the lips. While a lot of people seem to think this act is increasingly inappropriate as the daughter gets older, there is still a difference in opinion, despite the age of the daughter, about whether it is appropriate or not. Another example is that of Leona Dodd, walking naked about the house as she does her chores in the presence of her two young boys. People disagree a good deal on whether this kind of behavior is inappropriate or harmful.

Is the question of whether such behavior is harmful just a matter of one's point of view or opinion? Is this opinion dependent on the evaluator's own value system? I think not. I think we can do better than that. We can often, though not always, go beyond our individual value systems in making this kind of determination if we consider the cultural meaning of the particular act.

For example, if this act of doing one's chores naked occurs in a nudist colony or a hippie commune in which nakedness is common and expected, harmful effects are unlikely. The values of the family are supported by the surrounding values of the community to which the child is exposed on an everyday basis. In addition, if the child attends a school in that community rather than outside of it, then there will be no confusion of values that the child has to resolve by himself without community guidance. The differences in values between the hippie community and the larger community of which it is a part are differences that the family and the smaller community can help the child to negotiate.

Similarly, if a husband and wife living in Manhattan agree to walk about naked in the presence of their children because they want to instill certain values and beliefs, they might still get away with it without harming their children. But to do so, they must succeed in helping the children to negotiate the clash in values that will occur with the children's exposure to the wider surrounding culture. To the extent that the wider culture has more influence on the child than the values instilled by the family, or to the extent that the family fails to help the children to negotiate the incongruity in values, the children may experience stimulation and confusion which they cannot adequately channel and contain.

When the mother and father are separated and convey very different value systems, the naked mother who visits her boys on weekends has even less of a chance to cause no harm. There may be nothing inherently harmful in Leona's beliefs or in her acts of walking about naked. However, the more powerful influence of her husband, who has primary custody of the children, and the values of the surrounding community can easily render that naked behavior harmful to the children.

Despite her attempt to teach them that nakedness is normal, healthy, and not necessarily provocative, Leona's children may experience several negative effects. They may be aroused sexually by her nakedness, have difficulty understanding and resolving why she goes about naked, and spend an inordinate amount of time preoccupied by it when it would be healthier to spend their time in other ways. Her concept of boundaries is not congruent with her children's. Although she has no intention of blurring boundaries, boundaries are nevertheless blurred from the point of view of the children.

These same kinds of violations can be seen in a different type of situation, outside the family: that of a teacher and student having a sexual relationship. This kind of a relationship represents a blurring of boundaries and an exploitation of power. Even if the student were delighted with his luck, this would be an instance of sexual exploitation, whether the student was eight years old or 14 years old. But let us complicate the example further, rendering a judgment about potential harm less clear. What if the student is a 40-year-old woman taking a college course taught by a 36-year-old man? Not only is she older than he, but she argues that since they are both mature adults they would have fallen for each other wherever they had met.

While this is a definite possibility, it is more likely that they fell for each other precisely because she was his student. The closeness in age tends to obscure the very genuine complementary role relationship that may have fostered and enhanced the attraction between them. In the process of his teaching and her learning, she is dependent on him for a grade, deferring to him in ways that she would not have to were that not so. Her deference and dependence — and his responses to the situation — determine the kinds of interactions that occur and the overall intensity and complexity of the relationship.

She is dependent on him not only for a grade, but also for his wisdom. She is therefore likely to give his words more attention and attach to them more significance than she would if they had met in the fruit and vegetable section of the grocery store and found themselves discussing the increasing price of tomatoes. As he stands and walks about the classroom, he is a prime target on which to project fantasies of an ideal person.

While he might utilize this deference and dependence appropriately to facilitate the learning process, it is also common for some teachers to overly indulge themselves in this dependence, that is, to achieve a very personal and immature gratification that may be less available in other adult relationships, which are more symmetrical than complementary. The more interesting he is as he cavorts about the classroom and the more eloquent in holding forth his interesting ideas, the more she will hang on his every word and project on him fantasies of what a lover he could really be for her. Or a mother or a father or a friend.

This kind of intensity is not uncommon in student-teacher relationships, but it does not even have to be this intense to facilitate at least a mild degree of attraction — an attraction that would probably not occur in the market, the laundromat, a cocktail party, or a neighborhood barbecue. This attraction is often fostered to a mild extent even with students and teachers who are extremely careful to remain within their boundaries and who utilize the complementarity of their roles to enhance the teaching-learning process. To act on this attraction by establishing a sexual relationship is just as clearly an exploitation of power and blurring of boundaries as it is when the student is half the teacher's age, despite the fact that it might not be clear to the teacher and student.

\* \* \* \* \*

"But what if we end up married?" persisted the 40-year-old student.

"I'd congratulate you."

"But would you still consider me a victim of sexual exploitation? A happy victim?"

"A victim, certainly, and perhaps happy as well, for a time."

"What do you mean, for a time? It wouldn't last?"

"Who can tell what lasts and what doesn't? But the complementarity that brought you together would no longer exist in a formal relationship. That is, the course is over, and he's no longer your teacher."

"But it does still exist. He's like a mentor to me."

"So he keeps teaching, and you keep learning. But, as in any relationship, the same set of complementary differences that brought you together might drive you apart."

"What do you mean by that?"

"The quiet, introverted young man is drawn to the extroverted woman's spontaneity and bubbliness, while she is drawn to his slow obsessive logic and stability, which helps to anchor her. Later in their relationship, he can't stand her hysteria, and she thinks he's a boring stick-in-the-mud. She angrily tries to get reactions from him, and he responds with infinite patience and logic, which drives her even more hysterical."

"I get the point, but how does that relate to me?"

"The very thing you liked about your professor-husband, his fatherly wisdom, might drive you up the wall if he keeps expecting you to hang on his every word and keeps lecturing at you. He might not seem so very wise at all after a while when you find yourself noticing the bread crumbs stuck to the corner of his mouth instead of the insights he expects to illuminate for you."

"Okay, I can see that. But it still doesn't seem right to me that there's something wrong with a relationship between two consenting adults who go into it with their eyes open. What if I were aware of this blurring of boundaries and the exploitation of his power and consented to it anyway because the gratifications seemed worth the potential harm?"

"Well, assuming your eyes were open, then I suppose you would be giving informed consent. But were your eyes open, completely, at the time of consent? Was your consent adequately informed?"

"No, not at the time. How many people would be aware of all the potential harm? Even I wasn't, until you explained it. But is there any way at all that I could have entered this relationship without being an unwitting victim?"

"Yes, possibly. If you never took his teaching seriously and didn't feel dependent on him in any way, then it might be said that a complementary student-teacher relationship was never genuinely established."

"Do you mean if I never paid attention in class? Or didn't care how well I did?"

"Perhaps. Or if you were both neighbors who had only said hello to one another and then got to know each other in a one-night workshop where he was teaching photography and you were learning about it. The genuine student-teacher relationship would be very short-lived, and probably wouldn't have priority over the relationship established with him both before and after the workshop."

"So while harm could still be caused, it would be minimal."

"Probably."

"Let's go back to the college course. What if I were already in love with him before I took the course? Would there be any way that would harm me?"

"Only that you might not take him as seriously, or learn as much, as the students sitting on either side of you."

\* \* \* \* \*

On the one hand, age is a variable that can obscure an exploitation of power, as with our 40-year-old student. On the other hand, it can highlight such an exploitation of power while obscuring an identification of how boundaries may be blurred. Consider the 35-year-old woman who tries to justify her relationship with a much younger boyfriend.

\* \* \* \* \*

"It's not like I'm his mother or his teacher," she protests. "I met him in the laundromat. We got to know each other, and we have a lot to offer each other. I can see how it might screw him up if I was his teacher or something, but I'm not his teacher. I'm just his girlfriend."

"But what about his age?"

"He's 14. Big deal. Why should age matter? He's very mature for his age. He's kinder and more thoughtful to me than men twice his age. Believe me, I should know. I've been around the block a time or two."

"But has he been around the block, too? I mean, he's very young and inexperienced."

"Oh, he had sex one time before. He wasn't a virgin. He had a girlfriend his own age for a little while, but he said that the one time they had sex, it wasn't very good. If he's having sex with her, what's the difference if he has sex with me? What's so wrong with being older?"

"The difference is that you're much more experienced than he is, and you're more experienced than his previous girlfriend. You have the advantage on him. The result is that he thinks about sex all the time now. He can't concentrate on anything else."

"Well, I know that. I kind of like that about him, to tell the truth."

"He's too young to realize what he's missing out on."

"What, like football? How important is football?"

"Well, I'm not a football fan either, but he was. He ended up dropping out of football because of this. He was very good at football, and football was very good for him. Plus, his marks are dropping, and he hardly spends any time any longer with kids his own age."

"Don't you think he can make up his own mind what is good for him and what's not?"

"Yes, he has made up his own mind, but I don't think his judgment in this situation is very good. He doesn't have the kinds of life experiences that you have to give him a broader perspective to make a balanced decision. You have so much more experience and knowledge to help make decisions like this. He has very little. You have a great deal more power than he does, and I don't think you realize it."

"I don't agree with you. I may know a few things more than he does, but not that much."

"What if he was 13? Would that make a difference?"

"Maybe, maybe not."

"How about 12? What if he was 12, no, 11, or 10? If he was 10 years old, would you still feel comfortable having a romantic relationship with him?"

"What? You think I'm a pervert or something?"

* * * * *

The difference in power between these two people appears on the surface to be the only thing that has been exploited; it is not immediately apparent whether a blurring of boundaries also characterizes the relationship. This is even less apparent when considering differences in power and age between consenting adults. For example, what does one think when one encounters a fat, balding prosperous-looking gentleman in his sixties having dinner with a beautiful young model in her early twenties?

When his 30-year-old daughter joins them at the table, with an infant in arms, the 20-year-old newlywed says to her stepdaughter, "Can you show me how to feed the baby?"

"Sure, mom," says the gentleman's daughter with a laugh. "It's about time you showed an interest in learning how to feed your grandson."

This hypothetical role confusion is not due to a blurring or violation of boundaries in the same sense as has been described earlier. It is due, instead, to the different kinds of roles, expectations, and missions that tend to be attached to different stages in the life cycle. While it is possible for this kind of role confusion to enrich a relationship, it can also harm or pose certain difficulties for the relationship.

The prosperous gentleman might find it difficult to relate adequately to the newlywed's excitement at the news of her first pregnancy, having himself gone through a number of pregnancies with his first wife much earlier in his life, and having gone on to other stages in life where his interest is more focused on issues she can hardly yet conceive as being significant. She, on her side, may have little patience with those issues that are of more concern to him, such as his own mortality and impending death, and how to prioritize the time he has left. Each of them find themselves intruding upon, or aliens within, the other's boundaries of central interest. Nevertheless, each of them is capable, or has the right, to decide whether the advantages are worth the disadvantages.

They also have the right to decide whether the disadvantages of any exploitation of power are worth the advantages. Of course, it is possible that no exploitation exists in a situation like this. For example, it is possible that the old man and young girl are equal in intelligence, wealth, power, charm, wit, desire to be with one another, sexual attraction, and so on, with the only difference being in their age and beauty. However, it is more likely that the gentleman's greater age represents opportunities he has had to amass greater power or wealth than she possesses, and whose advantages she wishes to enjoy; in turn, her youth and beauty are assets he can enjoy only by a kind of purchase or exchange. She exploits him for his money, while he exploits her for her beauty and youth.

But this is not simply an exploitation. It is an exchange on the interpersonal marketplace, and it is possible for either of them to feel either that a fair bargain or a rough balance of power has been established or that the exchange has left one of them exploited, victimized, or cheated. Each of them is capable of weighing the advantages against the disadvantages, though some people are more capable than others.

This kind of difference in power between people, when it is exploited, is a matter of concern to us if the victim of exploitation is not capable of giving informed consent, such as when that person is a child. We need, then, to address whether the child requires protection from or a remedy to this kind of victimization.

However, when it involves individuals who are capable of informed consent, such as consenting adults, remedial or protective action would be presumptuous on our part, even when those individuals are not fully aware of the implications of their actions. For example, you wouldn't want to go knocking on some woman's door, uninvited, to point out to her that she is being sexually exploited. While we might, as individuals, choose to educate the public about exploitation and even to advocate in political arenas on such issues, it is outside our limits of expertise to suggest what needs to be done to rectify any harm that we believe we may have identified.

The focus in these examples has been not so much on severe cases of abuse and rape as on all those instances where differences in values and morals may play a role, that is, those instances where one person might consider an act harmful and another might consider it not harmful. It is important to show that one can negotiate the grey areas in some sensible and reliable ways to transcend one's own value system in arriving at a determination that a particular act occasioned some harm, and to identify not only whether some harm exists, but also what degree of harm.

There are important differences that we have determined here between a rape, which does a great deal of harm, and a sexually inappropriate behavior, which does minimal harm, or between a teacher's sexual exploitation of a 17-year-old student and that of a seven-year-old. We can examine these examples or those illustrations that opened this chapter and identify what harm, if any, exists in each of them; if we can't, because we lack adequate information to make this determination, we can at least be guided by the variables discussed here as to what kind of information we still need to seek.

With a reasoning procedure available to determine the degree of harm occasioned by a particular act, the logical next step in an evaluation is to suggest a means by which that harm can be remedied, reduced, or avoided. Suggestions of this kind comprise the recommendations that an evaluator makes to someone else—a therapist, an attorney, a child protective worker, or a judge. When one lumps all sexual offenses under the category of sexual abuse and considers all such acts equally harmful, then this kind of undifferentiated thinking can lead to the same kinds of protective or remedial measures being applied indiscriminately to all cases.

For example, prohibiting contact between parent and child and requiring both of them to receive therapy would be measures applied just as readily to Leona Dodd and her boys as to individuals involved in a violent rape. On the other hand, if one is able to differentiate between the harm occasioned by different acts, one is able to see clearly that these kinds of measures may be well matched to a rape case but constitute an absurd match to the needs of Leona and her boys.

These kinds of remedial or protective measures are absurd in the case of the Dodds, because first, they are not tailored to remedy or protect against the potential harm occasioned in this particular instance, and second, they will cause more harm than any that is occasioned by the alleged offense. Clearly, they are out of proportion to the need. It is necessary, then, to identify the needs—that is, what specifically needs to be done to rectify or protect against potential harm—and then to weigh the potential harm of this measure against the potential harm occasioned by the alleged offense. In attempting to utilize this reasoning process with the Dodds, we can first determine the potential harm of Leona's walking about naked in front of her boys.

Recall that she only sees the boys for visits, that she wishes to instill a healthy appreciation for the naked body, that her ex-husband who has custody of the boys has instilled opposite sorts of values, and that the boys are exposed to a wider culture in their school and neighborhood that supports their father's values. As a result, the boys are now confused and sexually preoccupied because the clash between the values to which they are primarily exposed and those of their mother has not been adequately negotiated. Despite Leona's good intentions and despite her right to try to instill in them whatever healthy values she wishes, she is unlikely to be successful at helping them adequately to negotiate the incongruity in value systems. To the extent that they cannot resolve this incongruity, they will remain confused and sexually preoccupied.

The confusion and sexual preoccupation constitute the specific forms of harm that can be identified here, and while this harm will vary in degree from case to case, it can be identified as relatively mild when compared to other kinds of symptoms occasioned by other kinds of acts. To protect against or remedy this harm it is necessary to identify needs, that is to say, what needs to be done to eliminate the harm. In this particular case, two possible needs can be identified: (1) the need to remove the incongruity in value systems and (2) the need of the children to have an adequate mechanism for negotiating the incongruity.

To meet these needs adequately, we can consider various possible remedial actions, first, to determine whether and how well these actions are tailored to meet the need, and second, whether they are likely to occasion more harm than the harm caused by walking about naked. In this light, consider the following possible remedial actions:

1. Terminate Leona's visitation, i.e., prohibiting contact between her and the boys.
2. Institute supervised visitation, i.e., permit visitation on the condition that a child protective worker will conduct surprise home visits, or that another adult will be present whose responsibility it will be to keep Leona's clothes on her body.

3. Postpone further visitation until Leona is able to get the therapeutic or educational treatment she needs to understand the harm caused to the children and, in addition, is able to agree to keep her clothes on.
4. Allow Leona to continue walking about naked during visits, but require the children to engage in therapeutic treatment that is aimed at reducing the symptoms of confusion and sexual preoccupation.
5. Require the children to engage in treatment aimed at teaching them to negotiate the incongruity in value systems, and require either Leona or her ex-husband or both of them to participate in this treatment.
6. Explain to Leona the harm occasioned by walking about naked and the reasons why, such that she decides that putting on some clothes is the most cost-effective solution for herself and her boys.

As can be seen, option #4 is respectful of both parents' value systems and therefore does no harm by intruding upon their autonomy as parents. It is unlikely to be effective, since the therapy will address only the symptoms rather than the reasons the symptoms exist. The rest of these options will reduce or eliminate the harm that has been identified, so they are all identical in this respect. However, these options vary both in how likely each is to eliminate the reasons for the symptoms and how much harm each causes by virtue of its intrusiveness.

The first option is obviously the most intrusive and harmful, trouncing upon the right Leona Dodd has to her own value system and thwarting the children's and Leona's needs to have contact with one another. This harm, in most instances, will clearly outweigh the harm caused by nakedness as well as the benefit of protecting the children from it. Similarly, supervised visitation, while less intrusive, is nevertheless intrusive enough to alter and contaminate the parent-child relationship and, in many cases, may be considered as harmful as, if not more harmful than, the effects of nakedness.

Contrast these remedies with option #5, which is tailored exceptionally well to the need because it specifically addresses the reasons for the existence of the symptoms. It provides a means to resolve the incongruity between value systems while at the same time respecting each value system. It is unlikely to be the option of choice because one or more of the necessary parties will probably not be willing to participate long enough in therapy for it to be effective. Even Leona herself will probably decide that it is not worth the trouble, should it be suggested by an idealistic evaluator who wishes to be respectful of her value system. The option is intrusive or harmful only to the extent that it is more trouble than it is worth and to the extent that certain individuals in the Dodd family might be forced to exercise this option against their wills.

The last option, #6, is obviously the most economical and effective in meeting the need. It eliminates the problem, and its only cost is that it compromises Leona's right to instill what values she wishes in her children. If this costs less to her than the cost of harm to her children and the cost, or bother, of therapeutic treatment, then it is likely to be the option of choice. On the other hand, she may fail to understand, or not agree, that there is any harm caused to her children. If she can't be counted on to alter her behavior, then the evaluator may need to consider a more intrusive and harmful remedial measure. In doing so, it is essential to weigh the harm of that measure against the confusion and sexual preoccupation and the benefits of eliminating those harms.

The process of weighing options can be made abundantly clear by the evaluator in his recommendations. When it is, it enriches the understanding of those who are the recipients of the recommendation and enables them to make informed decisions about how to best proceed. For example, it is important for the court to carefully consider the harm done to David Katz' 13-year-old daughter (illustrated at the beginning of this chapter) when he fondled her breast due to an overwhelming urge. It is important to look into the reasons why the urge was overwhelming and to address them. But it is equally important that in this case David inhibited any such urges on subsequent occasions and that the harmful effects to his daughter were minimal.

One needs to weigh the harm that might be caused to this child and to this family by exercising the full range of protective options, such as removing either the father or the child from the home, coercing the family into therapy of indefinite duration, and subjecting the family to repeated instances of investigation and litigation. Such measures can interfere with the child's academic performance, jeopardize David's ability to financially support the family, irreparably strain a marital relationship that initially had a good prognosis for improvement, and unnecessarily interfere with and contaminate a father-daughter relationship that, on the whole, may have been more healthy than unhealthy.

When this kind of weighing process is obscured, is not shared, or has not been attempted, then the identification of harm and the remedial action suggested are more likely to be undifferentiated, simplistic, and moralistic. The recommendation is then more likely to reflect the value system of the evaluator and lend itself more readily to a moral judgment on the part of the court or protective worker, rather than reflecting instead a ruthlessly thorough examination of genuine harm. Unfortunately, a termination of parental contact is all too common in cases like David's or Leona's; certain indicators representing red flags of alarm result in evaluators' making determinations between black and white, because they do not have the tools of thinking they need to differentiate among various shades of grey.

This chapter is an attempt to provide the evaluator with such tools: a differentiated way of thinking that can be brought to bear on the formulation of conclusions and recommendations. It is an attempt to convey the degree of power and choice the evaluator has in affecting the fate of a family: either to make a naive recommendation that causes extreme havoc and untold suffering or to make a suggestion more aptly tailored to the particular need.

* * * * *

"Wait a second."

"What?"

"You can't just close it like that. I want to make sure I understand the point you were making."

"Which point? I made many points."

"About harm."

"Well, what about it?"

"About being sure how much harm is caused by a sexual act."

"Yes, that's very important, but what about it?"

"I think what you're saying is that we shouldn't get all bent out of shape when the harm is minimal."

"Right. There are cases of minimal harm and cases of serious harm. We need to be able to differentiate between them."

"Because what needs to be done is different?"

"Yes, and because the remedies in each situation cost something."

"Cost something? What do you mean? Like the cost of making things worse by our remedies? Like to the Dodds?"

"Yes, exactly. And also the cost to us by applying the remedy. The cost to the agency. The time taken in supervision, following up on the situation, any special meetings that are called, time and energy taken to document what was done, and so on."

"I guess all that can take up a lot of time and energy, but the trouble it costs us shouldn't stop us from addressing the suffering."

"The time and energy aren't trouble for us. But the process is simply very wasteful when the harm is minimal and doesn't justify the cost. It might be better to spend those resources on more serious cases. We have people on our waiting list at the clinic who might be jumping out windows as we speak."

"Okay. I see that. I get the point. But which kinds of cases are the ones that aren't serious? Can you give me an example?"

"I've spent a good deal of this chapter talking about some of them."

"But nothing comes immediately to mind. Maybe because you spent the whole chapter talking about an awful lot of things. My mind is awhirl with thoughts and I can't keep them straight. Can you just remind me?"

"A therapist is caught flirting with a female client who sexualizes most of her interactions."

"That's kind of inappropriate, isn't it?"

"Yes, it is. Or a therapist who loses his temper and yells, 'You little motherfucker' when he's kicked in the shin by a child having a tantrum."

"He shouldn't have sworn at his client."

"No, he shouldn't have. And what about Andrea Katz, who is hardly bothered at all by the fact that her father touched her breast one time?"

"But you can't ignore it just because she didn't mind."

"You can't ignore any of these situations. You need to take appropriate actions in each of them."

"Well, in the first case, that male therapist needs some serious supervision if he's getting off on his patient's flirting. And the second case needs supervision and incident reviews."

"And maybe when the incident review form goes to the Office of Mental Health, they'll ask for even more investigation, and more meetings, and more write-ups, to be sure that appropriate action was taken. Meanwhile the therapist who got kicked in the shin and lost his temper for a second is scrutinized at great personal cost."

"I see your point. Too much time and energy can go into this."

"Yes, there are cases with higher priority than the kid who gets called a motherfucker by his therapist."

"But won't he suffer from being called a motherfucker? And doesn't that deserve our attention?"

"Yes, we need to attend to any of these cases. But we need to prioritize and to keep our perspective. That's my point. After all, how much pain is actually caused in these cases?"

"How can you really measure the pain?"

"You can't measure it exactly, not really, but you can compare it to the pain that people normally experience in everyday life."

"What do you mean?"

"Half the kids in America are torn between two divorced parents and a good portion of them suffer excruciating loyalty conflicts. A large part of their lives will consist of learning to live with this pain and to resolve these conflicts as best they can."

"But treatment is available for the effects of divorce on children."

"You're not getting my point. Treatment isn't always the answer. My point is that life is full of pain. Pain is inevitable. Extreme pain. Everyone you know will suffer all kinds of pain that nobody is going to jump through hoops to try to address. For example, everyone dies. And many of us don't want to. Should we all go into therapy for this? Everyone suffers the grief of losing someone they loved. Shall I go on?"

"But if the grief is too intense or prolonged, treatment is available for that, too."

"You're still not getting it. Maybe you'll get it if I use an example where it's the treatment that causes the pain."

"Now you've really lost me."

"Okay, stay with me now. You're treating a seven-year-old boy right now with an attention deficit disorder, aren't you? He was impulsive, distractible, tantruming, reading disabled, and engaged in socially inappropriate behavior with peers or anyone else."

"Yes, that's Billy all right."

"And what do you think would have been his future without treatment?"

"He would have kept getting in trouble, and when he was older he probably would have hurt someone or himself and gotten himself in really serious trouble. He still may. Medication and treatment might not be enough."

"And what's your focus in the treatment?"

"Monitoring the effects of medication, working with his teachers, helping his parents to understand him better and to provide him with more structure and clearer limits."

"But what has been your main emphasis? Where has most of your time and energy gone? How are most of your sessions spent with the parents?"

"On limit setting and structure."

"Why?"

"Because he ignores limits and rules. He forgets them because he's so distractible, and he ends up misbehaving."

"So what have you done about that?"

"Tried to get him to remember the rules."

"Making these rules vivid to him? So he's less likely to forget them?"

"Exactly."

"How? By just telling him? Reminding him?"

"Yes, there's some of that. I spend some time with cognitive restructuring techniques that help him to remind himself of the consequences of his behavior. But mostly it's making sure that he suffers when he breaks any rules. Making sure that the consequences of his misbehavior really matter to him."

"So what happens if he gets in trouble at school on the playground, like, for example . . . "

"Like inappropriate sexual behavior. Trying to pull down a girl's pants. That's something that happened."

"Okay, then, in that instance I suppose the parents administered some consequence. I can't remember what they did. But what happens if that consequence doesn't seem to have an effect?"

"Well, if you'd remembered, that's exactly what did happen. His mother told him that he couldn't watch television for the rest of the day because television is usually important to him, but it didn't seem to faze him much."

"So what do you do? If the punishment isn't potent enough, then it won't alter his behavior."

"I teach the parents how to up the ante. How to intensify the consequences until it does matter enough to him to make the right choices."

"Well, how did they do that?"

"Well, they saw that he wasn't too fazed, because he probably expected to play with his brothers or play with toys in his room. So they told him that he wasn't allowed to play with his brothers or with his toys. He wasn't even allowed to lie in bed because his mother was afraid he might fall asleep and miss the punishment. He had to sit at a desk and either stare into space or practice spelling words."

"And this was at your guidance."

"Yes, she called me when he got home from school to get my coaching on how to handle this incident."

"So what happened?"

"Well, while he was sitting at the desk, it finally dawned on him that he couldn't play, watch TV, or even sleep. When it finally hit him, I guess he began to sob uncontrollably. That's what they told me, anyway. At that point, the parents almost gave in and let him go play."

"But they didn't give in?"

"No, the whole purpose was to get him to suffer."

"How long did it last?"

"Till snack time, before bed."

"For a couple of hours?"

"Well, yeah, he sobbed off and on, and complained about how unhappy he was. But in the meantime, he practiced a lot of spelling words. He never seemed so in love with homework before. He kept asking for more."

"And, if I remember correctly, this has occurred many other times as well, where you teach him that intense suffering is in store for him. Wasn't there some incident with a broken toy?"

"Yes, he broke someone's toy when he was mad, and so he was timed-out initially. His father told him that this was the beginning of his punishment, because his father wasn't sure it would be potent enough by itself."

"Yes, that's the incident I remember. The time-out wasn't sufficient, right?"

"As it turned out, Billy didn't seem to be fazed by it, so his favorite toys were taken from him temporarily. His GI Joes. It was still uncertain that this was having an effect, so his father began slowly taking money from his piggy bank, to pay for the broken toy, a little at a time, right in front of him. He'd been saving the money for a really special toy that he wanted."

"What effect did that have?"

"As Billy watched his money disappear he kind of crumbled, broke down, and began to sob inconsolably."

"What else did they do then?"

"Nothing else. They had gotten to the point where they wanted to be. Inconsolable sobbing. They could tell they'd made a serious impression."

"And this was your intent? For him to suffer so intensely?"

"Yes."

"And it's not uncommon for these parents to inflict this kind of suffering on Billy? Where they get him to sob and to feel intensely miserable?"

"Well, it's less necessary than it used to be. Now it's only once in a while. Usually, frequent but smaller punishments keep him in line on an everyday basis."

"Like?"

"Well, like for minor things. If his mother is helping him with his homework at the kitchen table and he makes an angry face and stamps his foot, she doesn't even get into it with him because she doesn't want him to develop a negative attitude about schoolwork. She immediately sends him to the dining room to be timed-out until he feels ready to return with a positive attitude about getting the work done."

"But he might sit there daydreaming forever rather than come back with a good attitude."

"Yes, he might. But she goes in there to remind him that if another five minutes go by, she'll start confiscating his favorite toys, one by one. But that's his choice. He can sit there forever."

"Some choice. She's threatening to take his toys hostage and kill them off one by one."

"But it works. He comes back very quickly with a positive attitude. And he gets a hug when that happens. Generally he tries as hard as he can to avoid punishment and tries to do things that bring about rewarding consequences."

"Sounds like he can't sneeze without permission. The degree of structure here is unbelievable. It's more structured than a jail."

"Better than him ending up in a real jail later, isn't it?"

"But imagine the degree of stress this boy lives with. He walks around with memories of being tormented and constant worry about future torment if he makes one wrong move. You're creating an obsessive and worried child."

"Better than an impulsive and distractible child. That's my goal. And the approach is working, thanks to many of your own suggestions, if you'll remember. And you know very well that this approach doesn't consist only of punishment. It works so well because it's mixed with a lot of hugs and love and emotional bonding."

"Yes, I think what you're doing for Billy is wonderful. But what I want to focus you on is the degree of torment you've been inflicting on him."

"Torment?"

"Yes, it's incredible. You've become quite an artist at torturing children."

"Torturing children? That's a bit hard, isn't it?"

"If you were a sadist, or if Billy's parents were inflicting this pain on him in anger or frustration, then I'd say we had a serious case of emotional abuse."

"But it's intended to help him, not hurt him. And the parents aren't getting off on hurting him."

"I know, but the help that you're providing him requires the infliction of incredible psychological pain, extreme in degree and extreme in quantity. Probably more extreme than most spankings or forms of physical discipline."

"I guess it does. So? What are you getting at?"

"Picture, for a moment, the amount of pain you've inflicted on Billy. Okay?"

"Okay."

"How does it compare to the pain experienced by the boy who was called a motherfucker by his therapist? I mean, that kid was so angry that he probably doesn't even remember it was said to him."

"I guess there's no comparison between his pain and the pain that Billy experiences. But we can't just ignore what that therapist did."

"No, we shouldn't ignore it. But we can keep it in some perspective."

"By thinking of Billy's suffering."

"Yes. I think you've finally got the point I've been trying to make."

"Just don't get bent out of shape. Keep some perspective."

"Yes, that's all. That's all I was trying to say."

"Speaking of keeping things in perspective, aren't we getting off track here?"

"What do you mean?"

"Isn't this focus on my therapy case a little bit out of proportion to the points you're trying to make in this chapter? Aren't we spending an inordinate amount of time discussing it? Doesn't it distract from the points you want to make?"

"How can it distract? Most of your energy with Billy has been devoted to inflicting pain, hasn't it?"

"That's not exactly the way I would put it. But yes, I guess so."

"And this book is about abuse, isn't it? It's about the infliction of pain. Right?"

"Right. So?"

"So, the pain that Billy experiences at your hands far exceeds the pain experienced by some of the kids who have been sexually abused, kids who I've talked about here in this book."

"That's kind of weird to think about. I never thought about it that way."

"I wanted to spend the time to be sure that you did think about it this way."

"I guess it's simply the same point you keep making, over and over. I think I've got the point now."

"Good. Then I won't have to bore you with it again."

# CHAPTER 11

# *Formulation: Pulling It All Together*

"But Aaron, if I had to make a recommendation about David Katz and his daughter, what should I recommend be done about the fondling? You said in the last chapter that it caused only mild embarrassment."

"That's right. So?"

"Well, you said that removing the father from the home would be traumatic for the child."

"Yes, terribly traumatic, especially in view of what has been gained in the way of protecting the child from fondling. I mean, she might not even need any further protection from it."

"Right, that came across loud and clear. And you even went on to imply that less intrusive remedies might be harmful too, like counseling."

"That's right. Counseling might be unnecessary. The man feels so bad about it already that he might never do it again. His daughter might also be traumatized by a lot of talking about sex abuse when she's already successfully resolved for herself any problem it caused for her."

"But what if the fondling is due to a more severe problem that needs treatment? For example, what if she's a parentified child in the family and acting more like a wife than a child, and what if this could lead to more fondling? Maybe a progression to sexual intercourse?"

"Then you should say so if you think that's the case, and say what needs to be done. But just because a child is parentified doesn't mean that the parentification needs to be addressed in treatment."

"Why not? Shouldn't it always be addressed?"

"Sure, if you want to solve all the problems of the world. But a lot of children are parentified to some extent, and this parentification falls within the broad limits of normal without leading to serious problems or distortions in development. It's a question of perspective."

"Perspective again?"

"Right. You have to decide whether the parentification is serious enough to justify intervention, especially if these people aren't interested in your intervention."

"But how do you decide how important it is?"

"By looking at the interaction among a number of factors to make a more fine-tuned assessment. For example, if David's daughter had a relationship with a boyfriend that involved a lot of petting, how do you think her father's fondling would have affected her?"

"Well, I think it would have been more meaningful to her. She would have better understood its significance. So I think it might have been a lot more distressing to her than the mild embarrassment you talked about."

"Exactly. Or what if she had no special relationship with her father? For example, suppose he's an uninvolved father and she gets most of her affirmation and support from her friends and her mother. How would you say that the removal of her father from the home would affect her? Would she be so traumatized by it?"

"Probably not. She might be relieved."

"Right. Because the degree of distress she experiences is dependent on how the fondling interacts with levels of functioning in various areas of her life, such as peer relationships, heterosexual relations, impulse control, and so on."

"But you haven't explained all that—how you analyze the interactions among all those factors, how you pull it all together."

"I've explained a good deal of it in other parts of the book. For example, in Chapter 3, I talked about assessing all major areas of a child's functioning."

"But not like you're doing now. You haven't explained how you end up with an exact and precise recommendation that goes to the heart of the matter, one that tells exactly what needs to be done."

"That's right. That's what I was planning to do now."

"Oh. Sorry. Go on then."

"You can make a precise recommendation that goes to the heart of the matter when you've pulled together everything that you know about the case. This pulling together of everything is a complicated process; it's a way of thinking, a way of organizing one's thinking to make a problem understandable to yourself or to other people to whom you tell the story."

"Story?"

"Well, yes, to make it understandable, even to yourself, involves constructing a story. You make these people come alive in such a way that the precise reasons for the problem are illuminated so clearly that your recommendations are almost self-evident. But constructing a story like this requires that you direct your attention, and other people's, to certain things before others."

"You're losing me. This pulling together of information is like telling a story, right? And you need to direct attention to certain things before other things? Like what?"

"For example, would you first want to direct your attention to the question of whether counseling or removing David from the home is the more intrusive remedy? Or would you first prefer to know something about whom Andrea lived with, for example, if she comes from a family in which five older daughters had already been fondled by David?"

"Obviously, you'd want to know about her family first. It's important to know about the other five daughters to make a better decision about which remedy is more intrusive. Were there really five other daughters?"

"No, the five daughters are hypothetical."

"Your point, though, is that we need to figure out Andrea's story one step at a time, first things first, so we don't go off in our thinking on tangents—like debating about intrusiveness of a remedy before we know about five molested daughters."

"Yes. One step at a time. And each step in the story you construct constitutes an orientation or direction of your attention to particular information or to your own cognitive operations on that information."

"Like to the other five daughters. But what do you mean by cognitive operations?"

"Some of the steps I'm talking about serve to direct one's attention to certain kinds of conclusions, impressions, and other kinds of cognitive operations. And the entire series of orienting concepts pulls everything together."

"And this way of organizing your thinking occurs at the end point of the evaluation."

"Yes, at the end point, but ideally, as you get better at it, it can guide you from the very first moment of an interview."

"Like in organizing the written report?"

"That's right, or thinking out the case for yourself, or even in supervising someone else who is describing a case to you."

"So what are these orienting concepts, and how do you organize them?"

"They're not mysterious. You're well aware of them already. For example, what is the first—the very first—thing you would like to know about a case being presented to you? The conclusion? The history? What?"

"The presenting problem. That may sound simplistic, because the presenting problem isn't always the real problem that you end up working on, but it helps to orient you to the case. To orient you to what you need to do, like whom to interview first."

"Precisely. Who is complaining about what? Who is defining the problem? What is it you are being asked to do about it? There was a topic in Chapter 2, where I emphasized that you need to elicit from the D.S.S. worker the reason why he wants an evaluation."

"Right. Whether to address the question of if the fondling actually occurred. Or whether the fondling resulted in symptoms that should be treated in therapy. Or maybe whether to make a recommendation about if her father should be in the home or not. But Aaron, what if the problem, as it's presented, is so unclear or vague or so complicated that there is no clear focus?"

"Well, then, if it's possible and if it's desired by the presenter of the problem, maybe you can be helpful in articulating what the presenting problem should be, or what questions you think they should be asking, so that you can go about addressing those problems or answering those questions."

"That's right, you did talk about that already. So, what's next, then? Finding out more about when the problem first occurred and its duration and severity?"

"Perhaps, but I think you're getting ahead of yourself here. Don't you want to know first whom Andrea lives with? What her parents do for a living? How old they all are? Something about her neighborhood, how she gets along with her siblings, whether this is a chaotic and violent household, or whether it's a law-abiding, isolated family?"

"This is where you'd find out about the five other hypothetical daughters."

"Yes. Maybe you don't want to know all the details of all this right away, but you do need some broad demographic information, the broad brush strokes of the context in which Andrea's problem exists, the people and environment with whom she most frequently interacts. Your orientation can take on a slightly sharper focus when attending to these broad contextual features."

"Right. You do need to know that kind of thing first. It seems pretty superficial to want to know right away that it's a chaotic and violent household where neither parent holds down a job and all the kids are failing in school, but this kind of stuff helps you to rule out a whole bunch of other possible scenarios and focus on what is more likely to be relevant."

"Exactly, even though you need to recognize that such initial assumptions may be wrong."

"But Aaron, that almost sounds like a contradiction. Is it wise for us to make assumptions on the basis of these contextual features or not?"

"It's not really a contradiction. This orientation to the context in which she lives deploys your attention and energy to gaining a fuller understanding of what's unique to this particular case, so that as you proceed you're more likely to find out if an initial assumption was correct."

"Okay, then, what's the next step?"

"After that is when you consider the problem in more detail. You clarify it for yourself and understand its history."

"What? Like historical factors associated with it? Its onset? Its duration? Its frequency? Its severity? Those kinds of things?"

"Right. This further narrows your focus to the details of the case. I covered this in various sections throughout the book, for example in Chapter 4, when I talked about eliciting a description of the abuse."

"But what about all those cases where the issue is to determine whether the abuse occurred at all? And what if you're not sure it did occur?"

"In some of these cases, you may not get beyond this stage of an assessment, this clarification of the problem. The same thing happens in therapy when you can't achieve a mutual understanding with the client about what problems or goals you will work on together."

"So what do you do?"

"State that a lack of clarity exists about the problem. That perhaps one can go no further with the case. This can be done elegantly in the case of sexual abuse."

"You mean by looking at whether a statement is true or not?"

"Well, yes. To be more exact, by an analysis of the variables that help to discriminate between true and false statements. You may still be uncertain in the end but you will have elucidated your thinking for yourself or for others."

"Okay, but assuming that you think the abuse occurred, what's next?"

"To understand the problem in a multifaceted way, you will need to understand the larger history of the individual family in which the problem occurred."

"This is the history?"

"Yes, but not just any history. What you're after is history that is relevant to the problem."

"Then you mean just current history?"

"No, both current and past. Does the changing relationship between David and his wife over the years play some role in the fondling incident? Is there something about Andrea's early developmental history that is relevant now? You need to consider the broad routes that these people have traveled through life's stages and the specific details about the twists and turns in those routes that may have particular relevance to the presenting problem."

"But you don't really talk very much about how to take a history in this book. Is that because it isn't very important to you?"

"No. It's very important. How one goes about taking or examining someone's history depends on one's training and the theories one believes; these dictate the kinds of questions one will ask and what will be revealed. But this topic is addressed fully in other books, and I hope that there's no need to go into it here."

"But maybe there is a need to go into it. When you talk about history, are you talking about the facts or your conclusions about the facts?"

"There are no facts, as you call them. There are only conclusions, or perceptions of fact, whether these be yours or the client's. I suppose you can choose to write down everything the client says and consider that to be your history, but these are your client's conclusions, not the facts. I prefer to be more succinct and to summarize to myself what I think is the relevant history, and this is necessarily my own construction, my own assessment of what has been presented to me."

"How do you know when you've got enough history? I mean, you could go on forever, couldn't you?"

"You sure could, and many clinicians do. They assume that it will take many sessions to arrive at an adequate evaluation of the situation. As a consequence, they engage in interactions and activities with their clients which push them forward into a therapeutic direction. That is, they begin doing therapy before getting an overall look at the situation, only to realize later that they forgot to check out some important feature of the child's functioning, like how he gets along with peers."

"I guess I do that sometimes. It's hard not to."

"Of course it is. Once you establish more intense and ongoing interactions, it's hard to get the distance needed to ask the kinds of questions you would in an evaluation. To keep your evaluation from being contaminated by an ongoing relationship, you need to make a choice about when you will have enough information to figure out what to do about the problem."

"You're getting me confused. I thought that's what I asked already. How do you know when you've got enough?"

"When you've gathered enough information to formulate some conclusions about major areas of strength and dysfunction in the client and family."

"Like, what areas, specifically?"

"The ones you are already quite familiar with. All major spheres of life, a person's entire range of functioning. For example, how Andrea is doing with her peers, at school, with impulse control, and so on."

"Okay, I know what you mean, I do that in every evaluation, and you talked about it some in Chapter 3."

"Yes. These things are important because you need to know how her levels of functioning in any particular area interact with the presenting problem."

"Like we talked about earlier? If her peer relationships included a boyfriend who petted her, she'd react with more distress to the fondling than if she had no friends and was overclose with her father."

"Right. Some areas of functioning may play a role in causing the problem, some may be unrelated to the problem, and some may even be effects of the problem."

"But to know about an individual's entire range of functioning can take forever."

"Yeah, if you want to know every little detail about each one."

"So you don't need to know all the details?"

"No. You can check out lingering doubts later. During the evaluation you want an overall picture. And when a particular area is not problematic or not relevant to the problem, it often takes no more than a minute to check that out. And you can even be sloppy and omit looking into some areas, if you're willing to take a calculated risk that those areas aren't relevant."

"Okay, so after you've got an overall picture of strengths and weaknesses, what's next?"

"Next you figure out how important those are in relation to the problem. If Andrea has problems with peer relations, with parentification at home, with impulse control, with academic performance, and with everything else under the sun, do you try to help her solve every single problem?"

"No, I guess not, but it might be tempting to. Like before, I said that maybe the parentification should be addressed in treatment. But I guess you would want to consider it only if it related to the problem."

"That's right. In one case it might be related to the problem and in another case it might not be."

"So do you look at all these areas of dysfunction at the same time and check to see which ones are related to the problem?"

"That's right. All these areas of dysfunction twist into a unique perspective in relation to the particular problem. Once you've achieved this perspective, you might decide that there are many areas of dysfunction that you don't choose to address."

"For example?"

"Well, an autistic child might be having trouble getting to sleep at night. This causes some distress, but only a minimal degree. In other words, it's a mild problem and you may give him and his family some help in trying to solve the problem. But you don't necessarily have to try to solve all his other problems in life, such as his severe difficulties in relating to others, his poor academic performance, his communication difficulties, his impaired reality-testing, and so on."

"Why not? What if they relate to the problem?"

"Well, if they related, then you would try to focus on them in some way. But if they're unrelated, and if no one is asking for help in these areas, or if these dysfunctions are already being addressed in other ways, then it seems to me our focus is pretty clear."

"On the sleeping problem. And I guess Andrea would be another example like that, wouldn't she? The fondling was embarrassing for her and she got over it. So it was a mild problem, assuming it didn't cause significant dysfunction in major areas of her life."

"In order for it to be a mild problem, you would have to assume not only that the fondling had minimal effects, but also that the fondling itself wasn't the effect of major areas of dysfunction, for example, parentification, poor peer relations, and so on."

"Right, okay. And if it was this mild, there wouldn't be much of a problem to treat, especially if her father were sorry and you could count on him never to do this again."

"But what if D.S.S. removes her father from the home and this devastates her? She suffers in school, gets suicidal, and so on."

"I guess it doesn't sound like a mild problem anymore."

"No, it's been exacerbated by the solutions that were applied to remedy it, and now it may be quite severe, significantly affecting several areas of functioning. This is the perspective I am talking about. You have a number of areas of functioning to consider, and they kaleidoscopically shift into a particular set of priorities in each case, depending on how they relate to a particular problem."

"And this, then, helps you to figure out what to do about it."

"Yes. By helping you first to identify the factors that account for the problem."

"Is this another orienting concept in your construction of the story? Looking at the areas of dysfunction to find these factors?"

"Yes, and also looking at your clarification of the problem and your history. You're looking for factors that in some way explain or account for the problem. For example, a predisposing factor might be . . . "

" . . . the parentification of Andrea in her family."

"Right. And a precipitating factor . . . "

" . . . might be the fondling."

"And the father's removal from the home may be a factor that maintains or exacerbates the problem."

"But is it each factor by itself that is important? Like the fondling? That was a precipitating factor, but what if that same factor produced much more intense distress in another child with other strengths and weaknesses?"

"You're right. The effect of each factor on the child or family is just as important as the identification of the factor. The effect of the same factor might be different with different people."

"So you end up with a list of these factors and their effects. Does that adequately account for the problem?"

"To some extent. But the best understanding is achieved when you can formulate the way in which these factors actually combine with one another to account for the problem. It is in the combination or connections among the factors that a problem is illuminated in such a way that it provides direction for intervention."

"This is what you call the formulation?"

"That's right. It's the heart of the assessment. It's where you are heading from the beginning. And it's from the formulation that will emerge the precise interventions that will result in certain benefits to the child and family that address the presenting problem."

"What if it's a lousy formulation?"

"Then it will probably lead to a lousy intervention. But if it's adequate, then an identification of factors accounting for the problem, and how these combine with one another, can suggest precisely what needs to be done or what the child needs."

"Like, whether Andrea needs to develop better capacities for peer relationships, or whether this is unimportant because it's not sufficiently related to the problem."

"Yes, and more to the point, whether Andrea needs protection from fondling more than she needs contact with her father. Does she need to be deparentified at home? Or does the degree to which she is parentified fall within the broad limits of normal such that it would be intrusive and harmful for us to go knocking on her door to tell her she should be more of a child."

"So then we end up with a list of needs."

"Yes, the next orienting concept is a list of needs, of things that need to be done."

"Like to restore contact between Andrea and her father."

"Or to deparentify her."

"Or to improve her peer relations."

"Or to improve the spousal relationships between David and his wife."

"So your next step after that, your next orienting concept, is interventions?"

"Yes. The interventions that you can think of that will most aptly meet the needs. It is important to be precise about this. To say that needs will be met by weekly family therapy sessions says nothing at all. It is better to say what will be done specifically to meet the needs."

"What? Like saying that therapy will attempt to deparentify Andrea?"

"Exactly, and if possible, what behaviors you will prescribe and proscribe to bring that about."

"Okay, I got the idea. To meet her need for peer relationships, you'll teach her social skills. To meet her need for contact with her father, you'll advise the judge to send him home."

"Right. And it's useful here to keep in mind what your role is as a clinician in implementing these interventions. What is it that you are doing? In regard to the father's return home, you are advising or recommending. In the case of social skills, you are teaching."

"But what if teaching isn't the best way of going about it? Does this mean you have to start from scratch with your treatment plan?"

"Yes and no. Your interventions, if they are successful at meeting the needs, will have accomplished certain objectives or benefits, such as enabling the child to establish better relations with peers, or to feel affirmed and supported by her father, or to feel protected from the fondling, and so on. These objectives are implicit in the interventions you choose at any particular time to meet certain needs, and these objectives can be explicated to help you to determine how well your interventions are working."

"You mean like when the client doesn't understand the task or carries it out the wrong way, or the judge doesn't follow your recommendation."

"Right. You may need to modify your interventions in a more suitable way to accomplish the objectives. Teaching social skills may not be the best way to improve peer relationships. Perhaps systematic desensitization for social anxiety is better suited."

"So, are you saying that it's always necessary to articulate objectives? Are these behavioral objectives? That sounds like a requirement for an agency treatment plan rather than good clinical thinking."

"Objectives don't need to be articulated explicitly. Like I said, they are implicit in your identification of interventions to meet certain needs or, more exactly, they are implicit in the identification of needs. And you don't necessarily have to explicate them or even to think of them as behavioral or measurable objectives. They are simply the overall benefits or accomplishments that will accrue to the child or family as a result of intervention, which will enable them to accomplish the goal of eliminating or addressing the presenting problem."

"So the overall goal is to solve the problem."

"That depends. Is the goal to clarify the problem or to solve the problem? How many problems? Your goals will be different in every case. In one case it may be to improve peer relationships, in another it may be to improve Andrea's functioning with her entire family, in another it may be to protect her from harm, and in another it may be all of these."

"So the goals chosen will depend on the presenting problem and on who is defining it?"

"Right. Which brings us back to where we started. Is the problem the fondling? Or is it the distress caused by the father's removal from the home? Or both? Is the goal to eliminate the problem, diminish it, or to clarify whether indeed a problem exists?"

"What's next?"

"That's it, that's all."

"That's everything? That's how it's all pulled together?"

"Yes, except for how it's articulated. Is it an oral presentation? Is it just a thinking out loud to oneself? Is it a letter to the court? Or is it filling out an agency form for a treatment plan? The form it will take in its articulation depends on the particular needs at hand and on the capacity of the audience to digest the message."

"So in a letter to the court or to D.S.S., how much do you go into all of this? How extensive does it have to be? How long?"

"That will depend on the primary needs of the moment. It can be long or it can be short. But no matter how short it is, it can still reflect the comprehensive process of pulling it all together in the ways we've just discussed. Look at this example."

\* \* \* \* \*

Date: October 26, 1990

Honorable Joseph P. Peterson, Family Court Judge
County Courthouse
Troy, NY 12180

Re: Andrea Katz
Docket #: 727-Y-5511

Dear Judge Peterson:

I am writing in regard to the case involving Andrea Katz, age 13 (date of birth 3/16/77), who was referred to us by the court and by the Department of Social Services for evaluation and recommendation. The purpose of this evaluation, as I understand it from the D.S.S. worker, Scott Mason, is to determine whether Andrea was fondled by her father, whether symptoms exist that should be addressed with therapeutic treatment, whether the family will benefit from treatment, and whether contact (and what kind) should occur between Andrea and her father. To conduct this evaluation, I interviewed the D.S.S. worker, Andrea, her father, David Katz, age 35, and her mother Sharon Katz, age 33, in separate interviews on 10/26/90. In the paragraphs below I will summarize the highlights of the case and give my impressions and recommendations.

Andrea is a 13-year-old white female who lives in a lower middle-class neighborhood with hardworking parents and three younger siblings. The children are well behaved and all involved in extracurricular activities; father provides a good deal of parenting in the evenings, while mother is over-stressed with evening work. Father and Andrea are thrown together a good deal of the time in caring for the younger children.

Two months ago, while the two of them were watching T.V. after the younger children were in bed, Mr. Katz briefly fondled Andrea's breast; he admits to this now, though previously he had been denying it due to fear that he would never see his children again. At the time of the incident, he immediately apologized to Andrea and the incident did not occur again. They were both confused and embarrassed, but these feelings subsided in the next few days, and the overall trusting, warm relationship between them continued to predominate. However, the day following the incident, while Andrea was still preoccupied with her confusion, she articulated some of it to an acquaintance, who reported it to teachers. Eventually the case was hotlined and, in the process of investigation, Mr. Katz was asked to leave the home.

The fondling incident emerged in the context of Andrea's particular developmental history, the changing relationship of the spouses over time, and alterations in family roles and dynamics. Andrea was a quiet, overanxious child from infancy, to whom parents responded with overprotection; as a result, peer relationships were never adequately established, so that Andrea met her needs for affirmation primarily with her parents, and in recent years primarily with her father. The parents' relationship altered after the birth of their last child, with mother distancing from father in her preoccupation with the children, to which the father reacted with unexpressed jealousy, hurt, and anger. He focused his attentions instead on his oldest child, "daddy's little girl." Spousal distance and dissatisfaction increased after the youngest child was in school and mother returned to work to attempt to meet her own needs for career satisfaction. However, dissatisfaction with career, marriage, and family life resulted in depression, moodiness at home, and impatience with other family members. Father was the more available parent to the children, and he met his needs for affirmation in the companionship of his daughter rather than his wife, who he said could never "understand me as well as Andrea." No previous incidents of fondling or incest were acknowledged, father's sexual history reflects heterosexual orientations within normal limits rather than fixated or pedophilic orientations, and no history of incest or abuse is acknowledged by either mother or father in their childhoods.

The effects of the fondling had virtually disappeared within a week. However, ever since her father's removal from home, Andrea's condition has deteriorated. She feels responsible for the family disruption, doesn't understand the justification for father's absence, intensely misses her father's support, is extremely anxious, is declining markedly in school performance, and has been expressing suicidal ideation. Her mother is angry at Andrea for overreacting to father's removal from the home and is angry at her husband for jeopardizing the family's income and home. She wants her husband to return home and believes they can work out any problems they have in counseling. Father is fearful of losing his job as a consequence of frequent investigatory interviews and court appearances and of not making mortgage payments; he is intensely lonely, desperately wants to return to the home, and is willing to cooperate with directives for counseling.

The fondling incident can best be understood, I think, as a result of individual and family dynamics. Andrea's overanxious and shy temperament led to overprotection by her parents and a failure to develop capacities for peer relations, leaving her no network of support except within her family. She became overdependent on her father over the years as her mother became moodier and distanced more. As mother and father failed increasingly to meet one another's needs over the years, father became more dependent on Andrea for his need to feel special to someone. Her parentified role in providing him with affirmation, and helping him with the child care of the younger children blurred usual family roles to the point that he treated Andrea more like a loving companion than a daughter. It is quite understandable, then, that sexual feelings might emerge, and even be acted upon, in this context of blurred boundaries. When this did occur, Mr. Katz promptly inhibited himself from further acting out his needs in this way, recognized his error, and attempted to understand the sources of this error. Andrea, while initially embarrassed and confused, soon forgot about the incident. When D.S.S. learned of the incident, action was taken to protect the child, with good intentions and with a need to comply with legal constraints and procedures. However, the removal of Mr. Katz from the home has left Andrea with no support at all, made overt the covert conflictual relationship between her and her mother, brought about a serious deterioration in her overall functioning, disrupted the family, left it in disarray, and threatened its economic survival.

In view of this understanding of the situation, it is my opinion that Andrea needs to have contact with her father as soon as possible, that she needs support rather than conflict from her mother, that she needs to be deparentified in her functioning in the family, and that she needs skills and encouragement to develop sources of affirmation outside the family. Mother needs to directly address the source of her depression. Both parents need to address their dissatisfaction with their relationship and do so successfully enough that their own needs do not inappropriately impinge on Andrea or require her to meet those needs.

To address these diverse needs, I recommend that Mr. Katz be returned home as soon as possible, conditional on his and Mrs. Katz's cooperation and compliance with a D.S.S. service plan, which would include participation with a mental health treatment plan. These plans would be intended to ensure Andrea's safety from fondling or other inappropriate sexual behavior and to address and mitigate against the sources of such behavior. Therapy would probably be focused on improving the spousal relationship, altering the parenting and child roles in the family such that Andrea no longer played a parentified role in the family functioning, improving Andrea's relationship with her mother, establishing more appropriate boundaries between Andrea and her father, and helping Andrea to develop the skills she needs to establish a network of peer support.

I hope these observations and recommendations will be helpful in arriving at a disposition that is in the best interests of the child. Please call upon me if I can be of further assistance in this matter.

Respectfully,


Aaron Noah Hoorwitz, Ph.D.

cc: Scott Mason, Child Protective Service, Department of Social Services


* * * * *

"That example does help to bring it all together."

"Good, it served its purpose, then."

"But something bothers me about it."

"What?"

"It reads well, because you write a good narrative and tell a good story. But I'm not sure where all the sections are that we talked about — the presenting problem, the identification of factors accounting for the problem, the objectives, the . . . "

"You want me to show you. Here, I'll point to almost every section."

"But that's my point. *Almost* every section, not every section. It's hard to see clearly where each section is."

"That's because it's a narrative. I could have used headings. If I did, it would have helped you to see. But my main point was to show you how it can all be pulled together."

"You pull it together all right, but because it's a narrative you take a lot of liberties and do a briefer assessment. An assessment for treatment is more detailed and thorough. There's a lot missing in your letter. For example, there's nothing in there about impulse control, about whether developmental milestones were normal, and about a lot of other things. Did you ask about those things?"

"Yes, and I know the answers to those questions, but I don't think my audience is really interested. I don't think this particular audience, the judge, would understand the relevance of those particular features. So I included only those features that I thought would be clearly understood to relate to the problem."

"So there's really freedom here, in a letter to the court, that you don't have when you have to fill out an agency form for assessment and treatment planning. On agency forms you have to fill out things that may not be directly relevant to the problem and you have to go into a lot more detail about it. On an agency form, it's a lot harder to think clearly and to the point, the way you do in a narrative. I don't see you getting hung up on impulse control if impulse control is irrelevant."

"That's not true. You do get hung up on it, but you don't necessarily mention it."

"I don't get it."

"In a narrative you simply don't mention impulse control if it's irrelevant. But to decide if it's relevant you have had to consider it, and that means you have to ask questions to make a determination about it. You're still engaging in the same process as in any assessment for a treatment plan, you're still pulling it all together in the same way, but you're being selective in what you decide to impart about the whole thing."

"So you really have to think harder, and use your judgment, to decide what to include and what to exclude."

"Right, in the interests of telling a good story. But ask me about impulse control and I'll tell you all about it."

"Okay, but even though in some ways it's harder to write narrative, you have the liberty to pull it all together in your own way. If you had to write up an assessment and treatment plan on an agency form, I'm not sure you'd be able to pull it together at all. You might get in parts of it, but there might not be a way to include the most important parts, and there might even be an emphasis on the least important parts like goals and objectives. I don't see a thing about goals and objectives in your letter, yet the Office of Mental Health makes us write out objectives in meticulous detail in every treatment plan."

"The goals and objectives are implicit in my letter."

"But not explicit."

"Okay, your point is that pulling it all together the way we've talked about is possible in a narrative, but much less possible to do in a complete and succinct manner when utilizing an agency form."

"Right."

"I agree that some agency forms may be more difficult to use than others. But you would be attempting to accomplish the very same thing on an agency form for assessment and treatment planning as you would in my letter. I guess what we're talking about is how the process of pulling everything together can be done in different forms, different contexts, or for different audiences."

"But doesn't that make your thinking different?"

"Not at all. It's no different for evaluations for the court than it is for evaluations for treatment. You would still be organizing your thinking in the same way, pulling it together in the same way, and doing so just as thoroughly. It's all the same thing."

"That's hard to believe."

"You could write a cover letter that said something like this":

Dear Judge:

I'm recommending that Mr. Katz be allowed to return home on condition that he and his wife cooperate with treatment recommendations that are outlined on page such and such in the attached assessment. To summarize, the recommendations are as follows. For details and background, see attached.

"Then you would just fill out the agency form and send it along to court. Believe me, the thinking process involved is no different; it's only the context in which it occurs or the form that it takes that varies."

"I guess I'd have to see it to believe it. You'll have to show me."

"I will. Take a look at this form here."

**Table 3. Assessment and Treatment Plan**

---

**Client name:** Andrea Katz  **Age:** 13  **Date of birth:** 3/16/77  **Case #:** C-7718

**Responsible parent(s):** Sharon & David Katz

**Address:** 1357 Elm Street, Troy, N.Y. 12180  **Phone:** 270-3749

**Date of assessment:** 10/26/90  **Clinician:** Aaron Hoorwitz, Ph.D.

---

**Presenting problem**

Andrea is being brought to the clinic by her mother and father at the direction of D.S.S. as part of an abuse investigation. Her father is alleged to have fondled her breast on one occasion; he denies this. He is currently out of the home, but is participating in this evaluation. The reason for referral is to determine whether fondling occurred and, if so, determine its symptoms and effects on Andrea, make a determination of treatment needs and recommendations in regard to feasibility of family therapy and father's return to the home.

---

**Family constellation**

Andrea is the oldest child in an intact family. Father is David Katz, age 35, who works in a hardware store from 8 a.m. to 4 p.m. Monday thru Friday; mother is Sharon Katz, age 33, who works an evening and weekend shift in hospital's intensive care unit as an LPN. There are three younger children, Sarah, age 8, who does well in school and has no particular problems; Jonathan, age 7, who is learning disabled; and Joshua, age 6, who is doing fine in first grade.

---

**Describe overall features that help to provide an orientation to the family context**
*(Utilize only those cues below that are helpful)*

| | |
|---|---|
| *In-laws*<br>*Support network*<br>*Socioeconomic class*<br>*Neighborhood*<br>*How do family members get along with one another?* | Grandparents on both sides of the family live in another state, and there is very little outside support for the family. This is a hardworking couple, in a lower middle-class neighborhood. To their neighbors, family members appear to get along fairly well without violence, kids are involved in extracurricular activities, mother is overstressed with job and with learning disabled younger child, father is involved with the lives of the children and family. |

**Clarification and history of the problem**
*(Utilize only those cues below that are helpful)*

| | |
|---|---|
| *More than one problem?* | Andrea has been anxious, lonely, and suicidal for the past 2 months, due to father's removal from home by D.S.S., which in turn is due to his having fondled her, touching her on the breast over clothing on one occasion. He |
| *Onset?* | immediately apologized and has inhibited previous and subsequent urges to fondle. He and Andrea are overclose, due to her parentifica- |
| *Frequency?* | tion in the family. Effects of fondling consisted of mild embarrassment and initial preoccupation, leading to Andrea telling an acquaintance, |
| *Severity?* | who reported it to a teacher, leading to D.S.S. involvement and removal of father from home. Investigation and litigation are jeopardizing |
| *Duration?* | father's job and his capacity to make mortgage payments, further straining the marriage. Andrea blames herself for the family disruption, wishes she hadn't disclosed, and in- |
| *Changes in severity?* | tensely misses her father. She feels rejected by mother, who is impatient with Andrea's emotional reactivity in the past 2 months. |
| *Who wants what?* | All family members want reconciliation and will therefore cooperate with treatment. D.S.S. and Family Court seek validation of allegations and |
| *Who are the complainants?* | recommendations. |
| *Attempted solutions?* | Father attempts to inhibit urge to fondle, usually successfully. D.S.S. removed father from the home to protect child from abuse. |
| *Life events associated with the problem?* | See developmental history. |
| *Miscellaneous* | Father has been denying allegations, but admitted during this evaluation. His statement and Andrea's are congruent with one another; each are consistent, contain numerous confirmable statements, are redundant in detail, contain invariant positioning and sequencing of objects and events, and possess other qualities which render allegations credible. |

## Relevant developmental and/or medical history

*Check here (_____) if a medical condition is relevant to the presenting problem.*
*Check here (_____) if history is unremarkable or captured elsewhere in this document.*
*Cues below may stimulate ideas; they do not require responses.*

| | |
|---|---|
| *Pregnancy and birth* | Normal |
| *Postnatal adjustment* | Cuddly, attached easily, responded readily to feeding and sleeping routines. |
| *Early developmental milestones* | Reaching, sitting, standing, talking, walking and other milestones all within normal limits. Mom not threatened by child's independence at stage of rapprochement. Was noted at ages 3–4 that child was unusually anxious, shy, easily frightened. |
| *Illnesses or Accidents* | Usual childhood illnesses; no serious accidents. |
| *Significant life events* | Parents responded to constitutional shyness and anxiety with overprotection and sheltering. As a result, Andrea found it difficult to separate from mother in kindergarten. Continued to be shy, with no close friends, preferring to spend |
| *Stages of child's or family's development* | her time with parents. In latency stage (age 6–11), she became "daddy's little girl" as mom became preoccupied with younger children and dad reacted to mom's preoccupation with jealousy. After all the kids were in school, mom returned to work to achieve independence and to help family income, but this further polarized the spouses. Conflict between the couple was usually covert rather than overt, over failure to meet each other's needs. Mother's depression became chronic; she spent less time with dad and Andrea. Due to her evening shift, dad and Andrea took care of younger kids in evenings and did chores together, chatting with each other about their day. Each made the other feel special, being the only source of affirmation for the other. Mother's time at home was spent sleeping, in unpredictable displays of impatience with kids, and helping a learning disabled child with his homework. |

## Summary of Current Functioning of the Child

*Variables*                                 *Utilize space provided below to comment*

### Appearance:

*Strengths_____ No problems__X__ Minimal problems_____*
*Moderate problems_____ Severe problems_____*

### School or job performance:

*Strengths_____ No problems_____ Minimal problems_____*
*Moderate problems__X__ Severe problems_____*

### Peer relationships:

*Strengths_____ No problems_____ Minimal problems_____*
*Moderate problems__X__ Severe problems_____*

### Impulse control:

*Strengths__X__ No problems_____ Minimal problems_____*
*Moderate problems_____ Severe problems_____*

### Conscience and empathy:

*Strengths__X__ No problems_____ Minimal problems_____*
*Moderate problems_____ Severe problems_____*

### Avoidance of addictive substances:

*Strengths__X__ No problems_____ Minimal problems_____*
*Moderate problems_____ Severe problems_____*

### Avoidance of antisocial behaviors:

*Strengths__X__ No problems_____ Minimal problems_____*
*Moderate problems_____ Severe problems_____*

### Risk of suicide:

*Strengths_____ No problems_____ Minimal problems__X__*
*Moderate problems_____ Severe problems_____*

### Other significant mental status information:

Heightened anxiety, especially in last month. Confusion about resolving problems and increasing anger towards mother. Other than these, this is an intact child in regard to perception, intellectual capacities, orientation, and other variables relevant to mental status.

*Strengths_____ Minimal problems_____ Moderate problems__X__*
*Severe problems_____*

## Summary of Parental and Family Functioning

*Variables*          *Space provided below for comments*

**Food, clothing, and shelter:**

*Strengths_____ No problems_____ Minimal problems_X__*
*Moderate problems_____ Severe problems_____*

**Protection from abuse, neglect, and harm:**

*Strengths_____ No problems_____ Minimal problems_X__*
*Moderate problems_____ Severe problems_____*

**Guidance, supervision, and limit setting:**

*Strengths_____ No problems_X__ Minimal problems_____*
*Moderate problems_____ Severe problems_____*

**Nurturance and attachment:**

*Strengths_____ No problems_____ Minimal problems_X__*
*Moderate problems_____ Severe problems_____*

**Expectations matched to child's developmental limitations or unique needs:**

*Strengths_____ No problems_____ Minimal problems_____*
*Moderate problems_X__ Severe problems_____*

**Protection from family and spousal conflict:**

*Strengths_____ No problems_____ Minimal problems_____*
*Moderate problems_X__ Severe problems_____*

**Protection from disagreements about parenting:**

*Strengths_____ Minimal problems_____ Moderate problems_X__*
*Severe problems_____*

**Protection from parental instability or dysfunction:**

*Strengths_____ No problems_____ Minimal problems_X__*
*Moderate problems_____Severe problems_____*

**An enriching cultural and socioeconomic environment:**

*Strengths_____ No problems_X__ Minimal problems_____*
*Moderate problems_____ Severe problems_____*

**An environment free from drugs, alcohol, violence, and criminality:**

*Strengths_____ No problems_X__ Minimal problems_____*
*Moderate problems_____ Severe problems_____*

**Describe features of the child's or family's functioning which cannot be captured by the checklist summaries of functioning.** *Check here (_____) if this section is unnecessary. The cues below may stimulate ideas; they don't require responses.*

*Family's support network*

*Repetitive interactions, such as triangulation*

*Typical interactional postures*

*Complementary role relationships, e.g. pursuer/distancer, impulsive/obsessive*

*Alliances, conflicts*

*Boundaries, hierarchies*

*Map of family structure e.g.,* $\dfrac{M:C}{F}$

*Repetitive defenses and behaviors*

*Core conflicts*

*Quotes or behaviors that make individuals leap off the page*

*Interview behavior*

Spousal problem has something to do with complementary styles: Mrs. Katz is somewhat impulsive and extroverted; Mr. Katz is introverted and reflective. She was attracted to his stability, he to her spontaneity. Now she views him as a "stick-in-the-mud," while he views her as "hysterical and moody." She has always expected more expressions of affection and appreciation in the form of words, time with him, and flowers, candy, etc., and has not received these forms of affirmation because he affirms her by means of his earning capacity, the time he spends with the children and housekeeping chores, and his sexual interest in her. What he wants most is to feel valued by her, to feel "special," for her to think of him as effective, and to feel needed, but she has been so angry at him for so many years that she is unwilling to provide this affirmation.

## Prognosis Section

**Diagnosis:**

Axis I    309.28: Adjustment Disorder with Mixed Emotional Features
Axis II
Axis III
Axis IV
Axis V

---

**Seriousness of the *presenting* problem:** *(circle the number that is the focus of the treatment)*

10. **Dangerousness** or risk of hospitalization or placement
 9. **Serious** distress/disturbance causing **5 or more** areas of dysfunction in child's life
 ⑧. **Serious** distress/disturbance causing **3–5** areas of dysfunction
 7. **Serious** distress/disturbance causing **1–3** areas of dysfunction
 6. **Moderate** distress/disturbance causing **5 or more** areas of dysfunction
 5. **Moderate** distress/disturbance causing **3–5** areas of dysfunction
 4. **Moderate** distress/disturbance causing **1–3** areas of dysfunction
 3. **Minimal** distress/disturbance causing **5 or more** areas of dysfunction
 2. **Minimal** distress/disturbance causing **3–5** areas of dysfunction
 1. **Minimal** distress/disturbance causing **1–3** areas of dysfunction

| 1 | 2 | 3 | 4 | 5 | 6 | 7 | ⑧ | 9 | 10 |

**Scale of actual or estimated *responsivity to intervention***

***Please answer the following with numbers:  Yes = 2    Uncertain = 1 No = 0***

| | | | |
|---|---|---|---|
| Do the clients have the strengths or skills to benefit from treatment? | Yes 2 | Uncertain __ | No__ |
| Are the clients motivated to address the problem? | Yes __ | Uncertain 1 | No __ |
| Will the clients attend most scheduled appointments? | Yes 2 | Uncertain __ | No __ |
| Are the skills available in the clinic well matched to the problem? | Yes 2 | Uncertain __ | No __ |
| Can a viable therapeutic relationship be established? | Yes __ | Uncertain 1 | No __ |

Please total the above numbers in this space __8__ and circle this number on the above scale of *responsivity to intervention*.

**If helpful, please clarify your ratings below:**

Child's problem would be deemed minimal to moderate in regard to the molestation itself. D.S.S. protective measures have exacerbated the problem to the point that the child experiences severe distress.

## Formulation Section

| Factors predisposing, precipitating, maintaining, or otherwise accounting for the problem | Describe the specific effect of each factor on the child or the family |
|---|---|
| 1. Shy, anxious temperament may be a predisposing factor. | 1. Andrea developed an overclose relationship to father at the expense of establishing peer supports, which require more risk. |
| 2. Parents haven't been meeting each other's needs; mother is depressed, father needs to feel affirmed. | 2. Father seeks affirmation from Andrea, she steers clear of impatient mother, seeks to "understand" dad in ways mom can't. |
| 3. Father acted on sexual urge, fondled child, precipitating the present crisis. | 3. Confusion and embarrassment for both dad and Andrea; to resolve confusion, she talked about it to acquaintance, who reported it. |
| 4. Factors maintaining and exacerbating the problem are the state's solutions to the problem, litigation, removal from home. | 4. Dad's job and family home in jeopardy, family is disrupted and anxious, uncertainty about future and their relationships. |
| 5. Father's unavailability to Andrea, mother's exasperation with Andrea. | 5. Reduction in emotional support for Andrea and increased conflict between her and her mother. |

---

## Formulation (Describe how the *combination* of above factors account for the problem)

The parents' problems in meeting each other's needs, the mother's distancing, the father's seeking affirmation from Andrea, and Andrea's overdependence on the father are a combination of predisposing factors that resulted in a parentification of the child and a blurring of boundaries in the family. In this context of blurred boundaries and unmet needs for affirmation, a sexual urge on the part of the father was acted out to some extent, and then inhibited appropriately. This precipitated some mild confusion in Andrea, which, before it subsided, resulted in a disclosure. The resulting state intervention and investigatory process has neither protected Andrea nor remedied the predisposing and problematic family dynamics, but rather generated problems for Andrea and her family that traumatize her far more than the prior parentification of her role in the family or the embarrassment due to fondling.

**Identification of needs** *(i.e., needs of the child or what needs to be done, based on the factors identified above)*

1. Andrea needs protection from fondling and from abuse by the state; family needs to be reconciled; Andrea needs contact with her father.
2. Andrea needs support from mother rather than conflictual interactions.

3. Parents each have needs that can be met without involving child, i.e., father's need for affirmation, mother's depression and dissatisfaction with career.
4. Role expectations of Andrea in her family need to be altered; needs to be deparentified and treated as a child, not a spouse or a parent.
5. Andrea needs to feel less anxious in general and to have supports available outside her family.

**Interventions or tasks to meet needs** *(for each one, underline the word describing your method, i.e., teach, advise, advocate, etc.)*

1. Advised the court and D.S.S. that current remedial actions traumatize rather than protect the child; that dad return home with following intervention.
2. Educate mother about child's need for support; prescribe specific affirming activities, proscribe the rejecting behaviors and remarks.
3. Elicit from parents their decision to meet their own needs without involving Andrea, e.g., by following therapeutic directives and suggestions.
4. Give specific advice; prescribe and proscribe changes necessary in household routines and disciplinary practices.
5. Implement a behavioral plan for desensitization to anxiety-provoking situations and for teaching skills for peer relations.

## Objectives

*Underline each benefit to the child which is intended by each of your interventions, or write them in your own words in the space provided below*

### The child will:

1. be adequately nourished with food/shelter/clothing
2. be safe and secure from abuse and harm
3. compensate for deficits in stimulation, e.g., Head Start
4. follow directions when adequately limited and guided
5. feel affirmed/wanted when adequately attached and loved
6. be protected from overexposure to family conflict
7. be protected from overexposure to a parent's problem
8. be relieved from fullfilling unrealistic expectations or inappropriate roles
9. be relieved from painful emotions (anxiety, depression) when emotions and their sources are faced and explored
10. compensate for disabilities, e.g., with meds, tutoring
11. build skills for desired behavior, e.g., problem-solving skills, communication skills, coping skills
12. improve skills/capacities for peer relations
13. develop empathy, e.g., vicarious pain for pain of others
14. engage in desired behaviors, e.g., previously feared behavior, going to school, doing homework, chores
15. improve competence of performance at school or job
16. inhibit/be prohibited from suicidal behavior

## Goals for the presenting problem

*Which objectives will fulfill which goals? (Identify below, and write goals in your own words if necessary.)*

I. Improved school attendance or performance
a.) _____ b.) _____ c.) _____
d.) _____ e.) _____ f.) _____

II. Improved family relationships
a.) __2__ b.) __6__ c.) __8__
d.) __5__ e.) __7__ f.) _____

III. Improved relationships with others
a.) __9__ b.) _____ c.) _____
d.) __12__ e.) _____ f.) _____

IV. Control unacceptable behavior, i.e., antisocial, hyperactive, phobic, suicidal
a.) _____ b.) _____ c.) _____
d.) _____ e.) _____ f.) _____

V. Reduce painful emotions, i.e., anxiety, depression, anger, sadness, fear
a.) _____ b.) _____ c.) _____
d.) _____ e.) _____ f.) _____

VI.
a.) _____ b.) _____ c.) _____
d.) _____ e.) _____ f.) _____

VII.
a.) _____ b.) _____ c.) _____
d.) _____ e.) _____ f.) _____

VIII.
a.) _____ b.) _____ c.) _____
d.) _____ e.) _____ f.) _____

17. *inhibit/be prohibited from oppo-*
    *sitional, aggressive, antisocial,*
    *phobic, or other unacceptable*
    *behavior*
18. *change internal messages*
    *about self or others, e.g., ex-*
    *change fantasy for reality, im-*
    *prove self-esteem*
19. *better tolerate stressful situa-*
    *tions that won't change*
20. *receive additional evaluation of*
    *treatment needs*
21. _____
22. _____
23. _____

**Client and collateral agreements with plan**

**The role of other agencies in this plan** *(specify the expectations or agree-*
*ments you have obtained about what individuals from other agencies will do to*
*help with this plan, e.g., D.S.S., probation, courts, schools, etc. Check here*
*(\_\_\_\_\_) if this section is not applicable and explain why.*

1. Family Court Judge is asked to suspend litigation on condition that family
   complies with this plan.
2. D.S.S. agreed to monitor family's compliance with this and their own service plan, and to permit father's contact with daughter and with family according to therapist's discretion, if family complies with plan.
3. Samaritan Hospital outpatient mental health will treat Mrs. Katz's depression individually.
4. Our own agency will provide marital and family therapy and individual therapy for child.

**Which clients or complainants are in agreement with this plan?** Mr. and
Mrs. Katz are both in agreement with all features of this plan.

**Which clients disagree? Please explain why:** Andrea doesn't see the need
for desensitization or building social skills or altering routines at home but will
comply with directives so father will be returned to the home.

**Criteria for determination of progress and discharge planning**

**Progress towards goal (check here __x__ )   Competion of goal (check here _____) will be determined by:**

__x__ **indications of satisfaction from the complainant**

Mother and father each state that their needs are met by the other, or in other ways, that are tolerable enough for a satisfying and ongoing relationship with one another. Mother states that she enjoys spending time with Andrea, and that Andrea doesn't exasperate her enough to cause her to distance.

__x__ **prescribed degree of achievement is satisfied** *(e.g., child gets all B's in school; specify the criteria and levels).*

Andrea spends significant portions of her time with peers, e.g., at least one afternoon per week, or on phone in evenings instead of keeping dad company; mother's disciplining is no longer undermined by father; child no longer makes suicidal statements; parents are observed to engage in satisfying activities together.

__x__ **therapist's judgment that objectives or goals have been accomplished** *(elaborate if necessary).*

Father-daughter interaction is affirming to both but judged by therapist to be age-appropriate for child.

**Estimated duration of treatment**

__ < 3 mo.   __ < 6 mo.   _x_ < 1 yr.   __ > 1 yr.   __ can't be estimated because:

**This assessment and/or treatment plan constitutes the:**

_x_ **intake assessment**
__ **emergency assessment**
__ **initial assessment**
__ **initial treatment plan** *(to be completed within 30 days or 3 appointments)*
_x_ **comprehensive treatment plan** *(to be completed within 90 days or 11 appointments)*

**Messages to clinician treating the case if other than the clinician completing this assessment/treatment plan:** My own role on this case was to provide an evaluation and recommendation to D.S.S. and to the courts and to facilitate treatment if that was advisable or feasible. The clinician picking up this case has the option of doing a fresh evaluation and renegotiating with the court and D.S.S. or of utilizing the present assessment and treatment plan. If the second option is chosen, the clinician needs to review with the family members the interventions already provided, determine whether they have followed directives and suggestions, and revise interventions and tasks that are found to be ill-suited to meet objectives and goals. A. Hoorwitz, 10/26/90

**Revisions to plan at treatment team's review of plan:** This assessment and treatment plan will be used by the assigned clinician, Francis Tompkins. Modifications to the plan at our team's review of this case include the following:
1.) Determine whether Mr. Katz can play more of a role with the younger boy's learning disability, so that it doesn't all fall to the mother.
2.) Modify the behavior plan, with assertiveness training, which I am more familiar with; I am less familiar with desensitization techniques.
3.) Have Mr. Katz more thoroughly evaluated in regard to his urge to fondle, understand better what this is all about, especially if it turns out to be pedophilic in nature, and monitor it carefully.

**Review date:** 11/2/90

**When will case be reviewed next?** in 3 months: 2/2/91

**List other clinicians and individuals who helped to develop the formulation and treatment plan or were present at team review**

**Signatures** Francis Tompkins, M.S.W.
**primary clinician**

Lorraine Sanders, A.E.S.W.
**team leader**

William Murphy, M.D.
**psychiatrist**

Williams, Cohen, Hayes, Valente

## Concluding Remarks

"I can see what you mean."

"About what?"

"About pulling it all together. It's all the same, like you said."

"You mean you see the same thinking in this and in the letter?"

"Right. Like you said, the form it takes is different, but it's the same organization of thinking. I notice that you went into a lot more detail about treatment than you did in your letter to the court, with all the goals, objectives, specific interventions, and so on."

"Well yes, that's part of the point I'm making here. The context is different. The audience is different. A judge doesn't need to know all the treatment ideas in detail, but a clinician who has to treat the case might benefit from my thinking about it."

"I agree. It looks very helpful. Especially where you identify the objectives of treatment."

"The form itself was useful in helping to identify the relevant objectives."

"I could see that. All you have to do is underline the ones that your interventions are intended to accomplish. Writing goals and objectives of treatment is pretty much of a hassle in most forms I've used. It keeps me from thinking clearly about the case."

"I think maybe that's because most forms usually ask you to start with the goal in mind, then try to come up with objectives, and then methods and interventions. That sequence implicitly assumes that the flow of thinking should go from goals to objectives to methods. But that direction doesn't reflect the way a good teacher teaches or a good therapist practices therapy."

"That's it. That's what's different about this new form of yours. It reverses the flow. I'm not sure why, but somehow this reverse flow seems more natural: to flow from interventions to objectives to goals."

"Partly because it's difficult to identify a goal and then to articulate in advance all the objectives you need to accomplish to meet that goal. Two people may present with the same problem and have the same goal, for example to improve their academic performance. But the reasons for their problems are different. So you can't just come up with a set of objectives based on the goal."

"I see. The objectives will be different depending on the particular reasons for the particular problem."

"Right. The objectives flow from the idiosyncrasies of the problem, not from the goals. It's easier to say what you will try to do to address the reasons you've identified for the problem's existence than to predict in advance exactly what the objectives are to reach the goal."

"But that's what we're usually asked to do."

"And you can do it, but it's easier for your mind to do it in retrospect, when reflecting on what you already decided to do to intervene. It is at that later point, that point of psychological distance, that you can see most clearly what benefit will be accomplished if your interventions are successful."

"I think I see. You're saying it's easier for our minds to think of objectives when looking back, rather than in advance."

"Yes, the exact and appropriate objectives can best be identified on reflection or in retrospect. A good teacher has a broad idea of what needs to be done, but will be paralyzed and stalled forever if you force him to write out in detail all the possible objectives he needs to accomplish to reach his goal. Besides, you can't predict exactly what needs to be accomplished before reaching the goal. Sometimes you accomplish things you didn't even predict."

"That's right. Some of my best therapy occurs that way. Suddenly something occurs in a session and you seize the moment and capitalize on it. You know what needs to be done, but you can't formulate it as an objective in advance."

"Exactly."

"It seems to me it might be worth throwing out this idea of coming up with objectives. Seems like an empty exercise."

"It can be. You don't really need them. But as a concept they can have merit. After all, objectives or benefits to the client are implicit in everything we do."

"But haven't you just said that as a clinician in the field who has to make decisions from moment to moment, from session to session, and in the heat of the moment, it's easier to simply make a list of what needs to be done or of interventions to meet those needs?"

"Yes, but it is useful also to articulate in retrospect exactly what those interventions will accomplish if successful."

"Why? Why not just keep a running list of interventions or tasks or needs?"

"Because interventions are likely to change more rapidly than your objectives. When clients don't follow through with a particular intervention you can then use those objectives, which have a greater degree of permanence than your interventions, to review the efficacy of your interventions and to modify or revise them. When you review progress in therapy, whether it's a day after formulating your interventions or a month later, which are likely to remain the same? The specific interventions? Or the benefits intended by therapy?"

"The overall benefits, I guess. Interventions can change from week to week."

"That's right. Or from moment to moment during a session."

"So it's more natural to think of interventions first, of what needs to be done. Needs and interventions are more apparent to our humble cognitive capacities than are objectives."

"Right. Objectives are more apparent in retrospect or when one has some distance. Figuring out what to do is more natural in the field of action. But each is implicit in one another and each flows from the other, whether you are in action or reflecting on your action."

"So this form that you just used conforms in the way that it deals with objectives and interventions, to your way of organizing an assessment. It was easier for you to use than some other form you might get stuck with."

"Yes, it was. It conforms to good thinking; it even facilitates it. But that's why I used this form for illustration, rather than an inferior form, which would have required a lot of twists of thinking and writing to illustrate my thinking. My point was only to illustrate to you how a case can get pulled together in a similar way even in diverse contexts: in oral presentations, in a letter to the court, or in agency paperwork. My implicit point to you is to resist the temptation to be distracted by the surrounding context, by the task demands."

"But you just said you have to keep your audience in mind."

"Yes, by all means respond appropriately to the task demands of the peculiar context, but keep your thinking pure. The only thing that varies with the context is what you select to say or not to say, what you choose to emphasize or to leave out."

"But the way you think it out is the same."

"That's right."

"Okay, I think I understand that well enough. Can I bring up something else?"

"Sure."

"One of the objectives you identified was that the child be protected from abuse by the state. And you said the same kind of thing in your letter, but not quite as clearly. This brings us back to the question I had at the beginning: How do you decide in a specific case whether the particular intervention you have in mind is more harmful than the harm it's intended to remedy?"

"You mean Mr. Katz's removal from the home?"

"Yes, or the recommendation of family therapy and individual therapy? All of these remedies can be intrusive or harmful, and they also are intended to provide certain remedies for harm. How do you decide which to use in each case? Do you weigh those kinds of decisions when deciding your objectives?"

"No. Those kinds of decisions emerge from the formulation. The formulation is the heart of it all. It's where you're heading from the beginning, and it's from there that your recommendations emerge. It's clear in the formulation of Andrea's problem that the removal of Mr. Katz from the home is harmful, isn't it?"

"Yes, and probably unnecessary too."

"That's right. But isn't it equally clear that treatment is necessary?"

"But, Aaron, isn't it potentially intrusive and harmful as well?"

"Yes, but isn't it clear that the degree of harm it might cause is minimal when weighed against the harm that could be caused by avoiding treatment? The reasons that led to the problem, the parentification and the spousal conflict, might easily lead to further fondling, and these reasons can be successfully addressed in therapy."

"But you said earlier that parentification of a child might fall within the broad limits of normal, and that in some cases it would be presumptuous of us to go knocking on doors and telling people they should be different."

"That's right, but in this case the parentification is directly related to the problem. Was that unclear in the formulation?"

"No, it was crystal clear. And even if the fondling didn't occur again, I guess it was clear that the parentification and blurring of boundaries could cause serious problems for Andrea in the long run."

"Right. That's why the remedy of therapy was necessary but removal was not."

"But in another case, therapy might have been intrusive and harmful?"

"Yes, and that would have been clear from the formulation. Spousal problems, shyness with friends, and parentification might all exist, but if they are unrelated to the problem and if no one is complaining, then these factors might not be identified as necessary to address in any way."

"Okay, I grant that your formulation leads to an exact and appropriate recommendation in this case: in other words, let Mr. Katz come home but give them all therapy. But what if Mr. and Mrs. Katz had been unwilling to address their spousal problems and the parentification of Andrea in therapy?"

"Then removal of Mr. Katz from the home might have had to be seriously considered. The emphasis in the formulation would have had to be different. It would have focused on weighing the risks to Andrea of losing her father against the risks of leaving him at home with the situation unchanged."

"If he came home, the fondling might recur or Andrea's development might continue to be distorted by the parentification. But if he doesn't come home, then her anxiety would increase and perhaps she'd get more suicidal. Which would you decide?"

"In that event, perhaps it would be necessary to address her anxiety and loss in a different way than by bringing father home. I'm not sure what I'd decide because the situation would be different. Mr. and Mrs. Katz would be presenting a different picture than they do now and the problem wouldn't be the same as the one depicted here. But I assure you, the formulation would reflect those differences such that it would lead to a different set of needs and interventions and objectives than the formulation you see before you."

"Would the formulation look the same in the agency form and in the letter to the court and in an oral presentation at a conference?"

"Yes, pretty much the same, but very different from the formulation in the examples here."

"Well, I'm glad you gave two examples of the same thing. It helps me to see the similarity of thinking."

"That was the point."

"But it's hard sometimes to see the similarities because I get hung up on the differences in each example."

"But that's the point, too."

"I guess I know that, but could you do me a favor?"

"What?"

"Can you make me a list to help me remember all those orienting concepts that pull it all together?"

"Lists are kind of boring. It's all there in everything we've talked about."

"But I could get hung up on some heading in this last form that's not really one of the essential parts of a complete assessment. I might mistakenly get tied to some concrete feature of the particular context, to the form itself, when in fact that feature may be entirely unnecessary. A list would help me to abstract the distinguishing features from their distracting contexts."

"Okay, I'll give you a list. I hope it helps."

1. Statement of the presenting problem
2. Family constellation and context in which the problem exists
3. Clarification and history of the problem
4. Developmental and family history that is relevant to the problem
5. Assessment of overall functioning: areas of strength and dysfunction
6. Prioritization of dysfunctions with respect to the problem, to achieve perspective on the seriousness of the problem and the focus of treatment

7. Identification of factors accounting for the problem, selected from the history, from clarification of the problem, and from areas of dysfunction
8. Specific effects of each factor
9. Formulation of how these factors combine to account for the problem
10. Identification of needs, based on the formulation
11. Interventions, methods, and services that will meet the needs
12. Benefits or objectives intended by the interventions
13. Goals arrived at by the accomplishment of the objectives
14. Resolution of the problem intended by the goals

# CHAPTER 12

# What's Missing in This Picture: Offering Recommendations with Incomplete Data

"After that last chapter, I feel filled up. It'll take awhile to digest, so I might have more questions later. But something did bother me. The case of Andrea was pretty complete, wasn't it? You had all the information you could possibly need to formulate conclusions."

"Why? Do you think I missed something? I thought it was pretty complete."

"Well, that's my point, I guess. It was almost too complete. Is that typical? Do you always get all the facts you need? Or is crucial information sometimes missing?"

"It's often missing."

"Well, what do you do about it?"

"If it's possible or convenient to get the missing information, then by all means get it. But it's not always feasible."

"Does this happen a lot, or just occasionally?"

"More frequently than you'd imagine, I'm afraid."

"Then why didn't you say so before? Why did you spend so much time in the last chapter on a case where you had all the information you needed?"

"Because if you know what to do in an ideal situation, you'll have a better idea how to approach all those situations that are less than ideal, where something crucial is missing. In fact, it will enable you to identify what it is that's missing."

"Well, if these less than ideal situations are so common, don't you think you should explain how you go about figuring them out?"

"But you don't necessarily figure them out. Your problem is that you're missing something that prevents you from figuring them out, from formulating final conclusions. The problem before you is to try to crystalize what needs to be done next even though you can formulate no final conclusions."

"Well, how do you go about that?"

"The first thing you have to do is figure out what's missing in each case. Then you figure out what the advantage would be in having what's missing. You also need to figure out if there's any disadvantage in pursuing what's missing and whether doing so is reasonable and within your limits of expertise. And then you can utilize objectives to weigh the potential harm against the potential benefit of applying remedies that . . ."

"Wait, hold on for a minute. You're going too fast and you're getting too abstract on me. Could you give me a concrete example of what you're talking about?"

"Okay. A case I worked on yesterday is a good example. A teacher reported that one of her students told her that while her father was wrestling with her and tickling her, he touched her vagina, and digitally penetrated her. D.S.S. workers took an affidavit from the teacher and were prepared to go to court with it, but only if a mental health evaluation were to support the allegations. The teacher wasn't there for the evaluation because she was busy teaching and didn't want to be involved any further. In the evaluation, Teresa and her father both denied the allegations."

"Do you think Teresa was lying?"

"No, she explained in a very believable way that the teacher misunderstood her and put words in her mouth."

"Why was she so believable?"

"Teresa's statements were consistent and seemed embedded in a larger realistic context, she suffered no ill effects of alleged abuse, and the background didn't conform to scenarios typical of abuse. The only indication of abuse consisted of the teacher's statement, and she was not available for the evaluation, nor did she wish to be."

"So what did you do? How could you formulate any conclusions?"

"It wasn't possible for me to account for the discrepancy between the teacher's statement and the other statements available to me, so I couldn't formulate any final conclusions. In the absence of the teacher's statement, my tentative conclusion would be that there was no convincing indication of abuse."

"But what if the teacher were present?"

"Then it's possible, if the teacher were present, that my conclusion would be different."

"So what do you say to D.S.S. or to the court?"

"Exactly what I just said to you—and, moreover, that to pursue the question of abuse any further, the teacher would need to be examined in order to subject her statement to the same kinds of scrutiny applied to the statements by the alleged offender and the alleged victim. While this is an incomplete evaluation, my conclusions are potentially useful because they outline some options."

"To whom?"

"To the teacher, to D.S.S., or to the court. One option is to drop any further investigation. Another option is to pursue the matter. This option is available if the teacher feels strongly enough about it to subject herself to an evaluation, or if D.S.S. feels strongly enough about it to get the court to force her to do so. What is important here is to be clear about what is missing and to be clear with others about it."

"What's missing is the teacher."

"That's right. The person who is making the statement of the presenting problem. The complainant."

"Interesting that you put it that way, as if it's an assessment of a treatment case where the complainant never showed up. That's an important piece of a case to be missing. What other kinds of things are sometimes missing?"

"In a lot of other cases what's missing is exact knowledge of the extent of the abuse. You know that sexual abuse occurred, but you don't know how extensive it was, whether it was an isolated incident and mild in its effects or whether it was more chronic and traumatic for the child."

"But if you don't know the extent of the abuse, can you really formulate any recommendations?"

"Sometimes you can. Consider the case of Jane, a 12-year-old who alleged that her father had fondled her vaginal area numerous times in a period of a year, and that on many of these occasions he had penetrated her vagina with his finger. Also, she said that he had frequently forced her to put his penis in her mouth."

"What's unclear about that?"

"Well, you see, her father didn't deny abusing her, but he denied forcing her to engage in fellatio and fondling her vaginal area numerous times. He only admitted to fondling her breast, and only on three occasions. In regard to touching her vaginal area, he said he may have done that once, sort of by accident, but that she had pants on so that there couldn't have been any digital penetration. By the way, he said he was drunk on each occasion."

"Maybe he blacked out on the other occasions. And what did the medical exam show about penetration?"

"Maybe he blacked out and maybe he didn't. It was hard to tell. And the medical examination was inconclusive. But you're already getting hung up on whether he did it, and exactly what was it that he did. Aren't you interested at all in why he did what he alleges he did? In this case, the man has some awareness of his motivation."

"Okay, why did he say he did it?"

"He said he did it because when he's drunk, he gets jealous and lonely, because of his wife's intense preoccupation with her ex-husband. She not only is intensely angry at her ex-husband, but also sometimes openly flirts with her ex, and has even had discussions about reconciling with him, which this offender has overheard on the phone. He said the kids have also had trouble accepting discipline from him as a father figure, partly because his wife never provided any discipline, and partly because his wife has given mixed messages about this, sometimes insisting that the kids call him daddy and sometimes undermining his excessive disciplinary measures."

"So it's pretty complicated. You have a lot of dynamics here. Blending and stepparenting problems, spousal problems that predispose to abuse, etc."

"Exactly. And now, at the point of evaluation, the stepfather isn't sure he wants to come back into the home because he doesn't want to subject himself to further accusations. He's trying to cop a plea to a lesser charge so that he can do probation instead of some time. The mother is pressuring Jane to minimize the allegations because she wants the stepfather back."

"What's Jane want?"

"Jane originally wanted the stepfather out of the house because she resented his replacement of her own father. But now Jane fears her mother's anger and isn't sure what she wants anymore. Her statement is an undecipherable mixture of true and false recantations."

"So that's why you don't want to focus your energy on the question of what really happened. It can't be figured out. It's a waste of time."

"Yet, that's what everyone wants to know. Everyone is alarmed at the prospect of this guy making this little girl put his penis in her mouth. The D.S.S. workers and the court appear to be preoccupied with the question of what exactly occurred. In other words, how extensive was the abuse, and is it likely to occur again?"

"But with this kind of situation, everyone's lying, aren't they?"

"They all have good reason to, don't they?"

"Yes, they each have their own hidden agendas."

"Not so hidden, really. The stepfather has a clear enough agenda, to not do any time in jail, so he's probably minimizing what he did and won't budge. The mother's agenda is to get him back home, so she's probably distorting information too. And Jane is all mixed up, so she has mixed agendas. That's why her statement is a mixture of lies and half-truths."

"Even though it's clear she was abused in some way or other. God, what a mess."

"It is pretty much of a mess and it's probably not possible to say how extensive the abuse was with any degree of confidence."

"So what can you say?"

"You can say clearly that it's not clear what happened."

"But the reasons for its happening are fairly clear."

"Exactly my point. And this is what you need to articulate loud and clear. The formulation. The factors that led to the sexual abuse."

"What? You mean the stepparenting problems and family dynamics?"

"Yes, because from the formulation will emerge fairly specific treatment needs, as well as specific recommendations. These suggestions can be followed, even in the absence of a determination of what exactly happened, which may never be known."

"But won't the court be reluctant to allow contact between the offender and his family if they're not sure how extensive the abuse was? Won't they want a clearer determination of the risk of further abuse?"

"They want it, but it's not likely that it will be possible to obtain it, not when lies are flying fast and furious all over the place. But the court can get the same result by checking out how treatment proceeds. The process of determining whether the family members can respond positively to treatment gives them all a chance to show their true colors. A high-risk situation will become obvious and can be brought right back to court."

"So will treatment focus on the question of what happened? How extensive the abuse was?"

"No. That would be a terrible mistake. There would be no advantage in perseverating on that question. It just buys in to the panic and alarm everyone else is experiencing about the possibility of a high-risk situation. If the treatment focuses on the question of what actually happened, which the evaluation couldn't answer, then treatment will never get off the ground. It might as well not be started."

"So what are you saying? What should the focus be?"

"At this point, treatment needs to focus on helping the family members to function more effectively as a family, and if they can't succeed, you can go back to the court with that information. If they do succeed in resolving their problems, maybe later you'll find out what actually happened, but I'm not sure it will be all that relevant at that point."

"It might be relevant to Jane."

"Sorry. You're right. I'm overlooking that. The degree to which she was abused is extremely relevant to her own future, to her individual treatment, to her own prognosis. And maybe, if treatment is successful, you can find out more about this later. But my point was . . . "

"I see your point. You can say what needs to be done next without actually knowing whatever happened in the first place. I guess that's because your formulation helps you out there. But what happens if it's the formulation that's missing? Can you ever make recommendations when the formulation is missing?"

"Sometimes. There was a case recently that really frustrated me because the parents couldn't give me enough information about their marriage or their family life for me to figure out why the abuse had occurred."

"Were they trying to cover up?"

"No, they were being as open as they could. But due to a culturally impoverished background, they were unreflective and uninsightful people who didn't have any idea what factors pushed and pulled them through life. The abuse was mild, the father vowed never to touch his daughter Sarah again, and Sarah loved him and wanted him home. D.S.S. was monitoring the case very closely and was willing to do so indefinitely if I thought it would be okay for the father to go home. They just wanted the okay from me."

"What did you do?"

"Well, at first, I kept asking the father the same questions over and over again. What was going on in your head when you touched Sarah? What was going on in your marriage?"

"And what would he say?"

"He would keep saying he didn't remember. And that it wouldn't happen again."

"What did you say to that?"

"That it was all very well for him to say it wouldn't happen again, but it would help a lot more if he could give me some more information, because I needed to understand why it happened so I could be sure it wouldn't happen again. And he would say back to me, 'It won't happen again.' And I would say, 'But I need to know what to recommend so that the reasons for its happening aren't there anymore.' And he would say, 'It won't happen again.'"

"You were just beating your head against a wall."

"Yup. And I kept on doing it until I was satisfied that I wasn't going to find out anything more, no matter what tack I might take."

"Were they willing to engage in therapy?"

"They were hungry for it. They would jump through hoops if you asked them. All they wanted was to be together as a family again. They were willing to live for the rest of their lives with unannounced home visits by D.S.S. They were willing to engage in family therapy and group therapy and individual therapy and parenting classes and AA meetings and Alanon meetings and ACOA meetings and any other kind of therapy you could think of."

"For all the good it would do them. I doubt many therapists would keep them for long."

"Who knows? They might benefit from direct tasks and from hearing about others' experiences."

"So did you recommend something?"

"Yes, I did. Since the child seemed safe enough, with the D.S.S. monitoring, I recommended that the father be returned home."

"Even though you didn't figure out the reasons why the abuse had occurred? Or what needed to be done to address those reasons? So you'd have a basis to believe it wouldn't recur?"

"It would have been reassuring to have reasons to believe it would not occur again, but presumptuous to insist on those reasons as a condition for the father's return home. Maybe sufficient reasons existed, which I just wasn't very successful at uncovering. In other words, maybe it's more my fault than theirs."

"Do you feel like you've helped out in cases like this? That you've accomplished something?"

"Sure. Sometimes you accomplish something just by giving some closure or some direction for further action. Or even by helping others to think out a case, even if you didn't really discover anything new. Usually things are kind of in limbo and fraught with uncertainty. Sometimes you figure out hardly anything at all and yet you provide a useful service by explaining what you haven't figured out."

"Like what?"

"Like, let's see, like maybe in the case of a child by the name of Patricia, a very smart and verbal 13-year-old. Patricia first alleged that her father fondled her mildly on two occasions, brushing against her in a way that stimulated her. Then she recanted when she realized the extent to which her family life was disrupted by the investigation."

"But you could tell it was a false recantation?"

"Yes and no. While her recantation contained inconsistencies that suggested a false statement, she was very bright and covered herself pretty well with an intricate web of supporting statements. And she was so adamant in her denial that there would have been very little to go on in court."

"Wasn't there any other evidence?"

"No. An adjudication of abuse would have depended almost solely on my hints and suspicions. And keep in mind that I could have been wrong. I didn't think my hints and suspicions were solid enough to outweigh the detrimental effects of the state's intrusion into Patricia's life. And I had to make my lack of confidence very clear to the court and to D.S.S., and this very clarification resulted in the case being dropped."

"But what about the poor child? Did you really think you were wrong?"

"No. But even though I suspected that Patricia might have been molested, I doubted it had been very serious. I also explained that I believed Patricia was making her own very deliberate decision to tolerate any negative effects of the molestation rather than the more intense negative effects of state intrusion into her life."

"What did you think of her decision?"

"I thought it was an informed decision, and even a good judgment on her part."

"You didn't say that to D.S.S., did you?"

"Yes, I did. I wanted to point out that an option that was possible at this point was to pursue the investigation further, but that to exercise this option would probably harm the child and the family. In my opinion, the preferable option was to drop the matter and hope that the father would be put on notice and subsequently watch his behavior more closely."

"What if the child was affected by the molestation? What if she needed to talk about it with someone?"

"That's the unfortunate part of the whole thing. Patricia wouldn't really feel free to discuss any of it with a counselor because she knew that a counselor would be mandated to report it. I even pointed this out to her and commiserated with her and tried to advise her on ways to handle this problem."

"What did she say?"

"Not much. She had such a strong need to deny the molestation. So my discussion with her was more of a monologue than an exchange of ideas."

"Interesting case. But I've lost track. What was missing in this one?"

"Practically everything, except for a few hints and suspicions. But even so, I felt that there was a kind of closure brought to it."

"I can see that. I see that in all the cases you've talked about. In each of the cases, something important was missing: a formulation, a clarification of the problem, a statement of the presenting problem, and so on. But you went ahead and somehow found a way to make recommendations."

"Not final recommendations. Not confident ones. Perhaps tentative conclusions and cautious suggestions for some reasonable courses of action."

"Yes, that's what I mean. But how do you go about it? Can you articulate how these courses of action are derived? By what principles?"

"Yes, by crystallizing the problem that's laid before you and figuring out what needs to be done."

"Kind of like a formulation."

"Exactly, but let's not call it that. It'll only confuse matters. But in each of these cases, you can see that the horns of each dilemma are clearly outlined, or crystallized in such a way that possible courses of action suggest themselves."

"But how do you go about organizing or outlining the dilemmas so that those actions suggest themselves?"

"By looking at the ultimate benefits to the child that are relevant in each case."

"Benefits?"

"Or objectives."

"Objectives again?"

"Yes, like making sure the chid is safe from abuse."

"Or making sure the child remains safe from abuse by the state?"

"Yes. And other objectives may be relevant, too. For example, protecting the child from overexposure to spousal conflict."

"Or from disagreements about parenting. Or from being used in inappropriate family roles to meet parents' needs."

"Yes. Various objectives may leap out as relevant to the particular case even in the absence of certain crucial information. You then need to look at the ways you might accomplish these objectives, what remedies you might apply; then you need to look at the potential negative effects of these remedies, and weigh the positives against the negatives."

"You mean the way you've talked about already in the last few chapters?"

"Yes, but this time, let's use objectives and weigh them against each other in this balancing act."

"Okay, but don't get too abstract on me. Keep to concrete examples."

"Well, Teresa, whose teacher made the complaint, needs to be protected from abuse by her father, and she also needs to be protected from unwarranted abuse by state intrusion upon the integrity of her family. You need to weigh one objective against the other."

"Yes, I see that."

"Well, the only indication of abuse is in the teacher's complaint. It is up to the teacher to come forward or up to those who understand the constraints of the law to determine if the teacher's statement should be more adequately examined. As the situation stands, the child looks safe to me, and the teacher's statement is simply an isolated allegation that anybody might make about anybody. It deserves no more credibility than that, since an examination hasn't been made of the teacher's motives or other contextual features of her statement."

"Shouldn't you suggest that her statement be examined? That you interview her?"

"I suggested that this option exists. But it is outside the limits of my expertise to suggest that it would be best for this to be done. I'm not able to judge, in this case, whether it's best for the child for us to push further in this matter or to let the matter drop. My job is completed by suggesting that the option exists. And I do that by outlining the problem as I see it. Namely, that the complainant's statement of the problem has not been clarified because the complainant is not available to me. What I have said, basically, is that there is no presumption of credibility to the statement just because the statement is made by a teacher."

"So where does that leave you with your two objectives?"

"As far as I'm concerned, the child's need for family integrity is clear, whereas the need to be protected from abuse by her father is not supported by anything apparent to me."

"So what you're doing is balancing one objective against the other. Family integrity against protection from abuse."

"Sort of. But it's a little more complicated than that. I'm examining them and looking at the benefit and harm of trying to satisfy each objective."

"The benefits and harms of trying to satisfy each objective. Hmm. That's the main point? Again? Like in the last couple of chapters?"

"Yes. And it's a little more complicated in the case of Jane because there are not just two objectives but several."

"You mean the case where everybody is lying and you don't know the extent of the abuse?"

"Right, but in that case, remember, the formulation was clear. And it suggests several objectives. You tell me what you think they are."

"Okay, let's see. How about safety from further abuse, removal of the child from inappropriate family roles that meet the parents' needs, protection from disagreements about stepparenting issues, and things like that?"

"And what are the possible remedies you could suggest?"

"Well, I guess you'd suggest that the husband and wife work out their parenting problems, or their stepparenting problems, in marital therapy or family therapy. And that D.S.S. monitor the case closely. All the same things you recommended, I guess."

"Right, and those recommendations are all within our limits of expertise, within the domain of what we confidently know about the case."

"Yes, but don't these remedies intrude upon family integrity? What about the objective of preserving family integrity or protecting Jane from abuse by the state?"

"Yes, you need to balance that objective against the others. That's exactly what this case illustrates. Like all children, Jane has a need for family integrity, but family integrity will necessarily be limited in her case because her stepfather and her mother are not acting in her interest."

"You mean she loses the opportunity for full family integrity?"

"Yes. Family members are distorting information to an extent that doesn't allow us to permit them the degree of autonomy and integrity we might wish."

"You mean if they were more honest you might be able to do more in that respect?"

"Yes, one tries to preserve as much family integrity as possible, within certain feasible limits given the possible benefits and risks of preserving it. If they were more honest, perhaps we could do more. As it stands, the remedies we've suggested may be intrusive and potentially harmful to some extent. But is the potential harm any worse than the harm caused by the abuse?"

"No, I don't think so."

"And the possible benefits?"

"The prognosis is uncertain, but the possible benefits are extensive."

"That's right. This makes Jane's situation quite different from Patricia's who . . . "

"Patricia?"

"You remember, she recanted any abuse by her father."

"That's right, because she was devastated by the disruption to her family life that was caused by the investigation."

"Unlike Jane, Patricia had a whole lot to lose in the way of family integrity if we were to pursue the investigation or bring the family to court and try to mandate therapy—and not much to gain."

"But without pursuing it or requiring therapy or something like that, you left her totally unsafe. Do you have some kind of bias against separating families? I notice that in most of your examples, you leave the family intact. It seems the abuse is never bad enough to remove the child or to remove the offender."

"I don't think I really have the kind of bias you're suggesting. Are you asking whether I believe in family integrity so strongly that I leave children at serious risk for abuse?"

"Yes, when it would be a lot safer to split up the family."

"Well, I often leave children in families when there is a possibility of abuse, that is, when it's only a remote possibility. But when further abuse is probable, even if it's just mild abuse, then I'm quick to recommend that the offender be removed or that further contact be supervised."

"You are?"

"Yes. I don't fool around with a lot of obsessive indecisiveness if I think the risk of abuse is realistic or probable."

"Then why do most of your examples illustrate situations where your decision is to leave the family intact?"

"For a couple of reasons: because it's a harder decision to make, and because I want to offset the tendency among workers in this field to take the more conservative approach of separating families."

"I don't get it. What do you mean, it's a harder decision?"

"It's pretty easy to figure out what to do when the risk of abuse is realistic or probable. You remove the abuser, or you make sure someone is always present to protect the victim. But when the risk is more remote, it's more difficult to make the decision. Because of the difficulty of this decision, many workers in the field, including therapists and judges, are so fearful of being responsible for further abuse that they take the safer approach of separating families."

"Causing more trauma than the child experienced in the first place."

"Yes. And sometimes without an adequate basis to believe that the child was significantly abused. As a result, this panic about abuse has caused a great deal of stress to many children—and to many innocent alleged offenders as well."

"But it's hard to make that decision to leave a child in a home with an alleged offender. If anything happened, it's on your head."

"Yes, and anxiety about making that very difficult decision has wrecked many people's lives. That's why I take every opportunity to use examples that illustrate the process of thinking out exactly why I might recommend that the child stay at home with the offender."

"Which is what you did with Patricia. She might have been abused, but the investigation was wrecking her life, so she recanted. And so you let her stay at home, with no further protection from any possible abuse. It's still kind of hard to swallow that, you know."

"Pursuing the investigation or requiring therapy would have exacerbated the family disruption and solidified denial that anything had occurred. Besides, it's not clear whether there was an adequate basis for the court to even have the right to require them to do anything at all."

"But she continued to be at risk. You did absolutely nothing about the possibility that she had been abused."

"That's right. I'm afraid I was able to do very little. But in terms of her safety, I wasn't that worried. If the father had done something, he would be less likely to try it again, having been put on notice. Also, Patricia was now alert to sexually inappropriate behavior and more sensitized to take action to protect herself. She was old enough, smart enough, and big enough to protect herself fairly well. And finally, keep in mind, it never was clear whether her safety was in jeopardy."

"So, in this case, when you weighed family integrity against protection from sexual abuse, you didn't have much in the way of . . . "

"I had only hints and suspicions, while on the other hand, it was quite evident that harm was being caused by the intrusiveness of the investigation."

"I guess that's pretty clear. In fact, each case seems pretty clear to me now. I think maybe the objectives actually help me to organize my thoughts, to crystallize what needs to be done, the possible remedies to be applied."

"Right, they can help. It's another way of going about the process of weighing the potential benefit and the harm of each possible remedy against one another."

"And when you're done with this whole process, I guess the job is to explain it to the court or to whomever. Right?"

"Yes, you explain it in detail. You don't just give a recommendation, but, rather, you qualify it by explaining your thinking."

"You mean, you say that your conclusion is tentative, not final."

"Right, and you give reasons for your lack of confidence and your doubts. You outline with the utmost clarity what is missing in your assessment of the case and what this means. And when you've thoroughly described your thinking with ruthless honesty, you've given some closure to the case."

"You mean, helped others to think it out?"

"Yes, even if you didn't discover anything new. And you may have mapped for others a couple of reasonable courses to follow."

"Is that everything there is to it? Is that it?"

"Yes, I think so."

"Then why do I still feel a lack of closure? Like I'm left hanging. Like I'm missing a point somewhere. Or like there's something more I want you to say."

"Maybe it's the nature of these cases. They leave you with uncertain conclusions. And uncertainty and ambiguity are difficult to tolerate."

"Yes, maybe you're right about that."

# CHAPTER 13

# The Importance of Evaluation in Treatment

"Speaking of incomplete evaluations, there's another kind of situation that tends to produce incomplete evaluations."

"What situation is that?"

"Therapy and treatment situations."

"Treatment? Treatment produces incomplete evaluations?"

"In great abundance."

"What do you mean? How does it do that?"

"The urge to begin treatment, to begin helping, is a very seductive urge. To act on it prematurely can result in an incomplete evaluation."

"So what's so bad about that? In treatment situations, you have a relationship with clients and you're seeing them not only one time, but many times. You have lots of opportunities to compensate for errors."

"On the contrary, those relationships you're forming and the therapeutic activities you're engaging in with your clients are the very things that distract you from completing an adequate evaluation. They even distract you from the recognition that your evaluation is missing something essential."

"Are you saying it's because you're so caught up in the relationship? And in the therapeutic interventions?"

"Yes, and those interventions are based on an inadequate evaluation."

"So they're the wrong interventions?"

"Exactly. Your first step in treatment is to conduct an adequate evaluation. To figure out the problem and what to do about it."

"So, then, maybe the process of evaluation is just as important for therapy situations as it is for court consultations."

"Yes, because if your evaluation is incomplete or erroneous, you'll get off on the wrong foot, or go off in the wrong direction, and do something that may not be helpful at all in resolving the problem."

"But suppose the problem is clear. Suppose the child has been sexually abused, and you begin treating her for the effects of that. Where is it you might be going wrong?"

"Suppose this child who has been sexually abused also has other problems, for example, she's learning disabled and can't keep up with the class and it's causing her to hate school, to hate herself, and to act out. The symptoms that you thought were due to sexual abuse are really due to her learning disability, which you overlooked because the sexual abuse was most prominent in the picture and you didn't do a complete enough evaluation. You're off on the wrong track, right at the starting gate."

"And I guess the opposite situation could occur too. The child might appear to have a learning disability because of poor grades and low self-esteem and acting-out in school, but a complete evaluation might reveal that those symptoms are due to sexual abuse."

"Exactly. Sexual abuse and learning disability might both be in the background of the case. You can know how to intervene only if there is clarity in the beginning about which of these factors is the one that fuels and maintains the problem."

"Or that both factors contribute, but perhaps one more than another."

"Yes. That's possible too. The job of figuring this out is what evaluation is all about."

"It seems pretty straightforward when you describe it like this. What's the big problem? Why do therapists screw it up?"

"Because the capacity for evaluation in all of us is so fragile."

"The capacity for evaluation? I never heard it put quite that way. What do you mean by saying that this capacity is fragile?"

"I mean that it is extremely vulnerable to distracting influences. It is too easily deflected from its true course. It is too ready, too hungry to be seduced into unproductive efforts to be helpful."

"I guess that's probably the case for beginners, mostly, isn't it? It wouldn't be a problem for an old hand like you."

"It's always a problem, especially for an old hand like me. When you get too cocky, you get sloppy."

"You mean you still make this same mistake yourself?"

"Regularly. I could tell you a lot of stories that illustrate this mistake."

"Tell me one."

"I'll do better than that. I'll tell you two."

\* \* \* \* \*

## CASE 1: EMILY

Emily was nine years old when her mother called for an appointment. The complaint was that Emily was defiant, had frequent outbursts of temper, concocted incredible lies, and played one parent against the other by complaining to each about the stepparent in the other household. The first interview was with Emily, her mother, and her stepfather. During the interview, it emerged that Emily's defiance and misbehavior were a daily occurrence and certainly problematic to her parents, but that she also had more periods of pleasant than unpleasant behavior. In fact, she was a delightful, energetic child who performed well academically, was popular with her peers, and possessed extremely good impulse control in matters that were important to her, such as stamp collecting.

The history that was taken revealed some problems she had experienced adjusting to her parents' separation several years earlier. It was also mentioned that, at the age of five, she had been molested on several occasions by the boyfriend of a babysitter, that the molestation had been reported to the police when discovered, and that she had showed no signs of being adversely affected. What appeared to be quite prominent in the family's presentation at this point was that Emily's misbehavior was generating an escalation of conflict between the two stepfamilies and that her poor adjustment to each stepparent was probably a primary contributing factor to the problem. Also prominent in the family's story was that Emily's misbehavior was being mismanaged and maintained by faulty disciplinary practices. That is, her mother was inconsistently enforcing limits and was utilizing punishments that were not particularly potent.

Rapid diagnostician that I am, I informed the mother and stepfather that the first order of business would probably be to help them to fine-tune their disciplinary practices, and that the second order of business would probably be to get the two stepfamilies together to see what could be done about preventing Emily from playing one family against the other. The parents appeared to be delighted with the speed with which I was getting to the heart of the matter and were hoping to begin fine-tuning their parenting skills that very evening. I was more than happy to oblige them, but before proceeding with this intervention, I pointed out that it was my usual practice to interview the child alone in the first session. I assured them that the individual interview wouldn't take long in this case since I already had a pretty good grasp of what needed to be done.

When I met with Emily alone, I talked about a number of issues before mentioning the issue of her molestation. I was somewhat hesitant to mention it four years later because she might have forgotten it and to rehash it at this point might have caused her unnecessary pain. However, overcoming my reluctance, I did ask her.

"Oh, no, I didn't forget about it," she said. "I think about it all the time. It's hard to think about anything else."

"Oh, no," she responded to another question of mine. "It didn't just happen a couple times. He was doing it to me every day."

Every day, for a year's time. And not just mild touching or fondling.

"He made me put it in my mouth, every time. Till white stuff came out. I tried to spit it out, but he made me swallow it. He said he would kill my cat if I spit it out."

Emily needed to talk a great deal more about this issue that had appeared to have so little effect on her. Needless to say, I never got to fine-tuning any parenting techniques that evening. Nor did I in the next few meetings, which were devoted entirely to a continuation of that first meeting with Emily. In fact, as the effects of the abuse were therapeutically addressed in these next few meetings, her misbehavior declined dramatically and, to her parents, mysteriously. It was never necessary, as it turned out, to fine-tune disciplinary practices or to get the stepfamilies together to address blending and family systems issues.

## CASE 2: LISA

When Lisa was five years old, her parents brought her to see me because her Aunt Trisha had sexually abused her on one occasion. While babysitting Lisa, Trisha had taken a nap with her, during which she had engaged in a masturbatory experience in which she touched Lisa's vagina and gently influenced Lisa to touch her as well.

Prior to this event, Lisa's father had enjoyed a semiromantic relationship with Trisha, who was his wife's sister. Understandably, his wife had been quite jealous and somewhat unhappy with this state of affairs. She also had not been terribly happy about the fact that he was an alcoholic who spent most of his spare time drinking. Neither of these issues had been directly addressed by Lisa's parents in a conscious recon- sideration of the viability of their relationship, but the issues constituted significant strands in the fabric of the relationship.

The incident of sexual abuse had the effect of turning the father against Aunt Trisha and aligning himself with his wife to help the child through her traumatic experience. While the parents were preoccupied with helping Lisa, the father reduced his drinking to a level that was quite tolerable to the mother. As a result, it did not appear to me that drinking was a significant problem to address at that time. After all, both parents appeared to be doing everything possible to help Lisa, and here was a child who had been molested and was suffering from confu- sion about what had happened to her.

After helping the child with the effects of the molestation, I terminated with the family. Over the years, I remained a part of Lisa's life, running into her on the street, at school, and at community functions, where her mother reminded her that I was someone she could trust and talk to. Her mother also became aware, from public presentations I had made and from friendships with other clients of mine, that I was something of an expert in the area of sexual abuse.

When Lisa was nine years old, four years after I had last treated her, her mother called to say that Lisa's grades were declining because she couldn't concentrate in school. When her mother had asked Lisa what was troubling her, Lisa told her that she was thinking about Aunt Trisha again and wanted to talk to me about it.

"What's bothering you," I asked her during our first meeting.

"My aunt touching me. I keep thinking about it. It's like a bubble that gets bigger and bigger in my head. I can't stand it." A wonderfully descriptive metaphor, I thought, for the pain of her preoccupation.

"Tell me what's in that bubble that gets bigger and bigger. Do you remember anything more about what Aunt Trisha did? Tell me what you remember."

She remembered no more about it than she had four years earlier. Instead, she complained about it, saying, "Why did it have to happen to me? Why do I have to be different? Nobody likes me. Everyone knows I'm different."

"Different?"

"From other girls." She then rambled on about current events, telling me about difficulties with her peers, trouble concentrating at school, her wish to spend more time with her father, who was usually too busy drinking and arguing with her mother, and her daily squabbles with her younger brother.

"What about Aunt Trisha?" I gently persisted, bringing her back to what I thought was the underlying problem. After all, I knew a thing or two about sexual abuse; my job was to help her to look at the contents of that "bubble" that was getting bigger.

"It's all her fault," she complained. "Why did it have to happen to me? It didn't happen to all the other girls." She then launched into further details on difficulties she was having with peers at school, and then onto other current events in her home life.

The next session was just as frustrating as the first. She began by telling me that she was obsessed with the idea of hurricanes, fearing that a hurricane would strike the area and destroy us all. Like the bubble, I thought this an interesting metaphor for her preoccupation with the molestation. Again, I asked her to tell me about her memories of it, assuming that these replays or excerpts of the event were the disturbing contents of her preoccupation. Again, she didn't seem to connect to this question and went off on what I believed to be tangents about current events.

Gradually, after a few unproductive sessions, it dawned on me that what was bothering Lisa was not circumscribed to the molestation by Aunt Trisha. Lisa had been doing her best to tell me what was really on her mind, but I may as well have been wearing blinders as long as I persisted in the mistaken assumption that she was troubled by the sexual activities of the molestation. The specific sexual activities in themselves didn't trouble her. She was troubled not by the abuse itself, but by the idea of having been abused.

She was also troubled by the vague connection in her mind between Aunt Trisha and her parents' troubled marriage and her father's drinking. In some way, she viewed the event with Aunt Trisha as a precipitant for her current unhappiness with her family life.

Because I had extricated myself from the burden of family preconceptions about the effects on Lisa of Trisha's molestation, I was able to reflectively listen to her in such a way that the problem became clear.

\* \* \* \* \*

"Okay, so you're not thinking about Trisha's hand touching you, but still, something is bothering you. You're thinking about something."

"That I'm different."

"From other girls."

"Right."

"Because of how Aunt Trisha touched you."

"Yeah. Why did it have to happen to me? Why do I have to be so different?"

"So what goes through your mind is how different you are. From everybody else."

"Because I was touched."

"Because of what Aunt Trisha did."

"Yeah, and because I'm not normal."

"Not normal?"

"Because I was touched."

"Not normal because you were touched?"

"And because of everything else. Nothing's normal. I don't have a normal family. There's all kinds of problems and it's all because I was touched. Because I'm different."

"You're different because you were touched and that changed things somehow so that your family wasn't normal anymore. Is that what you're saying?"

"Right. Do you call it normal for your father to be drinking every day and yelling at your mother and me trying to stop it all by having a hyper and cutting my hand up and . . . "

"Whoa, hold on, you're losing me. You had a hyper and cut your hand? What do you mean?"

"Mom and dad were fighting about dad's drinking and he got in a car accident and then was trying to get in the car again and mom was fighting and trying to stop him, so I had a hyper and . . . "

"What's a hyper?"

"When you yell and scream and throw yourself all over the floor. And what happened was I put my hand through the window and got all cut up."

"So, when you cut your hand, did it stop them from fighting?"

"Yeah, they had to take care of me."

"So you got them to stop."

"Right. I always do."

"Always?"

"No, I can't always. Sometimes I can't think of ways."

"What else do you do to try to make everything at home more normal?"

"I try to be a little sweetheart all the time. Clean things up. Like a elf. Sometimes I get up early and sweep the floors so dad won't yell at mom about what a dump it is."

"You try to be an elf so everybody will be real happy and have no problems anymore."

"Yeah, but it doesn't work."

"It doesn't?"

"No. They still fight. And dad just keeps drinking beer. And he's drunk when I get home from school. I can't bring friends home. So I clean up."

"And you keep trying."

"You got to keep trying."

"And you keep hoping it will work. And sometimes it seems to work a little."

"Yeah, sometimes. But I never know what will happen next."

"You never know what it will be like when you get home from school. Like, maybe you're hoping dad will be fun and do something with you. Or maybe he'll be drunk and going crazy on your mom."

"Yeah, that's the worsest thing about it all. That's what I think about all the time. What will it be like?"

"Is that what you mean by feeling like your family isn't normal? And that you're different from other girls?"

"Yeah, that's it."

"What about Aunt Trisha touching you?"

"That's it too. I'm not normal."

"So what makes you feel so different? The fact that Aunt Trisha touched you? Or that you never know what's happening when you come home, with your father drinking and your parents fighting?"

"It's all of it, but mostly my dad's drinking."

* * * * *

## DISCUSSION

In Emily's case, I was on the verge of utilizing a very particular therapeutic intervention, that of fine-tuning disciplinary practices. This would have been time-consuming and only minimally productive in view of the more potent role of sexual abuse in that case. Had I been aware of the more potent role of sexual abuse, but judged it to be inaccessible to intervention, then I might have chosen to fine-tune the faulty disciplinary practices. While not the most important factor in accounting for the problem, at least the issue of discipline was one that was readily accessible to therapeutic leverage. However, I judged that the effect of sexual abuse not only was accessible to intervention, but would require no more time and effort to address than would the other factors. I was able to make this kind of judgment about which etiological factors to address first only when the evaluation was complete enough for me to be aware that sexual abuse was a factor to consider alongside the other factors.

In the case of Lisa, I also made a judgment, an extremely poor one, about which factors accounting for the problem I would address with a remedy. My efforts to treat her for the effects of sexual abuse were unproductive because Lisa was suffering more from her father's drinking than from what her aunt had done to her.

Both of these cases indicate the need to resist the urge to begin treatment until an adequate evaluation is completed. But what are the factors that seduce us into treating a case prematurely? Why don't we realize that the evaluation is incomplete? What interferes with a decision to make further inquiries, which would bring about a more adequate understanding of the problem?

One factor consists of the discomfort that we anticipate if we ask further questions. Therapists are often uncomfortable about sexual abuse and reluctant to cause pain by asking about it, as has been discussed a number of times in earlier chapters. This reluctance to cause pain, the reader will remember, was one reason that I almost failed to inquire further about Emily's molestation.

A similar kind of discomfort helps to explain why I failed to conduct a fresh evaluation the second time I treated Lisa. Instead of taking a fresh look at the situation, I plunged into treatment exactly where I had left off four years earlier, continuing the same kind of interaction with Lisa and her family that I had earlier established. I suppose I was embarrassed to let them know that I had forgotten some things about them and needed a fresh start, especially when they viewed me as a knowledgeable expert. I was also reluctant to focus on the drinking issue, even though there were more and more hints provided that the drinking played a more prominent role in the picture than it had seemed to four years earlier.

To focus on the drinking now would risk violating a mutual understanding that had been previously established by my interactions with the family. That is to say, it would have been uncomfortable to have to say to Lisa's father, "Say, let's take another look at that drinking of yours, even though we both sort of agreed that we wouldn't talk about it the last time you were here." It can be especially uncomfortable to do this when everyone is saying loud and clear that the problem is sexual abuse, not drinking.

Wasn't it clear to everyone that sexual abuse was the most prominent feature in this case and the relevant one to treat? And wasn't I the right person to deal with it, with a repertoire of methods ready and itching to be used for that problem? Likewise, in Emily's case, disciplinary practices and stepparenting issues had a more prominent place in the family's presentation than did the history of sexual abuse, which had been minimized in the presentation. Behavioral methodology seemed almost to cry out to be used to fine-tune disciplinary measures.

Idiosyncratic features of each case provoke or seductively invite certain ideas about treatment. When implementation of these methods is irresistible, we become distracted from the need to be complete in an evaluation, with the result that crucial information is obscured or unrevealed.

This urge to begin treatment is irresistible partly because we become enamored with our treatment ideas, with the idea that we thought them up. We presumptuously believe we have an exact grasp of what's wrong because those treatment ideas become the most salient objects of our attention, crowding out other considerations such as the need to seek further information. And we get too happy and excited at the prospect of a quick fix. In addition, requests for help by those in distress stimulate our desire to help, whether or not we know enough about the problem to begin to help effectively. They can push us forward to offer help before we are ready. In fact, when we are still powerless to help, we are often most desirous of helping and therefore most vulnerable to pretensions about having more knowledge and power than we yet possess.

These various factors can interfere with a decision to seek further information in any evaluation, whether it is a one-session evaluation for purposes of a court consultation or several sessions for the purpose of providing treatment. They are somewhat less likely to have as much power in one-time evaluations because the evaluator is under a heavy burden to economize his use of time. He must utilize the most fine-tuned evaluation techniques at his command to find out everything he needs to know before the client leaves, because he may never get another chance to do so. The factors that seduce one away from this evaluation mode have more power when the clinician anticipates seeing the clients again, when the purposes of the relationship are more open-ended, or when a previous relationship exists, as with myself and Lisa's alcoholic father.

As time elapses and the therapist engages with clients in one activity after another, sometimes in one session after another, it is inevitable that their activities with one another will commit them to certain implicit understandings about how time will be spent, what will be talked about, and so on. These mutual understandings and reciprocal expectations are barely accessible to our awareness due to their subtlety, complexity, and the rapidity with which they are implicitly established. But, while we remain hardly aware of their existence, they powerfully dictate our behaviors and render us less able to distance or break out enough from the forming relationship to take an overall and objective look once again at the relationship and at the case.

Although therapists often believe they can afford to wait to gather further information, they are less likely to do so in a precise fashion because of the implicit commitments and expectations that necessarily evolve in an ongoing relationship. Implicit understandings develop that inhibit the therapist from bringing up that nasty topic of sexual abuse, of drinking, or of something else. To bring them up will occasion discomfort—to the client or to the therapist or to both of them—and it is not polite to make people uncomfortable. It hurts us to hurt them. And they may not like us anymore. Therapists are not usually aware that they are laboring under these constraints; when they are made aware, in supervision, it is usually fairly easy for them to achieve the necessary distance from the relationship to ask the questions they already knew how to ask but did not.

When therapists notice that they are "stuck" or that therapeutic progress is "stalemated," but they are unsure why, they are wise to ask for help in supervision. When they do so, I usually ask some basic questions about the stalemated case, only to find that the impasse is due to the fact that an adequate evaluation wasn't completed and, as a consequence, therapy was prematurely initiated in an unproductive direction. In fact, this is one of the most common occurrences in supervision.

Although in each instance I may help the therapist to explore the unique reasons for this error, my most frequent piece of advice, which has become almost an echoing refrain, is to go back and complete the evaluation. Without having adequately figured out the problem and what to do about it, the therapist is a ship on the sea without a compass, and the client will benefit from therapy only with the greatest of good luck.

# CHAPTER 14

# *Conclusion: What to Do Last*

"It's astounding."

"What's astounding?"

"The mistakes you made in those cases. In the last chapter."

"What's so astounding about it?"

"That you would make such mistakes. With all your expertise and all your experience."

"Mistakes like that can keep you humble about your expertise and your experience."

"But it's hard to believe that you would be making mistakes like that."

"I make even worse mistakes than that sometimes."

"It almost makes me afraid that I might make those same kinds of mistakes myself."

"That was the point. It's supposed to scare you. It's supposed to humble you a little bit about all you think you've learned."

"But you've spent all this time building me up. Filling me up with knowledge. Teaching me to be more effective, to make better decisions, to do better interviews, to be a better clinician. Why try to scare me now?"

"Because it's important to be cautious about what you think you know."

"That's how we started out at the beginning. With you rubbing my nose in what I don't know. You made your point back then. Why do you want to keep making it now?"

"I need to keep making it because I think you're a little too cocky about what you think you've learned."

"Oh, no. Is this your way of trying to tell me that there's something wrong with my recommendations on that evaluation I did?"

"What evaluation?"

"The one I've been getting your help on. The one we started talking about a week ago, before I started reading this book. Remember? The one that's due in court tomorrow?"

"That's not what I'm trying to tell you. There's nothing wrong with your recommendations. That evaluation's fine."

"Then what's your point? I did it over just like you taught me, and I have lots of specific recommendations that you said looked very good."

"And they do look good. That's not my point. I'm trying to make a more abstract point, but you're staying very concrete about this. All you seem to want to know about is your case."

"That's right. It's due tomorrow in court. I have good reason to be concrete. I want some closure. I've done first things first, just like you taught me, and now I want to know if there's something I should do last, at the end. You seem to be implying that I've missed something."

"I've been trying to give you closure, but you keep confusing the general and the specific. In regard to your specific case, you did fine. It's done. Is that enough closure? Stop acting so paranoid about it."

"But you keep implying that I'm missing something."

"Yes, you are, on a more general or more abstract level. I had thought you were looking for closure not only on your case but to everything else you've learned here. But maybe you're not."

"That's not true. I was looking for closure on everything. My case and everything else you've been teaching, too. Go ahead and tell me what it is you think I'm not getting."

"I've been trying to tell you but you're distracted by worrying about your case."

"Then, say it to me again. Tell me what I'm missing. I promise not to talk about my case again. You were talking about what I've learned here this week, I think. Tell me what I'm missing here. Say it again."

"That you'd be wiser to be a little more humble about what you've learned here."

"You're not talking about my case?"

"For the last time, no. I'm not speaking about the specifics of a case. I'm speaking about generalities."

"But I don't get it. I did everything by the book. I read the whole thing from cover to cover."

"Yeah, in seven days. That's a lot to digest in seven days."

"But I did it, didn't I?"

"Did you? A lot of people can read. It's one thing to read some words, but it's another thing to really understand them."

"But I did understand them."

"And understanding them is not the same thing as digesting them."

"What do you mean by digesting them?"

"I mean internalizing the knowledge well enough to put it into practice, to understand hidden implications, and then to go beyond that knowledge and to question it and reframe it and discover new ways of thinking about the same things. That just doesn't happen in a week."

"You're saying I need to read this again?"

"It wouldn't hurt. And I think you need to be sure you've internalized it enough to . . . "

"But I think I have internalized it. Look at what I've already accomplished in a week. This knowledge has changed the way I do everything."

"Well, I'm glad it's helped, but . . . "

"No, you listen to me for a change. I think you're underestimating what I've learned here. I'm more effective in everything I do, not just sexual abuse cases. I'm able to figure out people's problems like never before, all kinds of problems."

"Well, I'm glad but . . . "

"And I'm able to stop clients in the middle of treatment and confront them, over and over again, until I understand exactly why they haven't followed my suggestions, or until I can clarify whether we have a mutual understanding . . . "

"Good, but . . . "

"And I've learned to strip my language of a lot of unnecessary therapeutic padding and say what I mean in simple language. And that's not all. I could go on and on. Would you call all this a superficial understanding of what you've been teaching?"

"Well, I can see that you've done more than just read it and understand it. You've digested it to some extent."

"Yes, and well enough to begin practicing it."

"Yes, and that's probably more than most people can do just from reading a book once, and in one week's time."

"But I've gone even further. Aren't you listening? I'm applying it to other cases of mine."

"Yes, you've taken this knowledge about sexual abuse and you've generalized it to other kinds of clinical situations. I agree that this is quite an accomplishment for one week of learning."

"But you're saying there's more?"

"Yes, there's more. The knowledge in each chapter has implications and ramifications that go beyond what I could include in those chapters. It takes time to discover the relevance of each implication."

"Like what? You're getting too abstract on me again."

"Okay. consider the case of a girl who was raped by her mother's boyfriend, repeatedly and violently, beginning at the age of 13. She's now 16 years old, legally married to him in another state, and totally in love with him. The jilted mother witnessed some of the rapes and has come forward now. She wants to testify against her former boyfriend."

"God, that's a good one."

"Do you put the guy in jail and put the child in therapy? Or do you congratulate them on their marriage and wish them good luck?"

"I'm not sure. You didn't exactly cover that kind of situation."

"But it was implied."

"Where?"

"It's in there."

"But you're saying that if I really understood everything in the book, then I should be able to figure out this case."

"Yes, exactly. Or other kinds of situations that aren't exactly spelled out."

"Like what?"

"What about doing therapy with a 60-year-old man who asks for help with a problem of impotence that he's experiencing with his 25-year-old secretary? Yet he claims he has no problem getting an erection with his 55-year-old wife. How would you feel about treating him for his problem?"

"Ha. That's a good one. I don't know if I can tell you, just like that. I don't even know if I'd consent to treat him. I have to think. There are too many ethical and social implications."

"That's right. There are serious and interesting implications to a lot of this knowledge you've been learning."

"And I guess it's not all spelled out."

"Of course it's not all spelled out. There are many hidden implications that you'll find useful if you take the time to discover them. You've learned a great deal, but you're approaching this knowledge as if it was concrete stuff to be put in your tool bag to be used as needed."

"But it is concrete, and very usable too. These are essential tools for the clinician. Are you saying I shouldn't use them?"

"No, by all means keep this knowledge in your back pocket and use it. But it's only knowledge; it's not real. It's there to be delved into, questioned, improved, and transcended."

"What do you mean, 'it's not real'?"

"You tend to reify this knowledge. You act as if it's as real as a screwdriver or a hammer. These are only constructs, convenient fictions, ways of conceptualizing."

"But they're not fictions. They're powerful ways of changing reality."

"They are stories and they can be revised. Improved."

"Do you mean I shouldn't take this knowledge so seriously?"

"Take it seriously but don't be too concrete with it. Learn it, and by all means learn it well. Go within it and then go beyond it. Transcend it. Find new twists to it."

"But that takes time."

"That's my point. It takes time to fully digest it and then to discover new ways to reframe it. Don't be so sure you have it under your belt yet."

"And this is your point? This is what you want to leave me with?"

"Yes. Keep on learning. Don't wed yourself so concretely to what you think you know at this point in time. Otherwise you'll find yourself in a unique and difficult situation, and you won't know what to do."

"So what I should do next is be sure I really understand it. Relearn it?"

"Yes, but not just this. Other knowledge as well."

"And then transcend it all?"

"You make it sound so simplistic. Just try to stay open."

"Question it?"

"Yes, but more than that."

"Reread it all?"

"Yes, but more than that, too. You're getting concrete again."

"What then? What is it you're telling me to do?"

"I guess I'm telling you to just remember that there's more to learn. That you don't know everything."

"Is that it? Is that all you're saying?"

"Yes."

"Well, I guess I know that."

"If you do, then you know everything you need to know."

# Acknowledgments

Special thanks to my wife Deborah for helping me to eliminate or revise sections of the manuscript that were either boring or difficult to follow. Discussions with her about the content helped me to bring a liveliness to the book that might not have otherwise existed.

I also thank Susan Barrows, of Norton Professional Books, and her assistant editor, Margaret Farley, for their patience, encouragement, and feedback. But most of all, I am grateful for their expertise in the editing of the manuscript.

Thanks are also due to those clinicians whom I have helped to supervise and train, and to those who have reacted to portions of earlier drafts.

Finally, I acknowledge the contribution made by all those I have interviewed over the years: the offenders, the victims, the falsely accused, and the relatives. I have learned a great deal from them all.

# Suggested Readings

Abel, G. G., Becker, J. V., & Cunningham-Rather, J. (1984). Complications, consent, and cognitions in sex between children and adults. *International Journal of Law and Psychiatry, 7,* 89–103.

Aber, M. S., & Reppucci, N. D. (1987). The limits of mental health expertise in juvenile and family law. *International Journal of Law and Psychiatry, 10,* 167–184.

American Psychiatric Association. (1987). *Diagnostic and statistical manual of mental disorders* (3rd ed., rev.). Washington, DC: Author.

Anderson, L. S. (1981). Notes on the linkage between the sexually abused child and the suicidal adolescent. *Journal of Adolescence, 4,* 157–162.

Arkin, A. M. (1984). A hypothesis concerning the incest taboo. *Psychoanalytic Review, 71,* 375–381.

Bagley, C. (1969). Incest behavior and incest taboo. *Social Problems, 16,* 505–519.

Bauer, H. (1983). Preparation of the sexually abused child for court testimony. *Bulletin of the American Academy of Psychiatry and the Law, 11,* 287–289.

Bender, L., & Blan, A. (1937). The reaction of children to sexual relations with adults. *American Journal of Orthopsychiatry, 7,* 500–518.

Benedek, E. P. (1982). The role of the child psychiatrist in court cases involving child victims of sexual assault. *Journal of the American Academy of Child Psychiatry, 21,* 519–520.

Benedek, E. P., & Schetky, D. H. (1987). Problems in validating child sexual abuse. *Journal of the American Academy of Child and Adolescent Psychiatry, 26*, 912–921.

Berliner, L., & Barbieri, M. K. (1984). The testimony of the child victim of sexual assault. *Journal of Social Issues, 40*, 125–135.

Boat, B., & Everson, M. (1986). *Using anatomical dolls: Guidelines for interviewing young children in sexual abuse investigations*. Chapel Hill, NC: University of North Carolina Press.

Boat, B., & Everson, M. (1988). Use of anatomical dolls among professionals in sexual abuse evaluations. *Child Abuse and Neglect, 12*, 171–179.

Bourne, R., & Newberger, E. H. (1977). Family autonomy or coercive intervention? Ambiguity and conflict in the proposed standards for child sexual abuse and neglect. *Boston University Law Review, 57*, 670–706.

Bresee, P., Stearns, G. B., Bess, B. H., & Packer, L. S. (1986). Allegations of child sexual abuse in child custody disputes: A therapeutic assessment model. *American Journal of Orthopsychiatry, 56*, 560–569.

Browne, A., & Finkelhor, D. (1986). Impact of child sexual abuse: A review of the research. *Psychological Bulletin, 99*, 66–77.

Burgess, A., Groth, A. N., Holmstrom, L., & Sgroi, S. (1978). Sexual assault of children and adolescents. Lexington, MA: Lexington.

Burgess, A., & Holmstrom, L. (1974). Rape trauma syndrome. *American Journal of Psychiatry, 131*, 981–986.

Ceci, S. J., Toglia, M. P., & Ross, D. F. (Eds.). (1987). *Children's eyewitness memory*. New York: Springer-Verlag.

Clark-Weintraub, D. (1985). The use of videotaped testimony of victims in cases involving child sexual abuse: A constitutional dilemma. *Hofstra Law Review, 14*, 261–296.

Cohen, A. (1985). The unreliability of expert testimony on the typical characteristics of sexual abuse victims. *Georgetown Law Journal, 74*, 429–456.

Cohen, R., & Harnick, M. S. (1980). The susceptibility of the child witness to suggestion. *Law and Human Behavior, 4*, 201–210.

Conte, J. R., & Schuerman, J. R. (1987). Factors associated with an increased impact of child sexual abuse. *Child Abuse and Neglect, 11*, 201–211.

Conte, J. R., Wolf, S., & Smith, T. (1989). What sexual offenders tell us about prevention strategies. *Child Abuse and Neglect, 13*, 293–301.

Corwin, D., Berliner, L., & Goodman, G. (1987). Child sexual abuse and custody disputes: No easy answers. *Journal of Interpersonal Violence, 2*, 91–105.

De Mott, B. (1980). The pro-incest lobby. *Psychology Today, 13*(10), 11–16.

De Young, M. (1982). Innocent seducer or innocently seduced? The role of the child incest victim. *Journal of Clinical Child Psychology, 11*, 56–60.

De Young, M. (1986). A conceptual model for judging the truthfulness of a young child's allegation of sexual abuse. *American Journal of Psychiatry, 56*, 550–559.

Elwell, M. E., & Ephros, P. H. (1987). Initial reactions of sexually abused children. *Social Casework, 68*, 109–116.

Everson, M. D., & Boat, B. W. (1989). False allegations of sexual abuse by children and adolescents. *Journal of the American Academy of Child and Adolescent Psychiatry, 28*, 230–235.

Everstine, D. S., & Everstine, L. (1989). *Sexual trauma in children and adolescents: Dynamics and treatment*. New York: Brunner/Mazel.

Faller, K. C. (1984). Is the child victim of sexual abuse telling the truth? *Child Abuse and Neglect, 8*, 473–481.

Finkelhor, D. (1979). *Sexually victimized children.* New York: Free Press.

Finkelhor, D. (1984). *Child sexual abuse: New theory and research.* New York: Free Press.

Finkelhor, D. (1986). *A sourcebook on child sexual abuse.* Beverly Hills, CA: Sage.

Finkelhor, D. (1988). The trauma of child sexual abuse: Two models. In G. E. Wyatt & G. J. Powell (Eds.), *Lasting effects of child sexual abuse* (pp. 61–82). Beverly Hills, CA: Sage.

Friedrich, W. N. (1990). *Psychotherapy of sexually abused children and their families.* New York: Norton.

Friedrich, W. N., & Reams, R. A. (1987). Course of psychological symptoms in sexually abused young children. *Psychotherapy: Theory, Research and Practice, 24*, 160–170.

Fritz, G., Stoll, K., & Wagner, N. (1981). A comparison of males and females who were sexually molested as children. *Journal of Sexual and Marital Therapy, 1*, 54–59.

Fromuth, M. E. (1986). The relationship of childhood sexual abuse with later psychological and sexual adjustment in a sample of college women. *Child Abuse and Neglect, 10*, 5–15.

Gale, J., Thompson, R. J., Moran, T., & Sack, W. H. (1988). Sexual abuse in young children: Its clinical presentation and characteristic patterns. *Child Abuse and Neglect, 12*, 163–170.

Ginott, H. G. (1965). *Between parent and child.* New York: Macmillan.

Goldstein, J., Freud, A., & Solnit, A. J. (1979). *Before the best interests of the child.* New York: Free Press.

Goodman, G. S. (1984). The child witness: Conclusions and future directions for research and legal practice. *Journal of Social Issues, 40*, 157–175.

Goodman, G. S., & Hahn, A. (1987). Evaluating eyewitness testimony. In I. Weiner & A. Hess (Eds.), *Handbook for forensic psychology* (pp. 258–292). New York: Wiley.

Goodman, G. S., & Reed, R. S. (1986). Age differences in eyewitness testimony. *Law and Human Behavior, 10*, 317–322.

Goodman, J., Sahd, D., & Rada, R. T. (1978). Incest hoax: False accusations, false denials. *Bulletin of the American Academy of Psychiatry and the Law, 5*, 269–276.

Gordon, M. (1989). The family environment of sexual abuse: A comparison of natal and stepfather abuse. *Child Abuse and Neglect, 13*, 121–130.

Gordon, T. (1975). *P.E.T.: Parent effectiveness training.* New York: New American Library.

Green, A. H. (1986). True and false allegations of sexual abuse in child custody disputes. *Journal of the American Academy of Child Psychiatry, 25*, 449–456.

Groth, A. N. (1979). *Men who rape: The psychology of the offender.* New York: Plenum.

Groff, M. G., & Hubble, L. M. (1984). A comparison of father-daughter and stepfather-stepdaughter incest. *Criminal Justice and Behavior, 11*, 461–475.

Guidelines for clinical evaluation of child and adolescent sexual abuse. (1988). Position statement of the American Academy of Child and Adolescent Psychiatry. *Journal of the American Academy of Child and Adolescent Psychiatry, 27,* 655–657.

Haugaard, J. J., & Reppucci, N. D. (1988). *The sexual abuse of children.* San Francisco: Jossey-Bass.

Herman, J. (1981). *Father-daughter incest.* Cambridge, MA: Harvard University Press.

Hoorwitz, A. N. (1982). When to intervene in cases of suspected incest. *Social Casework, 63,* 374–375.

Hoorwitz, A. N. (1983). Guidelines for treating father-daughter incest. *Social Casework, 64,* 515–524.

Hoorwitz, A. N. (1983). The visitation dilemma in court consultation. *Social Casework, 64,* 231–237.

Hoorwitz, A. N. (1989). *Hypnotic methods in nonhypnotic therapies.* New York: Irvington.

Hoorwitz, A. N., & Burchart, C. J. (1984). Procedures for court consultations on child custody issues. *Social Casework, 65,* 259–266.

James, K. L. (1977). Incest: The teenager's perspective. *Psychotherapy: Theory, Research and Practice, 14,* 146–155.

Jampole, L., & Weber, M. K. (1987). An assessment of the behavior of sexually abused and non-sexually abused children with anatomically correct dolls. *Child Abuse and Neglect, 2,* 187–192.

Johnson, M. K., & Foley, M. A. (1984). Differentiating fact from fantasy: The reliability of children's memory. *Journal of Social Issues, 40,* 33–50.

Johnson, T. C. (1988). Child perpetrators—children who molest other children: Preliminary findings. *Child Abuse and Neglect, 12,* 219–229.

Johnston, M. S. (1979). The sexually mistreated child: Diagnostic evaluation. *Child Abuse and Neglect, 3,* 943–951.

Jones, D. P. H., & McGraw, J. M. (1987). Reliable and fictitious accounts of sexual abuse to children. *Journal of Interpersonal Violence, 2,* 27–45.

Josephson, G. S., & Fong-Beyette, M. L. (1987). Factors assisting female clients' disclosure of incest during counseling. *Journal of Counseling and Development, 65,* 475–478.

Kempe, R. S., & Kempe, C. H. (1978). *Child abuse.* Cambridge, MA: Harvard University Press.

Kinsey, A. C., Pomeroy, W. B., Martin, C. E., & Gebhart, P. H. (1953). *Sexual behavior in the human female.* Philadelphia: Saunders.

Kiser, L. J., Ackerman, B. J., Brown, E., Edwards, N. B., McColgan, E., Pugh, R., & Pruitt, D. B. (1988). Post-traumatic stress disorder in young children: A reaction to purported sexual abuse. *Journal of the American Academy of Child and Adolescent Psychiatry, 27,* 645–649.

Knight, R. A., Carter, D. L., & Prentky, R. A. (1989). A system for the classification of child molesters: Reliability and application. *Journal of Interpersonal Violence, 4,* 3–23.

Lindberg, F. H., & Distad, L. J. (1985). Post-traumatic stress disorders in women who experienced childhood incest. *Child Abuse and Neglect, 9,* 329–334.

Loftus, E., & Davis, G. (1984). Distortions in the memory of children. *Journal of Social Issues, 40,* 51–58.

Lukianowicz, N. (1972). Incest—I: Paternal incest. *British Journal of Psychiatry, 120,* 301–308.

Lukianowicz, N. (1972). Incest—II: Other types of incest. *British Journal of Psychiatry, 120*, 308–313.

MacFarlane, K., & Krebs. S. (1986). Techniques for interviewing and evidence gathering. In K. MacFarlane, J. Waterman, S. Conerly, M. Durfee, & S. Long, *Sexual abuse of young children*. New York: Guilford.

Machotka, P., Pittman, F. S., & Flomenhaft, K. (1967). Incest as a family affair. *Family Process, 6*, 98–116.

Maddock, J. W. (1988). Child reporting and testimony in incest cases: Comments on the construction and reconstruction of reality. *Behavioral Sciences and the Law, 6*, 1–20.

Masten, A. S., & O'Conner, M. J. (1989). Vulnerability, stress, and resilience in the early development of a high risk child. *Journal of the American Academy of Child and Adolescent Psychiatry, 28*, 274–278.

McCarthy, B. W. (1986). A cognitive-behavioral approach to understanding and treating sexual trauma. *Journal of Sex and Marital Therapy, 12*, 322–329.

McCarthy, L. M. (1986). Mother-child incest: Characteristics of the offender. *Child Welfare, 65*, 447–458.

Mrazek, D. A. (1981). The child psychiatric examination of the sexually abused child. In P. Mrazek & C. H. Kempe (Eds.), *Sexually abused children and their families*. Oxford, UK: Pergamon Press.

Mrazek, P. B., & Mrazek, D. A. (1987). Resilience in child maltreatment victims: A conceptual exploration. *Child Abuse and Neglect, 11*, 357–366.

O'Brien, M., & Bera, W. (1986). Adolescent sexual offenders: A descriptive typology. *Preventing Sexual Abuse, 1*, 1–4.

O'Carroll, T. (1982). *Paedophelia: The radical case*. London: Owen.

O'Connell, M. A. (1986). Reuniting incest offenders with their families. *Journal of Interpersonal Violence, 1*, 374–386.

Parker, H., & Parker, S. (1986). Father-daughter sexual abuse: An emerging perspective. *American Journal of Orthopsychiatry, 56*, 531–549.

Parsons, T. (1954). The incest taboo in relation to social structure and the socialization of the child. *British Journal of Sociology, 5*, 101–117.

Pynoos, R., & Eth, S. (1986). Witness to violence: The child interview. *Journal of the American Academy of Child Psychiatry, 25*, 306–319.

Reinhart, M. A. (1987). Sexually abused boys. *Child Abuse and Neglect, 11*, 229–235.

Renshaw, D. C. (1987). Evaluating suspected cases of child sexual abuse. *Psychiatric Annals, 17*, 262–270.

Roe, R. J. (1985). Expert testimony in child sexual abuse cases. *University of Miami Law Review, 40*, 97–113.

Rosenfeld, A., Bailey, R., Siegel, B., & Bailey, G. (1986). Determining incestuous contact between parent and child: Frequency of children touching parents' genitals in a nonclinical population. *Journal of the American Academy of Child Psychiatry, 25*, 481–484.

Rosenfeld, A. A., Nadelson, C. C., & Krieger, M. (1979). Fantasy and reality in patients' reports of incest. *Journal of Clinical Psychiatry, 40*, 159–164.

Runyan, D. K., Everson, M. D., Edelsohn, G. A., Hunter, W. M., & Coulter, M. L. (1988). Impact of legal intervention on sexually abused children. *Journal of Pediatrics, 113*, 647–653.

Russell, D. (1982). The incidence and prevalence of intrafamilial and extrafamilial sexual abuse of female children. *Child Abuse and Neglect, 7*, 133–146.

Russell, D. (1984). *Sexual exploitation: Rape, child sexual abuse, and workplace harassment*. Beverly Hills, CA: Sage.

Sauzier, M. (1989). Disclosure of child sexual abuse: For better or for worse. *Psychiatric Clinics of North America, 12,* 455–469.

Schroeder, T. (1915). Incest in Mormonism. *The American Journal of Urology and Sexology, 11,* 409–416.

Schuman, D. (1984). False accusations of physical and sexual abuse. *Bulletin of the American Academy of Psychiatry and Law, 14,* 5–21.

Schuman, D. (1987). Psychodynamics of accusation: Positive feedback in family systems. *Psychiatric Annals, 17,* 242–247.

Sedney, M. A., & Brooks, B. (1984). Factors associated with a history of childhood sexual experience in a nonclinical female population. *Journal of the American Academy of Child and Adolescent Psychiatry, 23,* 215–218.

Sgroi, S. M. (Ed.). (1982). *Handbook of clinical intervention in child sexual abuse*. Lexington, MA: Lexington Books.

Smith, W. R., Monastersky, C., & Deisher, R. M. (1987). MMPI-based personality types among juvenile sexual offenders. *Journal of Clinical Psychology, 43,* 422–430.

Solin, C. A. (1986). Displacement of affect in families following incest disclosure. *American Journal of Orthopsychiatry, 56,* 570–576.

Sroufe, L. A., & Ward, M. J. (1980). Seductive behavior of mothers of toddlers: Occurrence, correlates, and family origins. *Child Development, 51,* 1222–1229.

Steele, B. F., & Alexander, H. (1981). Long-term effects of sexual abuse in childhood. In P. B. Mrazek & C. H. Kempe (Eds.), *Sexually abused children and their families*. New York: Pergamon Press.

Summit, R. (1983). The child sexual abuse accommodation syndrome. *Child Abuse and Neglect, 7,* 177–193.

Summit, R. (1988). Hidden victims, hidden pain: Societal avoidance of child sexual abuse. In G. E. Wyatt & G. J. Powell (Eds.), *Lasting effects of child sexual abuse*. Beverly Hills, CA: Sage.

Swanson, L., & Biaggio, M. K. (1985). Therapeutic perspectives on father-daughter incest. *American Journal of Psychiatry, 142,* 667–674.

Tedesco, J. F., & Schnell, S. V. (1987). Children's reaction to sex abuse investigation and litigation. *Child Abuse and Neglect, 11,* 267–272.

Terr, L. (1980). The child as witness. In E. P. Benedek & D. H. Schecty (Eds.), *Child psychiatry and the law*. New York: Brunner / Mazel.

Terr, L. (1981). Forbidden games: Post-traumatic child's play. *Journal of the American Academy of Child Psychiatry, 20,* 741–760.

Terr, L. (Ed.). (1989). Debate forum—Resolved: Child sex abuse is overdiagnosed. *Journal of the American Academy of Child and Adolescent Psychiatry, 28,* 789–797.

Tong, L., Oates, K., & McDowell, M. (1987). Personality development following sexual abuse. *Child Abuse and Neglect, 11,* 371–383.

Trepper, T. S. (1986). The apology session. In T. S. Trepper & M. J. Barrett (Eds.), *Treating incest: A multiple systems perspective*. New York: Haworth.

Troy, M., & Sroufe, L. A. (1987). Victimization among preschoolers: Role of attachment relationship history. *Journal of the American Academy of Child and Adolescent Psychiatry, 26,* 166–172.

Tsai, M., Feldman-Summers, S., & Edgar, M. (1979). Childhood molestation:

Variables related to differential impacts on psychosexual functioning in adult women. *Journal of Abnormal Psychology, 88*, 407–417.

Van Buskirk, S., Cole, C. (1983). Characteristics of eight women seeking therapy for the effects of incest. *Psychotherapy: Theory, Research and Practice, 20*, 503–514.

Van der Kolk, B. (1984). *Post-traumatic stress disorder: Psychological and biological sequelae.* Washington, DC: American Psychiatric Press.

Ward, E. (1985). *Father-daughter rape.* New York: Grove.

Waterman, J. (1986). Developmental considerations. In K. MacFarlane, J. Waterman, S. Conerly, L. Damon, M. Durfee, & S. Long (Eds.), *Sexual abuse of young children.* New York: Guilford.

White, L. A. (1948). A definition and prohibition of incest. *American Anthropology, 15*, 416–435.

White, S., Halpin, B. M., Strom, G. A., & Santilli, G. (1988). Behavioral comparisons of young sexually abused, neglected, and nonreferred children. *Journal of Clinical Child Psychology, 17*, 53–61.

White, S., & Quinn, K. M. (1988). Investigatory independence in child sexual abuse evaluations. *Bulletin of the American Academy of Psychiatry and the Law, 16*, 269–278.

White, S., Strom, G., Santilli, G., & Halpin, B. (1968). Interviewing young sexual abuse victims with anatomically correct dolls. *Child Abuse and Neglect, 10*, 519–529.

Wurtele, S. K. (1987). School-based sexual abuse prevention programs: A review. *Child Abuse and Neglect, 11*, 483–495.

Wyatt, G., & Mickey, M. R. (1988). The support by parents and others as it mediates the effects of child sexual abuse. In G. E. Wyatt & G. J. Powell (Eds.), *Lasting effects of child sexual abuse.* Beverly Hills, CA: Sage.

Wyatt, G. E., & Powell, G. J. (Eds.). (1988). *Lasting effects of child sexual abuse.* Beverly Hills, CA: Sage.

Yates, A. (1987). Should young children testify in cases of sexual abuse? *American Journal of Psychiatry, 144*, 476–480.